QUEEN VICTORIA'S OTHER WORLD

QUEEN VICTORIA'S OTHER WORLD

Peter Underwood

HARRAP
LONDON

First published in Great Britain 1986
by HARRAP Ltd
19–23 Ludgate Hill, London EC4M 7PD

ISBN 0 245-54355-4

Design by Michael R. Carter

Printed and bound in Great Britain
by Biddles Ltd, Guildford

For
MY MOTHER
Edith Mary Underwood
born in 1888 — a devoted
and knowledgeable royalist

CONTENTS

ILLUSTRATIONS

PREFACE

There have been far too many books about Queen Victoria and my only excuse for adding to the list is that there has never been one that explored her 'other world' — the world of the strange and the unusual, the world of death and its fascination for her, the world of the unseen and the paranormal that she could never resist.

This has not been an easy book to research, compile and write; some of those people I have approached have not gone out of their way to help me (on the excuse that I was walking a 'well-trodden path') but I think it has been well worth while. Certainly I know a lot more about Queen Victoria than I did before I wrote the book. Edith Sitwell, after writing a highly acclaimed tome on the Queen, always referred to her as 'that old bore', but I have found Queen Victoria to be a complex and interesting person who surrounded herself with equally interesting characters; she was not all good but, equally, she was not all bad; she was no genius by any standard but neither was she simple and easily deceived. In her early days and again in her later years she was disliked by only a handful of people who really knew her but she was loved by many, and she died happily — which may be the whole purpose of living.

It is a thousand pities that her exhaustive Journals are no longer extant as she wrote them. To achieve any sort of understanding today of Queen Victoria it is necessary to read between the lines of what remains of her own writings and what has been written about her. Some of this book, therefore, is assumption, but it is reasonable assumption based on extensive research.

Understandably, perhaps, I discovered almost as soon as I began to research Queen Victoria that there is no great desire anywhere on anybody's part to provide evidence to support the fact that she was deeply interested in the unusual, the macabre, the mysterious and the strange; in fact I had the distinct impression that there was something of a conspiracy of silence (once at the suggestion of the Deputy Registrar of the Royal Archives at Windsor I wrote to the Central Chancery of the Orders of Knighthood at St James's Palace on a particular query but I received no reply). Yet there is overwhelming evidence that as a fatherless and bewildered princess, as a quickly matured married queen and then for over forty years as a widowed and often lonely monarch, Victoria showed a healthy interest in apparently inexplicable phenomena and perhaps a less healthy interest in death.

Viewed from the Long Walk, the Victoria Tower of Windsor Castle can be seen on the extreme right of the battlements. On the right-hand side of this tower there is the big oriel window of Queen Victoria's private sitting-room. It was and still is a cold room (the Queen did not feel the cold and disliked fires). The enormous fireplace is carved with mysterious and jumbled mythological figures. On a table, in the middle of glass cases containing statuettes, plaster busts and a host of English and foreign souvenirs, Victoria displayed a sea of framed photographs, many of them obscured by those placed in a prominent position, several of which were of John Brown. On a little bamboo table stood a golden handbell which was used by the Queen when she wished to summon a servant. An enormous desk was more than half covered with framed portraits of Prince Albert, their children, grandchildren, German relatives and still more of the mysterious John Brown.

Here in this room the Queen was safe from interruption; only the ringing of her handbell would bring anyone hurrying into the room — except for John Brown, for here as everywhere else in the castle, John Brown might enter at any time unannounced and sometimes without knocking, even — perhaps especially — when he was in his cups. Any investigation of the interests of Queen Victoria has to take into account her domination by this Rasputin in a kilt.

The royal historian Hector Bolitho tells us that in 1883, when Queen Victoria was sixty-four, the four rooms she used at Windsor contained about 250 pictures, each a reminder of some cherished memory. Sometimes the servants would come upon the Queen walking about the rooms, fingering the objects she had hoarded over the long years: a silver teapot she had used as a child at Kensington; bundles of letters; dead flowers from occasions she remembered fondly; and the inevitable photographs. As each year passed all these souvenirs were carried from Windsor to Balmoral and then to Osborne in a time-honoured ritual. Among the odder mementoes still preserved at Windsor is the bullet fired by a would-be assassin at the Prince and Princess of Wales, Bertie and Alix, at the Gare du Nord, Brussels, on 4 April 1900. The gunman pulled the trigger of his revolver four times but two of the bullets failed to explode, one of the two that were fired broke the window of the compartment occupied by the royal couple, and the fourth (the one preserved at Windsor) was so close to its target as to pass almost between Bertie and Alix, striking the wall above their heads and richocheting back, burying itself in the cushions on the other side of the compartment. To many people at the time it was a providential escape. The Queen, however, did not believe in providence; to her it was a sign that her son and heir was not yet to die.

I should make it quite clear that I do not intend to derogate or discredit Queen Victoria or indeed any member of the royal family. I am a royalist and have a tremendous admiration for the royal family and all the valuable work they have done and are doing, but my particular interest is the realm of the paranormal and, in the present work, to explore the not inconsiderable interest that Queen Victoria had in the same subject; my aim then is not to produce a rounded picture of Queen Victoria and her glorious reign but to highlight the interest and involvement she had in ghosts and haunted houses and the whole world of the unexplained.

For the purposes of convenience I have looked separately at relevant aspects, such as her youthful encounters with the occult, her visits to haunted properties, her friends and acquaintances with similar interests and experiences, her alleged involvement with Robert Lees, the medium, her undoubted interest in the Jack the Ripper murders, her obsession with omens and superstitions, her fascination with death. Since the early environment is important in any assessment of a person's inclinations and approach to life's mysteries, I have dealt first of all at some length with her mother, Victoire, Duchess of Kent, who had a profound and considerable influence on the impressionable Victoria.

It is difficult precisely to describe what exactly Victoria was so interested in as far as the other world is concerned. Was it proof of life after death that she was seeking? Was it belief in a spiritual apprehension of truths intellectually incomprehensible? Was it yearning for the mystical and the inexplicable in a world that was fast becoming commercialized and machine-minded? Was it simply that the symbolic, the esoteric, the mysterious intrigued her as it has intrigued so many people from all walks of life over the centuries? Perhaps it was all of these things or none of them; perhaps it depends on what is meant by mystical — one of Queen Victoria's eminent biographers finds a belief in fresh air 'a trifle mystical'!

Prince Albert, who helped to cultivate the Queen's inquiring mind in matters of a physical nature, was in the habit of walking with her up and down the terrace at Windsor for hours on end, discussing with her the afterlife, what it was really like and whether those already there could contact those still on earth. In 1861 the Queen wrote to her eldest daughter: 'I feel now to be so acquainted with death — and to be so much nearer that unseen world.'

Not long before his death the Prince Consort told the Queen: 'We don't know in what state we shall meet again; but that we shall recognize each other and be together in eternity I am perfectly certain.' Through forty years of widowhood, in a changing world, Queen Victoria believed utterly that it would be so. Let us hope they found each other in that other world.

Peter Underwood

The Savage Club
Berkeley Square
London W1

ACKNOWLEDGMENTS

The literature about Queen Victoria is vast and the textual sources from which I have drawn information for further research are too numerous to be listed here. They include contemporary and subsequent newspaper reports, magazine articles and correspondence spanning a century, communication with librarians and curators in this country and abroad, and examination of more than a hundred books and anthologies, the chief of which are included in the Select Bibliography at the end of this volume. To all those writers whose work has helped me to explore the hidden world of Britain's longest reigning queen I owe a debt of gratitude as I do to the many people who have helped me. There are too many, I fear, to name individually; but I gratefully acknowledge the patience, encouragement and understanding of my wife Joyce Elizabeth.

CHAPTER ONE

QUEEN VICTORIA'S MOTHER – A POWERFUL INFLUENCE

Princess Charlotte, Princess of Wales, the young wife of the penniless Prince Leopold (the younger son from a small German duchy, and related by marriage to Queen Victoria's mother Victoire) plunged the whole nation into sadness when, at the age of twenty-one, the apparently healthy and fit Princess died within hours of giving birth to a large but stillborn son.

Sir Richard Croft, the accoucheur, committed suicide three months later and the widowed Leopold of Saxe-Coburg never really recovered from the shock. The Princess's father, the Prince Regent, was prostrate with grief and the whole country joined him in mourning the double tragedy at Claremont; an unprecedented demonstration of national mourning. Claremont House at Esher in Surrey was afterwards described as being 'full of affecting memories and mementoes' of poor Charlotte.

A former lady-in-waiting to the Princess's mother, Lady Charlotte Bury, was only one of many people who regarded the two deaths as prophetic. 'This national calamity', she wrote in her diary, 'is the forerunner of many future woes.' And so it turned out to be.

A curious and little-known reminder of the tragic Princess Charlotte lived for most of Victoria's life at Nunwell on the Isle of Wight in the person of Charlotte Maria Oglander — although she does not appear in the official genealogical table of the Oglander family; in her generation there is only mention of her two brothers, William and Henry. Her father, Sir William Oglander, sixth baronet, was married to Lady Maria Fitzroy, eldest daughter of the fourth Duke of Grafton. She had been a lady-in-waiting to the much-loved Princess Charlotte, whose death in November 1817 seems to have thrown a strange cloud over the child born to Lady Maria in March 1818.

The baby girl, named Charlotte after her mother's royal mistress, seems never to have really grown up. Physically she developed into a woman but mentally she remained a child. She lived all her life and died, not long before Queen Victoria's Golden Jubilee, at Nunwell where she would wander listlessly and aimlessly through the still rooms and quiet gardens of Nunwell House, hand in hand with her nurse. And, it seems, her ghost has wandered there ever since her death. A long-standing housekeeper reported repeatedly hearing and feeling the presence of Charlotte, or 'Little Missy' as she was called. Sometimes she could be heard crying in the night and sometimes crying in the daytime; those who knew Nunwell had no doubt about the presence of poor Charlotte, long after she was dead.

Even as the coffins of the young Princess Charlotte and her baby were being buried in the family vault at Windsor, with some ceremony and amid genuine sadness, not a few members of the court were gloomily discussing the frightful political and dynastic implications which now faced the country.

That year, 1817, King George III was seventy-nine years of age; he was generally considered to be deranged, 'an old, mad, blind ghost . . . immured with his keepers at Windsor Castle' (as Alison Plowden puts it in her volume *The Young Victoria*, 1981). Although the King and his ugly little German wife produced no less than fifteen children, of whom twelve were still alive, with the death of Princess Charlotte the King did not possess a single legitimate grandchild. His five surviving daughters were either spinsters or childless, and since the youngest was over forty there seemed little hope that they would produce offspring; and his sons appeared to be even less promising.

The Prince Regent was fifty-five and long estranged from his wife. This once handsome young man was now a wreck — a bloated mockery of the promise he once held in royal circles; it seemed almost laughable that the man known as Prinny would ever father another child. His surviving brothers were all middle-aged and always seemed to be hindered and embarrassed by debts and scandals: 'the dregs of their dull race', Shelley called them; but the continuation of the House of Hanover depended upon the seven unpromising Princes.

The two who were married were Frederick, Duke of York, and Ernest, Duke of Cumberland. The reputation of the former had been tarnished by his alleged connivance in selling commissions and stories involving his mistress Mary Ann Clarke; at fifty-four his future looked bleak. His wife was Frederica, Princess Royal of Prussia, a somewhat eccentric person, who if we are to believe contemporary reports, rarely went to bed and lived out her life among innumerable dogs, monkeys and parrots whose penetrating smell and perpetual barking and screeching filled her days.

Ernest, Duke of Cumberland, was a man of sinister reputation and hideous appearance who was commonly regarded as the ogre of the family. He was credited with a wide variety of crimes and not a few vices. At forty-six he had recently married the widowed Princess of Solms-Braunfels, whose own reputation, as one writer has put it, 'was none too fragrant'. The couple had no living children, a single daughter having been born dead.

Augustus, Duke of Sussex, had already taken two unofficial wives by this time and he was only forty-four; by the first he had a son and a daughter but since neither union had had the King's consent and were therefore legally void, their children could not be in the line of succession to the throne.

Then there were the three bachelor Princes of whom William, Duke of Clarence, was already fifty-two. A friend of Nelson and best man at the naval hero's wedding, he had taken up with an actress named Dorothea Jordan who had presented him with no less than ten little FitzClarences. His brother Edward, Duke of Kent, aged fifty, had made a life in the army and found a mistress with whom he had lived in apparent content and some happiness for more than a quarter of a century. Lastly there was Adolphus, Duke of Cambridge, at forty-three the youngest and perhaps the best bet from the old King's point of view for Adolphus, unlike his brothers, was not known to be in debt and he had, as far as we know, acquired no extra-marital encumbrances; he was fond of playing the violin, liked to wear an unbecoming blond wig and tended to talk too much but otherwise harmed nobody.

The *Morning Chronicle* went straight to the heart of the matter and declared that the earnest prayer of the nation must be 'that an early alliance of one of the unmarried Princes may forthwith be settled'. As if in response, the three unlikely suitors seem to have hurried to obey the call. It was an undignified spectacle with stout, balding and listless-looking men jostling for the lead in a race to be suitably married and quickly produce an heir to the throne of England.

The youngest, Adolphus, was the first to make a start. He proposed to Augusta of Hess-Cassel within a fortnight of his niece's death and he was accepted. His two unmarried brothers were not far behind. William left Mrs Jordan after twenty years of idyllic happiness and proceeded to make a spectacle of himself by pursuing just about every English heiress he could think of before, bluff as ever, he approached Princess Anne of Denmark and then, with some excitement, the Tsar's sister; but he could not persuade either to take him seriously. He eventually returned to Bushey Park and to his many sons and daughters of whom he seems to have been genuinely fond. Suddenly, in the middle of 1818, it was announced that he was to marry Adelaide of Saxe-Meiningen and he duly did so. Now, surely, an addition to the royal house would be provided before very long. But, in spite of William's proven procreative ability, it was not to be.

Edward, a humourless man whose harsh discipline in his chosen military career caused him to be known as the most hated man in the army, had an exaggerated idea of his own importance and he exuded a righteous air that infuriated his father who called him 'Simon Pure' while diarist Charles Greville made no bones about his hatred of the man, calling him 'the greatest rascal that ever went unhung' and 'by far the worst of the family'. In fact the Duke of Kent could be a charming host and an agreeable friend but his brutal severity brought to an abrupt end his military career when he provoked a mutiny in Gibraltar and the unhappy man was recalled to England under a cloud.

Once settled in England Edward installed a mistress in a luxurious house in Knightsbridge before moving with her to a retreat in the then rustic village of Ealing, Castle Hill Lodge, a pleasant but somewhat rambling property which he proceeded to alter to his satisfaction with military precision but without regard to cost. The completed house was a gaudy showplace with coloured lights, musical clocks and mechanical birds; concealed faucets produced fountains and waterfalls, ornamental windows looked out on neat lawns. The renovations and innovations put Edward in debt to the tune of some £200,000 and his creditors became anxious. The Duke opted to live abroad for a while and settled on Brussels where the cost of living was, at that time, as low as anywhere in Europe.

Unwilling for his exile in Belgium to be a lonely one Edward shared his home and bed with the by now middle-aged lady who was known in the family as 'Edward's French Lady'; officially she was described as Madame de St Laurent. She was said to come from an aristocratic Catholic background and to be the widow of a French-Canadian officer. It seemed possible that Edward had met her in Canada where he spent some time during his army service. According to some sources the Duke married her and they had several children whose descendants were the rightful heirs to the English throne, but much of this is disproved by recent research which reveals that Mademoiselle Julie de St Laurent was the daughter of a French civil engineer and had been procured by a certain M. Fontiny to 'act as required' for Prince Edward. She had been a pretty girl, even-tempered and intelligent without being cunning or unscrupulous. A purely business arrangement seems to have developed, as time passed, into a tender liaison. In fact they never married, nor did they have any children, which was fortunate for as things now stood Edward, Duke of Kent, needed to look for a wife. His eye fell on Princess Katherine Amelia of Baden (over forty and described as 'odious') and also on the recently widowed Princess of Leiningen, Victoire Marie Louise, just thirty, the mother of two children and sister of Princess Charlotte's husband, Leopold of Saxe-Coburg.

Before she married Emich Charles, son of the Count of Leiningen-

Dachsburg-Hadenburg (who could trace his ancestry back for more than seven hundred years) the name of the seventeen-year-old Victoire had, it has been said, been on the list of princesses offered to the conquering Napoleon who was at the time considering replacing Josephine in favour of a grander marriage partner. At all events the idea came to nothing and Victoire married Emich Charles. This contract of marriage is still preserved at Amorbach in a red velvet-covered book with silver seals. Emich Charles, twenty-three years older than Victoire, was said to be of uncertain temper but for a time at least the couple shared a love of music and would play duets and sing together. They had a son Charles nine months after the wedding and a daughter Anna Feodorovina (known as Feodora) three years later. Seven years on, Emich Charles, Prince of Leiningen, died of pneumonia.

Victoire eventually agreed to marry Edward, Duke of Kent, after having met him only once. In spite of his military training he did not have the courage to inform his mistress of the fortuitous turn of events but as soon as she heard she accepted the inevitable, retired to her home in Paris where King Louis XVIII bestowed on her a courtesy title, Comtesse de Montgenet, and as far as we know she and the Duke of Kent never met again although they certainly corresponded and he always expressed an interest in her welfare.

Victoire Marie Louise, who was to become the mother of Queen Victoria, was the youngest daughter of Francis and Augusta of Saxe-Coburg-Saalfeld, and she was born on 17 August 1786, an inauspicious date. Frederick the Great, King of Prussia, founder of the fortunes of the House of Hohenzollern, the German hero of his age, had died on the very day on which Victoire entered the world. It was a coincidence which was to mar her childhood birthdays, for her grandmother, whose sister had been the wife of Frederick the Great, would never allow Victoire's birthday to be celebrated on a day which was devoted to the memories of her illustrious brother-in-law.

Victoire and the Duke of Kent were married in Ehrenburg Castle, in the atmospheric Giant's Hall with its heavily-painted ceiling supported on the shoulders of a number of twice-lifesize giants. Afterwards they travelled to England where a second marriage ceremony took place in the drawing room at Kew Palace.

The Duke, like his future daughter Victoria, was very superstitious and never forgot a prophecy that he had been told many years before. A Gypsy had impressed on him, when he was in Gibraltar, that he would one day have a daughter who would become a great queen. He died while this was still highly unlikely and when his daughter was only eight months old.

Victoria's father seems to have been a strange man: strong, obstinate, a harsh disciplinarian, fond of animals (a trait which Victoria inherited) and of young people (which only surfaced in

21

Victoria in later life), intelligent and highly eloquent. Although the diarist Greville called him 'the greatest rascal' and confidently waited for the 'bad blood' to come out when Victoria came to the throne, the Duke had remained loyal to the same mistress for twenty-seven years and there seems little doubt that his wife, Victoria's mother, loved him; but he was not a happy man.

Financial difficulties had always been a problem and his marriage to Victoire did not help matters in that respect. In fact Edward was deeply in debt less than two months after the wedding when the couple left England and set out for Amorbach. They broke their journey at Vakenciennes where the Duke of Wellington had his headquarters, and at Aix-le-Chapelle where a European summit conference was being held, and they visited one of Victoire's sisters, Juliana, in Switzerland. They eventually arrived at Amorbach at the end of October. Notwithstanding his financial straits the Duke began to make many costly alterations to the Amorbach property, building new stables, constructing walls around the gardens, and installing an improved heating system. Then, in the middle of November, the Duchess informed her husband that she was pregnant.

The year 1818 had been good for royal weddings and when 1819 dawned it looked as though it would be a good year for royal births since no less than three of the Duke of Kent's sisters-in-law were also due to give birth. The 'three Cs', the Dukes of Clarence, Cumberland and Cambridge, were happy enough for their royal offspring to be born abroad, in Germany, but the Duke of Kent was determined that his child should be born in Britain. The problem, as always, was money.

The Duke wrote a long letter to the Prince Regent's Private Secretary with news of the forthcoming confinement, probably in the coming May, and expressed his hope for assistance; in particular he desired the loan of the royal yacht for the Channel crossing and the use of accommodation at Kensington Palace for the necessary period.

Unfortunately the tone of the Duke's letter irritated his brother the Prince Regent who found the subject of royal marriages and royal births distasteful — doubtless due to his own unhappy marriage and now childless condition. He made it very clear that he had no intention of helping and went out of his way to draw attention to the fact that his brothers were quite content for their offspring to be born abroad and he could see no reason why Edward and Victoire should not do the same.

The Duke of Kent, disappointed but penniless, told himself that some solution might still turn up. In common with many members of the royal family before and since, right up to the present day, he set great store by what he learned from visits to fortune-tellers and other practitioners of various methods of divination: he had been told that he would live by the sea in England and that he would die there. So, in spite of present disappointments, Edward, Duke of Kent, kept an optimistic outlook; not without cause was it said that he possessed 'an unshakable belief in the future'. 'My brothers are not as strong as I am,' he was in the habit of saying to anyone who would listen to him. 'I have led a regular life, I shall outlive them all; the crown will come to me and my children.' Such an attitude at this time, loudly proclaimed for all to hear, hardly helped to improve the poor relationship that existed between him and his brothers although his robust and strong appearance lent persuasion to his oft-repeated boasts.

Edward tried to borrow from his Methodist friends who were becoming increasingly influential and only too keen to embarrass the profligate Prince Regent. The Duke managed to raise a sufficient amount to pay off some of his more impatient creditors and just about have enough for the journey to England. Armed with this slender ammunition he again wrote to his brother and threatened to bring his pregnant wife over on the mail boat and to take meagre lodgings. The Prince Regent, annoyed but, not for the first time, out-manoeuvred, made available with bad grace the royal yacht and also apartments at Kensington.

By the time all this was sorted out Victoire was entering her eighth month of pregnancy and her mother made no secret of her apprehension about the journey her daughter was proposing to make — some four hundred miles over very bad roads, followed by a sea crossing that was often choppy and stormy. By contrast Victoire herself, 'thoroughly happy in her new married life', was actually looking forward to the journey. At the tearful parting of mother and daughter, the Dowager comforted herself with the conviction that her daughter was indeed happy and contented and she was able to write: 'Kent makes an excellent husband.' Indeed Edward does seem to have been most solicitous over the welfare of his wife and he is credited with remarking that her condition caused him 'hourly anxiety'.

When they eventually set off on 28 March 1819 he had acquired a well-sprung phaeton, a light open carriage drawn by a pair of horses, which he drove himself. Behind them in a 'baroutsch' travelled the Duchess's old friend and lady-in-waiting Baroness Späth and Madame Siebold the midwife. Then came the Duchess's empty but covered post chaise to which the expectant Duchess could transfer if the weather was inclement; and following that came another post chaise for her daughter Princess Feodora and Feodora's governess. Next came the servants and the baggage train carrying the Duchess's own bed and bed linen and her precious pet birds and lapdogs. Bringing up the rear was Dr Wilson, the Duke's personal physician, who had attended the Duchess 'to perfection' from the beginning of her pregnancy. An Englishwoman, coming across the entourage, described it as an 'unbelievably odd caravan'. The weather was exceptionally kind to them and there were no accidents. 'Providence,' wrote the Duke at the time, 'absolutely prospered our undertaking.' Providence did not, however, appear to favour the Duchess of Clarence whose daughter was born the day after the Kents set out and lived only seven hours.

A month after leaving Amorbach Edward and Victoire were installed in the south-west wing at Kensington. The rooms had stood stripped and empty for several years and were in a poor state of repair but the Kents were delighted. The Duchess's rooms looked out over the lush trees and green grass of the park with the quiet waters of the Round Pond in the foreground. The Duke immediately set about improving the décor, several thousand pounds being lavished on furniture from one Bond Street store alone, and it is as well that he lost no time in doing so for during the evening of 23 May the Duchess went into labour.

At 4.15 the following day, as a grey dawn broke over the silent park outside, a vigorous baby girl made her appearance into the world. The distinguished witnesses assembled included the Duke of Wellington, the Duke of Sussex, the Archbishop of Canterbury, the Bishop of London and the Chancellor of the Exchequer. In accordance with time-honoured custom the newly-born infant was presented to the Privy Councillors. They and the physicians present signed the certificate of birth and asserted to the perfectly healthy appearance of the child. Contrary to one legend that became widely circulated in later years, there were no complications at the birth. The Duchess fed the child herself and while this was considered rather middle-class and decidedly out of date in some circles, it met with general approval. The Duke, who had personally supervised practically every detail of the surgery and its routine, found the 'process of maternal nutriment most interesting in its nature . . . .'

Although the Kents had naturally hoped for a boy they took comfort in the knowledge that their legitimate offspring took precedence over any of the Duke's younger brothers and that the little Princess whom they looked on with such pride and joy was fifth in line to the throne. Only three middle-aged uncles (the Prince Regent and the Dukes of York and Clarence) and her own middle-aged father stood between her and succession. The Dowager Duchess Augusta of Saxe-Coburg-Saalfeld put into words the thoughts in many royal heads: 'She is destined perhaps to play a great part one day — the English like Queens.' Even the Duke himself, although in public careful to admit the possibility of the Duke of Clarence's producing an heir, was often heard among friends to introduce his little daughter as the future Queen of England; so in spite of what has been written to the contrary, from her earliest years Victoria must have been aware of her potential destiny.

Yet always there seemed to be difficulties and hostilities surrounding the Kents and their daughter. Even the baptism of the innocent infant was not without problems. The Regent found himself unable to prevent the child being born in England and he accepted the invitation to be a god-parent along with Tsar Alexander of Russia, the widowed Queen of Württemberg and the Dowager Duchess of Saxe-Coburg-Saalfeld, but he resolutely set about ensuring that the christening was as inconspicuous an event as he could make it. He decreed that the ceremony should take place at Kensington on 24 June and he gave the parents just two days' notice. He insisted that the guest list should be restricted to a few close relatives — the Yorks, the Gloucesters, Princess Augusta, Princess Sophia and Prince Leopold. The Duke of York was to stand proxy for the Tsar and the Duchess of Gloucester and Princess Augusta for the two god-mothers. The occasion was to be a private affair and this being so the gentlemen were to wear frock coats; there were to be no uniforms, decorations or gold lace, and so on and so on.

The names that the child should have caused further wrangling and hostility. Edward had already submitted his choice, Victoire Georgina Alexandrina Charlotte Augusta, but at the eleventh hour he was notified that Georgina was unacceptable. The Regent indicated that he did not choose to 'place the name before the Emperor of Russia's and he could not allow it to follow'. The message added that he would indicate his approval or otherwise regarding the remaining names at the actual ceremony!

So, in the Cupola Room at Kensington Palace, amid crimson velvet draperies hastily borrowed from the Chapel Royal, the family gathered for the 'happy' event. The silver-gilt font had been brought from the Jewel House at the Tower of London and the service, conducted jointly by the Archbishop of Canterbury and the Bishop of London, began with nothing further having been said about the names the infant was to bear. Standing poised over the font with the child in his arms the Archbishop intoned 'Name this child' and turned inquiringly to the only sponsor present in person. 'Alexandrina' came the prompt and curt reply. A disconcerting pause followed before the Regent vetoed the names Charlotte and Augusta. The desperately unhappy parents asked that another name be added and suggested Elizabeth; this too was refused. Having made it clear that he would not allow his niece to bear any of the traditional royal names, the Regent, glaring at the distressed and disturbed Duchess of Kent who was weeping with frustration and embarrassment, suddenly said brusquely, 'Give her the mother's name also then, but it cannot precede that of the Emperor.' So, as Alison Plowden puts it in her volume *The Young Victoria*, 'in an atmosphere heavily charged with rancour and wounded feelings, and to a background of its mother's sobs, the baby was baptized Alexandrina Victoria'.

By the time she was three months old the 'lovely little darling' of her parents was perhaps 'rather more a pocket Hercules than a pocket Venus'. She was already nicknamed by the Dowager Duchess of Saxe-Coburg-Saalfeld 'the little Mayflower'; it was the first of many nicknames that Victoria would be known by until towards the end of her long life she was known to everyone (outside her hearing) as 'the old Queen'.

Meanwhile the Prince Regent lost no opportunity to publicly express his dislike for his brother Edward and for the baby Victoria. When he saw the Kents with their young daughter at a review on Hounslow Heath he was heard to ask, angrily and loudly: 'What business has that infant here?' and at one foreign reception he went out of his way to cut his brother dead. But Edward had other fish to fry; he was determined to secure a niche for his wife and himself in England and he had no doubt that their daughter would one day be Queen.

The Kents continued to occupy apartments at Kensington Palace and there the proud parents would often display their daughter to admiring passers-by in the Park; there too they would give dinner parties and musical evenings; and from time to time they would visit Uncle Leopold at Claremont with its sad memories and Windsor with its haunted apartments. The Kents seemed at this time to be a perfectly happy family and there is little doubt that the Duke was a changed man and was now a model husband and father. The Princess Feodora grew to love her stepfather and was to say, years later: 'I loved him dearly; he always was so kind to me.'

Happiness does not pay bills, however, and Edward was finding it exceedingly difficult to make ends meet. He was eventually forced to the conclusion that on an income of around £14,000 he simply could not manage to live in London. They explored Torquay, Teignmouth and Dawlish without success but at Sidmouth they found Woolbrook Cottage, a Gothic-style romantic property sheltering in a wooded valley and only a couple of hundred yards from the beach. They decided to take up residence but not before the Duke celebrated his fifty-second birthday. 'Drina', as the infant Princess was sometimes called in her baby days, dressed in white with bows of red and green ribbon (a portion is still preserved at Windsor Castle) and now six months old, was made to appear to make a presentation to the Duke; his stepdaughter Princess Feodora sang for him and his stepson Prince Charles of Leiningen wrote a letter to his 'dear father' in English from his school in Geneva.

Edward tried his best to raise capital and settle the debts that worried him but Coutts Bank were no longer willing to accommodate him; Castle Hill Lodge (his only remaining disposable asset) might fetch £35,000 with the contents, but there was no immediate buyer in the offing; plans for the sale of the property by lottery had fallen through and a tontine was now under consideration. The idea was that five hundred members of the tontine would each buy a share and as each died his portion would be divided among the remainder and eventually the last survivor would become the owner of the property. If each member put up one hundred guineas it was calculated that the Duke's financial problems would be solved but the matter dragged on and on and eventually, leaving the matter in the hands of a committee, the Duke and his family took off for the West Country.

They spent a night at Windsor which at this time was rife with stories of ghosts and ghostly happenings, especially in the vicinity of Curfew Tower. Today hundreds of visitors each day walk up and down the main staircase where occupants of the castle maintained they heard phantom footsteps. The tower, built in 1319 and situated over the castle dungeons, has a gruesome history. Prisoners used these stairs to reach a small door in a wall where there is a drop of more than a hundred feet to the ground. From a beam above the doorway hung the hangman's noose and it was here that those who were to die were hanged and their bodies left hanging as a warning to others; small wonder that slow and dragging footsteps have been heard there for well over a century and a half. On at least one occasion the Duchess of Kent claimed to have seen a ghost at Windsor Castle.

The Kents also broke their journey at Salisbury where they spent two days with Edward's old tutor Bishop Fisher. Salisbury, with its white birds that circle the cathedral tower before the death of a bishop, was the subject of a strange phenomenon then which is still occasionally reported to this day. For two hundred years a wire noose hung over St Ormond's tomb, which also apparently contains the remains of a murderer, Lord Stourton, who was hanged by a silken noose in the market place in 1557. The wire replica was removed in 1780 but periodically thereafter there have been those who maintained that they still saw the luminous outline of the ominous noose.

Edward and his family reached Woolbrook Cottage on Christmas Day. They had hardly settled in when a potentially lethal and profoundly disturbing incident took place. Three days after their arrival the seven-month-old child was lying in the arms of her nurse when a shot broke the windows of the nursery and a bullet whistled past the baby's head. The culprit was not the expected anarchist or hired killer but merely a boy potting at chattering sparrows outside the cottage! The shot that shattered the window missed the little Princess by a fraction − it was close enough to tear the sleeve of her nightgown. However, although the Duchess was understandably 'most exceedingly' alarmed, the strong and healthy child showed no signs of being any the worse for the near fatal accident. The boy, who had been hastily captured, was released from custody at the Duke's request and let off 'upon a promise of desisting from such culpable pursuits'. Today the window is marked by a coloured pane of glass.

It was the Princess's first brush with death — the subject, more than any other topic, that was to interest her and influence her life and actions more and more; there were to be at least seven serious attempts on her life when she became Queen. At the moment however the child was busy cutting her first teeth 'without the slightest inconvenience'; 'she seems almost too healthy' some people commented.

Within days a spell of severe winter weather made the cold and cramped cottage seem cheerless and depressing and within a week the whole family was far from well. Colds and headaches were the order of the day and even the usually happy baby was fretful with a sore throat. The robust Duke suffered a trying gastric attack for which he blamed the Sidmouth water but on 7 January he insisted on his customary walk with his Irish equerry, Captain John Conroy of the Royal Artillery, and he returned thoroughly chilled. Next day the chill had moved to his chest and his doctor prescribed calomel (a preparation of mercury used as a purgative) but the Duke thought a good night's rest would set him to rights and he refused any medication. He was rarely ill and had long held valetudinarians in contempt.

By morning he had a high temperature and the Duchess insisted that he remain in bed. The doctor was called again and looked worried; pneumonia had developed. During the next four days the doctors did what they could but at that time their skills were virtually limited to 'cuppings' and 'blisterings' which only drained the strength from the patient. The Duke grew worse and worse; he had a high fever, complained of pains in his chest and vomited violently. There could be no disguising the fact that Edward was seriously ill.

Bleeding was practically the only remedy then known for such maladies and when this brought no relief the Duchess, who for five days did not leave her husband's side, not even to change her clothes, became frightened and wrote urgently to Sir David Dundas, the senior royal physician, begging him to come at once. Sadly, the request came at a bad time, for the old King George III was ailing and Sir David could not leave him. He sent Dr Maton instead and the fight was on between Edward's remarkable constitution and will to live and the deadly and still mysterious pneumonia, against which the skills, such as they were, of medical science seemed helpless.

Loyal Victoire was thoroughly sickened by the practices inflicted on Edward by the doctors and she insisted on giving him his medicine with her own hands but soon there was hardly anywhere on his body which had not been 'touched by cupping, blisters or bleeding'. Still she nursed him devotedly through the long days and even longer nights.

Soon six pints of blood had been taken from him and he was often delirious, racked by exhausting coughing and by an excruciating pain in his side from which there seemed no escape, other than brief spells of unconsciousness.

Prince Leopold had been sent for and Edward's friends, Generals Wetherall and Moore. Prince Leopold's secretary and companion Dr Christian Stockman was a qualified physician and, after he had examined Edward on 22 January 1820, he had no option but to tell Victoire that 'human help could no longer avail'. As if to give a lie to his diagnosis, that evening Edward rallied for a short while, spoke lucidly and, supported by Captain Conroy and General Wetherall, managed to sign his will in which he appointed the Duchess, his wife, sole guardian of the infant Alexandrina Victoria. He died at ten o'clock the following morning, Sunday, 23 January 1820, with his wife kneeling beside his bed holding his hand.

Forty years after the event Princess Feodora wrote to Queen Victoria, her half-sister: 'I well remember that dreadful time at Sidmouth. I recollect praying on my knees. Our dear Mama was deeply afflicted, but very resigned, and careful not to do you any harm by giving way too much to her grief.'

From the moment of Edward's death the traditional paraphernalia of royalty, which he had scarcely known during his life, was brought into play at Woolbrook Cottage. In the biggest room of the house, its walls hung with black cloth and lit by great candles, the coffin stood on raised trestles, covered with a velvet pall. At the head of the coffin, on either side, were plumes of feathers, and right and left stood three large wax tapers in solid silver candlesticks five feet high. For nearly a week the room was open to visitors who entered by one door and left by another when paying their respects.

In the midst of all this the question uppermost in the thoughts of the Duchess of Kent, and even more so in the mind of her brother Prince Leopold, a man of great political shrewdness, was the future of the baby and her mother. Prince Leopold, for all his thoughtfulness and kindnesses, was a mean man (according to the memoirs of his mistress Karoline Bauer, at night he placed two little gold clamps between his back teeth to protect the enamel, in case he ground his teeth while asleep) but he had no doubts about the present problem: whatever happened, his sister and the baby must make their home in England. Not only was this what Edward would have wished, it was essential for the future of the little fatherless Princess. The Duke of Kent had left 'nothing in the world but debts' and the past months had clearly shown that the Duchess could expect only the 'greatest animosity' in high places. It is fortunate that Leopold was a determined man; as he was to remind his niece in later years, 'I know not what would have happened to you and your Mama if I had not then existed.'

Prince Leopold did not exaggerate. The sad and grief-stunned Duchess, widowed for the second time, mother of a baby girl who might one day be Queen of England, discovered that she did not have sufficient ready money to leave Sidmouth, so it was fortunate indeed that her brother was willing and able to take charge.

As Woolbrook Cottage (today the Royal Glen Hotel) swarmed with surgeons, embalmers, undertakers and officials going about their grim tasks, Leopold lost no time in getting the woman and child away from the doom-laden property that the Kents had moved into with such high hopes only a few short weeks before. Now it was 'melancholy Sidmouth' that the sad little funeral cortège left on 26 January, 'a bitter cold and damp day I shall not easily forget' wrote Leopold later. 'I looked very sharp after the poor little baby, then about eight months old.' Seen off by an immense concourse of silent and curious spectators the sorrowful party set out slowly for Windsor, making overnight stops at Bridport, Blandford, Salisbury, and Basingstoke; and at each place crowds gathered, bells tolled and windows were shuttered. It must have seemed to Leopold like the sadness that was expressed on the death of Charlotte. The journey was a bad one and 'poor little Vickelchen' was very upset by the 'frightful joltings'.

The death of the Duke of Kent was a shock and the outside world treated it with astonished and stunned sadness but to Victoire it must have seemed a crushing blow. She, as well as everyone close to the Duke, knew his faults: he was pompous above all but he was also self-centred, careless in money matters and brutal and tyrannical in military matters. Yet he was not without intelligence, he was a fluent and graceful public speaker, he inspired affection, he could be a charming host and a loyal friend, and there could be no denying that to his wife he had been the kindest and most thoughtful of husbands. She was sadly grieved by his death. Now back at Kensington, but all alone in a foreign land with a baby girl, she faced an uncertain future and she was still finding it very difficult to learn the English language. The child of her beloved Edward, Alexandrina Victoria, 'Dear sweet little Vickelchen' as her mother called her, had quickly recovered from her sore throat after leaving Sidmouth and, small as she was, already seemed to be showing signs of wanting to get her own way. From her earliest moments of consciousness, according to the Duchess of Clarence, the baby 'Drina' was continually shown pictures of her father, so much so that once when her uncle William entered the room wearing his Star decoration, it reminded the child of the portrait she had seen of her father and she stretched out her arms to him exclaiming, 'Papa! Papa!'

Denied by court custom and etiquette from the consolation of attending her husband's funeral in St George's Chapel on 11 February, the Duchess of Kent, 'sick at heart and very lonely', sat in isolation with her thoughts while the immense coffin, said to have been seven feet long and weighing more than a ton, was with some difficulty lowered into the family vault. Afterwards the widow received visits of condolence from the Dukes of York and Sussex, while the Duke and especially the Duchess of Clarence became regular callers.

Comforting as it was to be able to talk the same language to the Duchess of Clarence and eager as she was for a real friend at this time, Victoire was aware that Adelaide could mean frustration for her since she was the only person in a position to affect Victoria's place in the line of succession to the throne. Adelaide, Duchess of Clarence, knew what it was to have problems. She had to put up with her husband's eccentricities, his riotous bastards, and her own inability to bear another child after the death of her first. Yet for her to have a baby was the last thing the Duchess of Kent wanted now that her daughter had been quickly raised from fifth to third in the line of succession, her grandfather having died within a few weeks of her father.

George III died at Windsor Castle, the victim of porphyria, a disease not identified at that time. He had lived at Windsor for years, shut away from the world, his brain undoubtedly affected. His gloomy rooms overlooked the north terrace and he was in the habit of standing at the window, during fleeting moment of normality, and watching the Palace Guards pass below. Sometimes he would even raise his hand in acknowledgement of the Guards' command 'Eyes right'. After his death on 29 January 1820 and while his body lay in state elsewhere in the castle, the routine changing of the Guard took place and as they passed the King's old rooms, the Commander of the Guard automatically looked up and to his surprise saw the bearded and unmistakable figure he knew so well. The contingent of Guards followed his command 'Eyes right' and the figure at the window made the customary response. Sir Owen Morshead, a later Royal Librarian, recounts the story in his erudite study of Windsor Castle. The officer concerned was William Knollys, who became Comptroller to the young Prince of Wales, later Edward VII, to whom Knollys related the experience as he did to the Prince's second son who became George V. Other stories of the ghostly presence of George III in Windsor Castle include the sound of his voice muttering, 'What? What?', a familiar exclamation of the King.

On the death of George III, the Prince Regent, who had held that position for nine years, became George IV. Vain and fat, he alarmed the royal family by almost immediately becoming very ill with acute inflammation of the lungs and for a few days the whole country held its breath. As Princess Dorothea Lieven put it, 'Heavens, if he should die! . . . such a catastrophe . . . father and son, in the past, have been buried together . . . but two Kings!' Henry Brougham (who was later to describe Victoria as 'the heiress presumptive of the British throne') said the King was 'as near death as any man ever was before' and his 'precious life' was only saved by the letting of a hundred and fifty ounces of blood. At all events the King recovered and Victoire was forced to think once again about her future and that of her baby daughter.

In view of her constant money worries (her only source of income would be the £6,000 jointure voted by Parliament at the time of her marriage to the Duke) and the indifference of the English establishment to her and the Princess, she felt she would be better off among friends in Germany and indeed there is no doubt that George IV would have liked nothing better. He let it be known that it was his 'great wish' that Victoire and the child should leave the country; otherwise he would not give the Duchess any money at all. But Prince Leopold told her she must live in England. Not only was it Edward's wish that the child should be brought up in an English environment but, perhaps of more consequence, it was vitally important that she should have such a background if she were ever to become Queen of England.

The King had little choice but to allow Victoire to retain the Duke's apartments at Kensington Palace but he saw to it that she was left without 'furniture, plate, linen, wines, horses, carriages or in fact any one of the materials of an establishment', and she was obliged to purchase such items as were necessary at an expense of £12,000. Half this sum the Duchess of Kent borrowed at interest, guaranteed by Prince Leopold. The Prince, still drawing the annual pension of £50,000 settled on him when he married Charlotte, now settled on his sister and her daughter an allowance of £3,000 a year. Needless to say his actions on behalf of the Duchess of Kent did not endear him to the King or help relations between the English royal family and the Coburgs.

In the spring of 1820 the Duchess gave up the guardianship of her son Charles, whom she had left at school in Germany, and resigned herself to Kensington, then little more than a rural suburb with orchards and market gardens. The palace, once the favoured residence of William and Mary and of Queen Anne, had become unfashionable and harboured such royal retainers as the enormous Duke of Sussex and the sad Princess Sophia (fourth daughter of George III) living in self-imposed seclusion and never able to forget the scandal of her illegitimate child.

Alison Plowden calls Kensington Palace 'this slumbrous, ghost-ridden retreat' and so it was and perhaps still is. For years the ghost of George II was reportedly seen from time to time at one of the windows. He and his consort Caroline of Anspach were devoted to the palace and during his last years especially the ailing King would often raise himself to gaze from the windows of his room at the curious old weathervane with its conjoined cyphers of William and Mary, high up over the main entrance to the palace, hoping for winds from the right quarter to speed the ships conveying long overdue despatches from his beloved Hanover. The despatches arrived at last but too late for the King who died on 25 October 1760, still struggling to watch the weathervane; and today when there are strong winds blowing, the ashen face of the King is still sometimes reportedly seen gazing up at the weathervane as he did so many years ago. There is still an air of sadness about the old palace, which Prince Charles and other members of the royal family refer to as 'the aunt heap', and it is not difficult to imagine that the ghost of the old King returns from time to time to the room in which he died. When Princess Margaret, who has lived for many years at Kensington Palace, was once asked whether she had ever seen the ghost of George II she replied, 'I'm afraid not, but I live in hope.'

Victoria's earliest memories of the 'poor old Palace' (as she called it) were of herself crawling along a yellow rug laid down for that purpose — and of being told that if she cried or was naughty her Uncle Sussex would hear and punish her; consequently, said Victoria years later, she always screamed when she saw him!

By the summer of 1820 the Duchess of Kent began to emerge from the traditional seclusion of mourning; she was granting interviews, meeting people and invariably she proudly presented the royal baby to all and sundry. Some of the visitors were less than enchanted; Harriet, Countess Granville, went as far as to say: 'Well may they call it the *Roi* George in petticoats; it is so fat it can scarcely waddle.'

In the December of that year Adelaide, Duchess of Clarence, gave birth to a premature daughter and the King allowed the child to be given the names Elizabeth and Georgiana with the mother's name following; there was none of the opposition that faced Victoire and Edward when they were christening their baby daughter. For a few short months the baby Princess Elizabeth replaced her cousin of Kent in the royal succession and then she died. Four months later Adelaide too was dead, seemingly quite unmourned, and for a while there were fears that the Duke might take as a new wife a young bride capable of producing an heir and possibly eliminating Victoria from any possibility of succession, but the Duke of York found a married lady more captivating and less of an encumbrance and gradually the threat receded.

After the death of 'the erring' Caroline the King too seemed set upon acquiring a new wife but, as Dulcie M. Ashdown has pointed out, 'the pleasures of his mature mistress proved too strong a hold on him — nevertheless, there were always rumours circulating as to his prospects, which were to disturb the Duchess of Kent until George IV breathed his last', some ten years later.

Meanwhile the Duchess of Kent lived on at Kensington Palace, her life and thoughts centred on aspirations for the little Princess and, with the fulfilment of such hopes, reflected grandeur for herself. In all probability and throughout all her years the Duchess had no wish to be unkind; she seems always to have loved Victoria but it is obvious that she never understood her.

Among those in the young Princess's immediate circle who were also to influence her in one way or another were Louise Lehzen, the daughter of a Lutheran pastor, who had been chosen by the Duchess of Kent to be governess to Feodora, the Duchess's daughter by her first husband Emich Charles, Prince of Leiningen, and it was always understood that the shrewd, dark-haired and devoted Lehzen (as she was always known) would in due course take over the charge of the little Princess Victoria; and coming more into the picture following the death of the Duke of Kent, there was the Irishman John Conroy, good-looking, plausible, and completely unscrupulous. His devotion lay in the advancement of John Conroy; his inclinations lay towards the still very attractive Victoire (he was only two months her senior). There is a story that on his deathbed the Duke of Kent seized his equerry's hand and entreated him never to desert the Duchess and her child, Princess Victoria. It is a story that Queen Victoria emphatically denied — although on what authority is not recorded for she herself was of course a small babe at the time. At any rate Conroy became Comptroller of the Household of the Duchess of Kent and his determination to further his ambitions and feather his own nest is quite obvious from his actions. His deceitful and disgraceful behaviour towards the Princess Victoria was only crowned when he was dying. Then, according to his daughter-in-law, Mrs Henry Conroy, he had the audacity to gaze at a portrait of Queen Victoria and sink back on his pillows for the last time saying: 'I did my duty!'

Conroy, who had a family of six children to support, was the Duchess's close confidant and in the years that followed there were many in high places who believed that he became her lover. Indeed when the Princess Victoria was ten years of age she had an unmistakable indication of the extent to which her mother had fallen under John Conroy's spell when the middle-aged and much-loved lady-in-waiting Baroness Späth was dismissed. She had been with the Duchess for a quarter of a century as friend and companion. She had helped the Duchess after the deaths of each of her husbands; she had travelled with the Duke and Duchess to England and had watched at the bedside of the dying Duke at Sidmouth. During the early days at Kensington — so full of anxiety and poverty — she had loyally remained at her mistress's side, uncomplaining and always ready to help with sympathy and kind words and deeds. Now, all of a sudden it seemed, she was too German, her manner left much to be desired, she spoiled the infant Princess, and she talked too much. Perhaps the real reason lay in the latter criticism for no less a person than the Duke of Wellington was among those who were convinced that the young Victoria had witnessed 'some familiarities' between her mother and Conroy. She told the Baroness Späth what she had seen and heard and the Baroness went as far as to remonstrate with the Duchess on the subject. The consequence was that Baroness Späth had to go and it was not for want of trying that Lehzen did not go at the same time.

The dismissal of the Baroness added weight to the whispers of an improper relationship between the Duchess and Conroy but if Lehzen was aware of the affair, as must seem likely, she was wise enough to keep quiet; she was, in the words of a contemporary witness, 'prudent enough not to commit herself'; to keep apart from petty feuds, jealousies and intrigues that seethed and smouldered beneath the surface of Kensington Palace. Lehzen stayed on for the time being. She succeeded in obtaining the powerful protection of George IV and later William IV and although the Duchess of Kent and in particular Conroy were by no means happy at her continued presence in the palace household, there was little they could do in the matter. In 1827 the King, with a rare sense of fairness, created Lehzen a baroness and Conroy a Knight Commander of a Hanoverian order.

That an affair of some sort existed between the Duchess of Kent and John Conroy seems highly likely. Victoria, when she was Queen, once said to Lord Liverpool, regarding Conroy, that she 'knew things of him which rendered it totally impossible for her to place him in any confidential situation near her . . . things which entirely took away her confidence in him . . . things she knew herself without any other person informing her.' And diarist Charles Greville says that the early exclusion of Sir John Conroy seems to prove that Queen Victoria believed Conroy to be her mother's lover.

By all accounts Conroy had a coarse, familiar manner with women; he was certainly dishonest, and he struck up an intimate relationship with the tragic Princess Sophia, the King's sister whose youthful 'fall from grace' had probably contributed to her unbalanced character. Conroy's friendship with her was described as 'chère amie' and it was through her good offices that Conroy was knighted.

George IV's own disastrous marriage had caused embarrassment and awkwardness to the country time and time again. It is said that when he first set eyes on Caroline of Brunswick, he called urgently for brandy; while the bride always swore that the groom spent their wedding night lying on the floor in a drunken stupor. They had separated within months of the wedding and from her house at Blackheath she provided endless fodder for the gossip-mongers. Abroad she turned up at parties in a state of near nudity accompanied by a handsome Italian gigolo, and in June 1820 her arrival at Dover, bent on claiming her rights as the Queen Consort, convulsed

35

the country with reverberating scandal and culminated in a trial.

Caroline was staying in South Audley Street when disorderly crowds, most seeing her as the persecuted victim of an unpopular administration, demonstrated, smashing windows and blazoning such slogans as 'No Queen, no King!' and generally making their cause so noisily obvious that the King, irritable with gout, promptly retreated to Windsor. From there he offered a compromise settlement, which was refused. Hoping at last for a divorce, the King flatly refused to recognize Caroline as his consort and threatened to abdicate before he allowed her name to be included in the liturgy. The Government, under Lord Liverpool, had no option but to bring in a Bill of Pains and Penalties, designed to prove Caroline's adultery with her Italian paramour and so dissolve her marriage and deprive her of her title. The subsequent 'trial', which settled nothing, did not improve the image of the royal family in the eyes of the populace but soon afterwards Parliament decreed that the Queen not only be excluded from the Prayer Book but also from the coronation — a magnificent event that is chiefly remembered for the ludicrous spectacle of Caroline trying repeatedly but unsuccessfully to gain admittance to Westminster Abbey.

Soon the Duchess of Kent and her two daughters spent two months at Bognor, described at the time as a 'secluded watering place', gathering 'a store of health for the ensuing winter'. The Princess Victoria is said to have much enjoyed 'a regular course of sea-bathing'. She evidently thought more of that 'watering place' than did her grandson George V who convalesced at Bognor and whose dying words are said to have been 'Bugger Bognor'.

The Duchess of Kent was shrewd and capable and did everything she could to ensure that she gained the Regency and to protect her daughter. There is little doubt that she was led to believe that the Duke of Cumberland (a possible alternative Regent) actually had designs on Victoria's life. Such fears were encouraged by Conroy.

Conroy attempted to further his aims of power by making sure that there was a complete rift between Kensington and the court. He hoped to do this by feeding the frightened and bewildered Duchess of Kent with all manner of tales purporting to suggest that the Duke of Cumberland had designs on Victoria, thus persuading the Duchess, who had no reason to love her English relations, to avoid the court. The Duke, it was said, was hatching a plot to remove the only life that stood between him and the throne and it was thought that he would seek to weaken the little Princess's health with small doses of poison, introduced into her food by a bribed servant, so that the public would become accustomed to the idea that she was a sickly child; then at the right moment Cumberland would have her kidnapped and she would surface at court before declining in health, to no one's surprise, and finally dying.

The Duchess was horrified, for the Duke of Cumberland with his horribly scarred face looked just like a murderer. Had he not allied himself to a twice-widowed German princess who was rumoured to have murdered her previous husbands? Furthermore he was said to be vicious, incestuous, perverted, and reactionary.

Conroy was helped by exaggerated newspaper reports about the Princess's childhood ailments. For example her legs and feet were said to be so diseased that walking was almost impossible. To counteract such rumours Conroy and the Duchess made sure that the Princess took exercise in public, and day after day the Duchess and her daughter would walk from the gates of Kensington Gardens to Apsley House and back in full view of the public.

Apsley House, presented to the revered Duke of Wellington by a grateful country, now houses the Wellington Museum. In the days when the Duke was so unpopular that he was totally besieged, he had iron shutters fixed over his windows which he kept fastened for the rest of his life. One night the worried Duke was preparing for bed when he said he met a ghost, dressed in outsize armour, walking along a passage at Apsley House, a figure that he recognized as Oliver Cromwell. The figure seemed to be pointing a warning finger towards the crowds outside and the Duke decided to change his mind about the Reform Bill that was making him so unpopular and he persuaded the Lords to let the Bill pass. Years later, when he knew of Victoria's interest in such matters, he told her of his one memorable encounter with a ghost at Apsley House.

Quoting private information from a descendant of Queen Victoria, Hector Bolitho believed that Cumberland was capable of any crime and that he may even have engineered the deaths of Princess Charlotte and her baby. Bolitho accepted that Cumberland was almost certainly responsible for the murder of his valet in St James's Palace; a murder that gave rise to a horrific ghost story that Victoria never tired of relating to her grandchildren.

The murder came to light when the blood-drenched figure of little Sellis, Cumberland's Italian valet, was found propped up in bed with his throat cut from ear to ear. It seems that Cumberland, on the night of 31 May 1810, returned to his chambers at the palace after a visit to the opera and a night of debauchery. Almost immediately the sounds of shouts, cursing and scufflling were heard by the startled servants, but they were used to such sounds and disturbances and they knew better than to interfere. After a while things quietened down and then the Duke called for Yew, his other valet. Yew found Cumberland standing in the middle of the room, cool and composed, but his shirt-front was covered with blood and his bloodstained sword lay on the floor at his feet.

Cumberland stated that he had been set upon as he had entered the apartment and had only succeeded in driving off his assailant at the expense of being seriously wounded himself and he instructed Yew to fetch the distinguished physician Sir Henry Halford at once. The doctor arrived within minutes and found, to his surprise in view of what he had been told, that the Duke's wounds were superficial in the extreme, the only deep cut being on the Duke's sword hand.

By the time the wounds were dressed to the Duke's satisfaction and the room had been restored to its accustomed elegance, more than two hours had passed since Cumberland had returned to the palace and he now asked Yew to fetch Sellis. Yew's sworn statement tells of him going straight to Sellis's room and there finding the valet propped up in bed against the headboard, his head almost severed from his body by a frightful gash, and a razor, saturated with blood, at the opposite end of the room — too far from the body to have been used by Sellis himself or to have been thrown away by him in such a condition.

At the subsequent inquest Cumberland maintained that Sellis had tried to murder him and had then committed suicide; an unlikely suggestion in view of the fact that while the Duke was large-boned and heavy, Sellis was small and slight. Cumberland had seduced Sellis's daughter who had committed suicide when she found that she was expecting his child, and in order to silence the indignant manservant it seems that Cumberland had attacked the poor man while he was in bed, holding him by the hair with one hand while he cut his throat with the other. He had then gashed himself with the razor before throwing it down and returning to his own room to disarrange the furniture, bloody the sword and generally act as though he had been attacked. Cumberland was disliked in London before the Sellis affair, and although the matter was hushed up as much as possible, afterwards he was openly booed in the streets and so hated that he hardly dared to show his face in public.

And the haunting? Well, from time to time scuffling noises, the sound of two men cursing and the sickly-sweet smell of blood is said to return to the area of the palace once occupied by Cumberland and his servants, and sometimes the awful spectre of Sellis with his throat cut, body and bedclothes drenched with blood, has been encountered at St James's Palace, which is so full of history that it would be surprising if it did not harbour a dozen ghosts.

Small wonder that Victoria's mother was terrified for her daughter's safety and it is a fact that the little Princess was kept in isolation from all but the Kensington circle; she slept in her mother's bed, and continued to do so every night of her life until she became Queen; she was never allowed a moment's solitude and was accompanied everywhere and at all times. Her Journal, which she faithfully kept every day, was noticeably lacking in anything of which she thought her mother might disapprove. It was a difficult childhood by any standards.

George IV died on 26 June 1830. The 'Prince of Pleasure' was mourned by few and certainly not by the Duchess of Kent who knew the power of his spite and the hurt of his tongue. The new King, William IV, was far more preferable. Having no legitimate children of his own — although numerous bastards — he was prepared to welcome the young Victoria and her mother to court and to acknowledge the former as his heir. Nonetheless the Duchess of Kent and John Conroy still only felt secure as long as they maintained their hold over the Princess and they would not allow her any sort of independence or let her make friends with anyone who might be unfriendly to them. She was guarded every moment; she could not walk up or down stairways without her governess holding her by the hand; and the educational curriculum was so strict and severe that at the age of twelve Victoria was on the edge of a nervous breakdown. Interestingly enough, Prince Albert followed in the same mould. He held the key to the nursery quarters on his chain and oversaw every hour of the working day, setting standards in education which his eldest son could never attain.

Victoria must have been aware of being between two opposing factions and it could well be that this was the beginning of her inner conflict and outer stoniness which was foreign to her nature and undoubtedly damaging. Her Uncle Leopold had become King of the Belgians and the young Princess, who had once shown her spirit by being adept at creating and enjoying tantrums and storms, now dreaded the scenes created by her mother. Her only outward reaction seems to have been silent withdrawal, the patience repeatedly advised by Lehzen. But bitterness and resentment were building up behind the passive exterior.

The impassiveness and withdrawal extended to her relationship with the new King who was irritated by the apparent rejection of his friendship, but he had matters of state on his mind — a general revolution was a distinct possibility at this time and his coronation was in the offing.

This event provided yet another opportunity for the Duchess of Kent to attempt to exert her somewhat limited power in the royal hierarchy. Learning that Victoria's place in the procession at the coronation would be after the King's brothers, she demanded that as heir presumptive Victoria should precede the royal Dukes. When they would not give way, she announced that neither she nor her daughter would attend the coronation. The official reason given, that it would be too much of a strain on the Princess's health, did not fool anyone and the national papers were full of the 'systematic opposition' on the part of the Duchess of Kent to the feelings of the King, some pointing out that while her not being present was merely disrespectful, the absence of the Princess Victoria 'cannot fail to be considered by the public as indecent and offensive'. The Duchess of Kent was doing her daughter and herself no good; the Duchess was openly referred to as 'a tiresome devil' and Victoria, in the very centre of all this wrangling, was of course the person who suffered most. 'Nothing could console me,' she wrote years later. 'Not even my dolls.' While Lehzen comforted the girl as best she could the newspapers questioned the Duchess of Kent's 'advisers', by which they meant John Conroy, who the growing Princess knew well enough was as much to blame as her mother.

In later years Victoria was to refer to her 'sad, dull childhood', and perhaps it was in many ways. It was certainly a curious and unsettled one and if, as some authorities assert, many of the emotional problems of the adult stem from a childhood inability to establish consistent and good feelings towards those in authority over them, perhaps Victoria's later problems in facing and accepting the death of Albert do indeed spring from that odd upbringing at Kensington Palace. But Victoria's childhood memories also included pleasant occasions — those daily outings, for example, when she became one of the sights of London, a bonny child with glowing cheeks and prominent blue eyes, often appearing with Dickey, a donkey presented to her by the Duke of York. Sometimes she would ride the animal and at other times drive it harnessed to a little carriage. On other occasions she would be seen running briskly hand in hand with Feodora, the Princess's fair hair blowing in the breeze; and she would brightly pass the time of day with anyone she met. Another lasting memory of Victoria was her fourth birthday when her uncle King George IV presented her with a miniature of herself set in diamonds.

Another happy memory from her childhood days must have been summer holidays at Tunbridge Wells or Ramsgate; running and playing on the sands; walking and running in the shallow sea (wearing thick boots over her shoes!) and, very occasionally, being allowed to play for a little while with other children — as long as they were the children of gentlefolk.

While visiting Tunbridge Wells the little Princess may have seen her first ghost. The common there has been haunted for more than two hundred years by a singular apparition and I am told that such a figure was encountered by the royal party one afternoon. The form is that of a tremendously broad person, clothed in a long grey gown with what look like frills around the bottom. It is thought to be the ghost of a local character, enormous Mary Jenings, a drunkard who died when she was about thirty in 1736. She was described by a contemporary as 'not unlike a barrel'.

Victoria rarely forgot or forgave. Soon after her accession as Queen she sent for John Conroy, consoled him with a pension and expelled him from her court. 'How is it possible,' she pointed out to Lord

Melbourne, 'that I can have any confidence in my mother when I know that whatever I say to her is repeated immediately to that man?' A month later the Queen moved to Buckingham Palace. It should not be overlooked that Victoria's mother (as D. M. Stuart points out in his *Mother of Victoria*, 1941) had 'quite a pretty psychological problem of double-personality' and it is a fact that before 1829 and after 1840 we look in vain for the arrogant and scheming woman friend of John Conroy and find instead only 'the gentlest creature one can ever imagine'. In a letter dated 27 March 1861 Queen Victoria wrote to Crown Princess Augusta of Prussia after the death of Victoire: 'To lose a beloved mother is always terrible . . . but when you consider that this mother has lived for no one and nothing but me, that for forty-one years I have never been separated from her for more than three months, that she was the gentlest, most tender and loving creature that one can ever imagine, and that her heart, like none other, was always full of loving kindness.' Read in association with some of the terrible things that Victoire did to her daughter one begins to feel that the Duchess of Kent was not the only one with a psychological problem.

Louise Lehzen had replaced the governess 'Boppy' (Mrs Brock) when Victoria was five and over many years had become a power to be reckoned with; she could do no wrong in her mistress's eyes. Victoria's marriage changed all that. Lehzen never got on with Albert and little more than two years after the wedding Lehzen, who in more than twenty years with Victoria had never even taken a day's holiday, was sent packing to Bückeburg where she had a sister. Heartbroken as Lehzen must have been, she still thought first of her dear Victoria and slipped away without saying 'Goodbye' in order to spare the Queen any distress. Victoria wrote that she did feel sad but agreed with dearest Albert that it was perhaps 'for our and her best'.

In the early days Lehzen could see that the fatherless child whom almost everyone worshipped was being thoroughly spoiled. Victoria had the well-known Hanoverian temper and 'overflowing animal spirits' (as Alison Plowden has put it) and from time to time the sweet little girl was likely to burst into a screaming fit or a violent explosion of rage in which, it was noticed by the more observant, Victoria herself took more than a little pride.

Later in life Victoria took as much pride in being different from other people; in being something of a mystery; and in herself endeavouring to unravel some of the mysteries of life and death. Perhaps after all she had her mother to thank for that adventurous and inquiring and determined attitude.

CHAPTER TWO

ITINERARIES AND INTRIGUES – EARLY INTERESTS AND DIFFICULTIES

One of the places Princess Victoria was taken most frequently for 'long walks' as prescribed by her doctors, during her youth, was Hampstead Heath. She was usually accompanied by the two daughters of John Conroy, Jane and Victoire, Lady Flora Hastings (who was to be the cause of great anguish to Victoria some years later and whom she regarded as one of Conroy's spies) and 'dear Lehzen'.

Victoria was frequently bored on these walks but she never tired of visiting the quaintly named 'Spaniard's Inn', then a modest, creeper-covered house with an atmosphere that reeked of colourful figures such as Dick Turpin and exciting times such as the threat of the Spanish Armada.

The Spaniard's Inn seems to have strong connections with Dick Turpin. Legend has it that many a time he used the cellars of the inn to evade the Bow Street runners, and the little window in the staircase is reputed to be the one through which food was passed to him as he lay in hiding. When I was there a few years ago the inn had on display a number of Turpin mementoes including the knife and fork he was using when he was eventually captured and the leg-irons in which he was confined before his execution.

All this interested Victoria intensely but she was even more intrigued by the undoubted fact that successive occupants of the house and later landlords at the inn all heard unaccountable sounds resembling horses' hooves, especially at dead of night. And then there were the stories and the mysteries associated with the wonderful old house. No one seemed to know where it got its name; possibly from the Spanish Armada, for it is thought to date from the same year as that event; possibly because the Spanish Ambassador to James I stayed at the house; or possibly from two Spanish brothers who lived there years ago and who fought a duel over a girl, a duel that saw the death of one of the brothers. One authority on inn signs, G. J. Manson-

Fitzjohn, says in his *Quaint Signs of Old Inns* that before the premises became an inn it was a house used as the Spanish Embassy and the 'dark-complexioned Spanards so impressed themselves on the minds of the natives of Hampstead' that they always referred to the house as 'The Spaniards'. Nor did the young Princess Victoria disbelieve the many reports, some ten or more by 1836, that the ghostly form of Dick Turpin riding a phantom Black Bess had been seen galloping across Hampstead Heath towards The Spaniards.

As a young girl Victoria accompanied her mother on several 'journeyings' to see something of the land and the people she would in all probability reign over; excursions that took her to places like Leamington Spa, Birmingham, Gloucester, Bath, Devizes, Salisbury, Southampton and Portsmouth.

One 'royal progress', as it was called, headed for Wales by way of St Albans, Dunstable, Stoney Stratford, Towcester, Daventry, Braunston, Dimchurch and Coventry. At St Albans Victoria would have been told one of the oldest recorded ghost stories in the county, dating from the fourteenth century, when a monk of the Benedictine Order of St Albans Abbey encountered a ghost in the Chapter House. A 'horrible thing', it is recorded, was sitting on the Abbot's throne, a spectral form that claimed to have once been a monk itself but now suffered eternally for indulging in three sins, slander, lying and quarrelling. After intimating as much the fiendish form then 'rose up' and disappeared from the Chapter House. There is no doubt that such stories delighted Victoria and had their effect upon her; certainly, all her life afterwards she was averse to slander, lying and quarrelling.

The young Princess with her inquiring mind would have been fascinated to hear that phantom monks had been seen at the old abbey, sometimes in broad daylight, and that the sound of chanting and the singing of Matins had been heard at the odd time of two o'clock in the morning. She would have been interested too in the sounds of battle that were heard at Battlefield House. St Albans was the scene of the first of the battles in the Wars of the Roses and on 22 May 1495 the Yorkists and Lancastrians met face to face, with between them Battlefield House near the Lancastrian defence line. The Yorkists, led by Warwick, won that battle and captured King Henry VI in the process. An Elizabethan half-timbered house was built on the site of the former property and there, it was said, the sound of galloping horses, the clash of steel and other sounds of primitive combat were heard for centuries afterwards.

At Dunstable Victoria would have heard the story of Sally the ghost witch. According to local legend she was troublesome enough when alive but even more so after her death! She was burnt alive and died with a curse on her lips. Before long her ghost reportedly returned, manifesting in the old Priory Church of St Peter, founded in 1131, where she became such an annoyance that a 'ghost catcher' was employed who, with great difficulty it is said, eventually succeeded in luring the ghost witch into a bottle which was quickly corked. The ghost catcher warned the assembled monks that 'if the bottle is broken, out the wicked ghost shall flee, and shall plague you ten times more than she ever did before'. The bottle, with Sally's ghost inside, was buried in the Priory churchyard and the story goes that years later, when the place of burial had been forgotten, burials were no longer made in the churchyard for fear of accidentally breaking the bottle and releasing the ghost of the witch.

At Stoney Stratford inquiries would have elicited the fact that a house nearby, once an inn, had long been haunted by a phantom man on horseback and a pair of lovers. Elsewhere on her journey the Princess Victoria would have heard various and equally intriguing ghost stories: at Shrewsbury and at Welshpool, where the Earl of Powys waited to greet them, they would have heard the famous ghost story associated with the Red Castle, that enormous, impressive, gloomy and atmospheric castle reputed to harbour several ghosts.

Later, at Caernarvon, the royal party was met by a happy crowd of onlookers and by the firing of a salute, arranged by the Corporation as their carriage was accompanied into the town.

After a couple of months in Anglesey where the Princess much enjoyed the riding and sailing, the royal party returned home by way of Chester with its holy River Dee that never claimed a sacrifice and never hides a drowned body and the seventy Wishing Steps that lead up to the town walls. To ensure that a wish comes true or that they will enjoy a happy love affair, girls make a wish at the bottom of the steps and then run up and down the steps without drawing breath. Victoria merely looked with interest at the Wishing Steps and opened the Victoria Bridge over the river.

After somewhat strenuous visits to the Devonshires at Chatsworth and the Shrewsburys at Alton Towers the party paid a state visit to Oxford where they were 'most warmly and enthusiastically' welcomed by the undergraduates.

At Oxford Victoria would have heard of the haunted reputation of Manchester College, among many others. When I was there lecturing a few years ago I heard all about the stories of the ghost of Bishop Bonner, Chaplain to Cardinal Wolsey, and of an unidentified Grey Lady in Room 29. Among other 'curiosities', the Princess saw at the Bodleian Queen Elizabeth's Latin exercise book written when she was only thirteen — the age of Victoria herself during that visit to Oxford, which probably encouraged her in what was to become a lifelong habit, keeping a Journal.

During one of her later 'journeyings' Princess Victoria was drawn in an open carriage, escorted by the Dorsetshire Yeomanry, through enthusiastic crowds to stay at Lord Ilchester's seat, Melbury, with its two lions standing upon their gate-piers at the entrance to the drive: lions, the young Princess was fascinated to learn, that were reputed to come alive at midnight and go for a drink in the lake! Did she recall those lions and their drinking habits and the saying about 'When the lions drink, then London is in danger' thirty years later? For when the Thames Embankment was built in the 1860s, lions' heads were incorporated on the walls of the embankments so that when the Thames is in flood these lions may indeed be said to be drinking!

More than once the royal party went to the Isle of Wight and when they did so they usually made their headquarters at haunted Norris Castle near Cowes. Here, for many, many years, there were reports of the ghostly footsteps of an elderly butler shuffling along a certain passage; most often the sounds would be heard when any visitors to the castle were at dinner and the youthful Victoria must have hoped they would be heard while she was there. On one occasion when the footsteps were plain and unmistakable it is reported that an intrepid admiral and his wife left the dinner party and quietly made their way to the haunted corridor but all they saw was an empty passageway although the sound of footsteps could still be heard perambulating there!

By 1834, when Victoria was fifteen years old, the Duchess of Kent was still treating her as a young child with no mind of her own and no say in such matters as her own ladies-in-waiting. Without consulting Victoria or anyone else the Duchess, together with Lehzen and the Conroys, decamped for a long holiday in Tunbridge Wells. In fact, Victoria enjoyed it immensely, not only the town itself but the surrounding villages as well. There Princess Victoria would have heard, with undisguised glee, about the ghostly headless horsemen that haunted a pathway in the area of Rusthall that was occupied by Cromwellian forces during the Civil War; of the property in Southborough haunted by the ghost of Queen Caroline, the unhappy wife of George IV, who stayed at the house with her little daughter the Princess Charlotte late in the eighteenth century; of the spectral monks of Bayham Abbey; and of mysterious Scotney Castle and its singular ghost.

In November the whole party moved to St Leonards-on-Sea where they stayed at the St Leonard's Hotel, now the Royal Victoria Hotel. When I stayed there in 1985 the manager was good enough to provide me with copies of material pertaining to the royal visit and he allowed me to examine various artefacts, including the Visitors Book where, after her signature, Victoria had added the rather pathetic: 'Sorry to go'.

One author writes of this royal visit as 'one of the greatest events in Hastings' history' and the residents certainly went out of their way to make the visit a memorable one. A royal salute was fired from the East Hill and they were welcomed by the Mayor, William Scrivens. A grand procession was formed, headed by horsemen and trumpeters, with the Mayor leading and members of the Corporation behind the royal carriages; a huge gathering of the town's inhabitants followed and the band of the local Friendly Society.

The following day an address was presented by the Mayor hoping that the 'genial climate of the neighbourhood would induce the party to make a lengthy stay' and assuring them of the town's loyalty. In reply the Duchess of Kent said:

> The Princess and myself feel most grateful for such marks of intent and regard, which your Loyalty to the King leads you to evince towards us, as Members of his Family. My maternal feelings, and those I owe to the country, warmly respond to the interest you express for the Princess: Providence seems to have destined Her to fill a great Station; (you will believe how anxiously I pray it may be at a very distant day;) and if She should do so, I am confident that She will always feel and act as a Constitutional Sovereign, called to preside over the destinies of a free and loyal People.

That night there was a public dinner at the Swan Inn and an exhibition of fireworks, mostly rockets but including an unusual 'vertical coloured wheel which changed to a boa constrictor in pursuit of a butterfly in white and yellow lights', surrounded by crimson wheels and ending with a 'variegated wheel, changing to a Royal Star, surmounted by a Ducal Coronet, and the initials of their Royal Highnesses, surrounded by alternate crimson, green and purple Suns'.

During this visit an accident happened that could have altered the course of history. The carriage containing Princess Victoria, her mother, the faithful Lehzen and Lady Flora Hastings (Victoria's recently appointed lady-in-waiting) was proceeding along the promenade when the horses suddenly took fright and bolted, completely out of the postilion's control. After galloping some distance, to the distress of the occupants and to the horror of bystanders, one of the horses became entangled in the traces and fell, slowing the carriage to such a speed that a workman on the scene, one Thomas Ranger, ran up and seized the other horse and brought the carriage to a stop.

For a few moments there was a danger that the kicking and struggling of the horses might overturn the carriage but a gentleman, Peckham Micklethwaite, appeared on the scene and helped Princess Victoria and her mother and the other occupants out of the swaying carriage as fast as he could. Victoria's first thoughts seem to have been for 'poor dear little Dash', her pet dog who was understandably terrified. The Princess took him in her arms and ran away from the mêlée, calling to the others to follow her. As the traces were being cut, one of the horses escaped and bolted off down the road, while the royal party took refuge behind a wall.

Altogether a very frightening experience and Victoria recorded later that they all felt 'most grateful to Almighty God for His merciful providence' in thus preserving them 'for it was a very narrow escape'. Could it have been this 'narrow escape' that heightened Victoria's awareness to the nearness of death, one wonders, and to an even greater interest in what lay beyond?

Thomas Ranger was warmly thanked and disappeared, which is perhaps just as well for it seems that he was a shoemaker by trade, a publican in practice and a noted smuggler *sub rosa*! Micklethwaite, however, was careful to make sure that the royal visitors knew his name and where he could be found; indeed it is said that he pressed his claim for some notice to be taken of his action on the Prime Minister to the extent that he asked for a knighthood. At all events, four years later he was created a baronet. Later it is recorded that he became a prominent figure in the county, even rising to High Sheriff for Sussex.

The following month the Duchess and her daughter became patrons of the Society of St Leonard's Archers and the following year they presented an embroidered silk banner, designed by the Princess, as well as two challenge cups, the Royal Victoria prizes, for the highest scores each year. After her succession to the throne Victoria continued her patronage and gave permission for the society to bear the title The Queen's Royal St Leonard's Archers. In 1840 Prince Albert also became a patron.

For her sixteenth birthday — about which Victoria wrote: 'How very old that sounds, but I feel that the two years to come till I attain my 18 are the most important of any almost . . .' — the Princess received a stream of callers and dozens of wonderful presents including lockets from Feodora, a gold and turquoise bracelet from Uncle Sussex, a 'very kind' letter from the Queen and a prayer book presented by 'a bookseller of the name of Hatchard'.

The time had come for Victoria to be confirmed and although this sacred occasion was marred by provocation and blatant breach of etiquette by her mother, eventually Victoria prepared herself for the 'special occasion', among her solemn declarations being 'to try and comfort my dear Mamma in all her grief, trials and anxieties, and to become a dutiful and affectionate daughter to her . . .' In the event Princess Victoria was 'frightened to death' and almost 'drowned in her own tears'; nor was she pleased when she learned later the same day that in future she was to keep her beloved Lehzen 'at a distance'. There was also mention of the fact that she would remain under the 'guidance' of her mother until the age of 'either eighteen or twenty-one'. Royal personages had always come of age at eighteen; was her restricted life to be extended beyond the usual?

The year 1835 saw the Kents on another of their 'journeys'. This time, after strenuous travelling which upset Victoria, who had been feeling poorly before they set out, the caravan reached York, which was somewhat further north than royalty usually travelled at this time. There, at that notoriously haunted town, Victoria would have heard more about ghosts and ghostly happenings in a few days than she had heard in her whole life up to that point.

In his *Ghosts of an Ancient City*, John Mitchell recounts the stories associated with Holy Trinity Church, Micklegate, with its three distinct and daytime ghosts; the old Mansion House with its ghost of a man in working clothes; a ghostly funeral; the Lady in White at All Saints' Church; a phantom duellist; the sounds of murder at the mansion in Spurriergate; three headless ghosts; the music-loving ghost in the Shambles; the Grey Lady of the Theatre Royal; several ghosts at the King's Manor; the ghost children of Bedern; Nance, the helpful ghost; haunted Beningbrough Hall; the ghosts of the Treasurer's House; and many more. Indeed one writer has said that most of the streets of York have their own particular ghost and certainly the official residence of the Archbishop, just outside the city, has a strange story associated with it that Princess Victoria would have thoroughly enjoyed.

The Elizabethan house, long since demolished, has been described as a house of baronial dimensions and, like Glamis, had a peculiar secret that was passed on to the head of the family, generation after generation, and was known to no one else. It seems that the last holder of the secret died suddenly before being able to pass it on. Following a curious custom that is to be found in many parts of the world, the coffin of this lady was passed out through a hole made specially in the wall of the estate, after which the hole was bricked up. This was supposed to prevent the ghost of the departed finding its way back to the ancestral home. A few nights after she had been buried a member of the family was awakened by the sounds of hurrying footsteps and sobbing. The time was past midnight and he got out of bed to see whether anything was visible that might account for the very frightening sounds. It was a cold night with an almost full moon and as he looked out of the window he saw clearly the figure of a woman on the other side of the estate wall. She had long hair that hung down over her white dress and with a sudden feeling of horror he recognized his recently dead relative. As he watched, the figure passed to and fro, back and forth, as if seeking a way back to the house. The sight was distressing as well as frightening and the reluctant viewer returned mournfully to his bed.

Thereafter, it was said, the same ghostly figure was seen on numerous occasions by many people and although the lady never found her way through the estate wall and back into the house, the unease and distress caused by her frequent appearances resulted in the remaining inhabitants eventually leaving the house and later, some time after Victoria's visit, having it demolished.

After visiting Castle Howard and attending a music festival at the haunted York Minster, where Victoria found Handel's *Messiah* 'heavy and tiresome', the party proceeded to Harewood House and then to Wentworth, passing through Leeds, Wakefield and Barnsley, all full of cheering crowds, waving flags and pealing bells. The Princess, however, found this particular journey irksome and it was noticed by many observers that she looked pale, nervous and that she was unusually quiet.

On they went to Belvoir Castle and Burghley House where a grand ball was held but Victoria excused herself on account of a 'dreadful headache' after the first dance and she went to bed. Then on they travelled to Peterborough, Wisbech and King's Lynn where the loyal inhabitants unharnessed the horses and themselves drew the royal carriage round the town! On to Holkham Hall where a magnificent dinner was prepared but again Victoria retired early to her bed, being 'considerably fatigued'; however there was not far to go now and after a brief visit to the Duke and Duchess of Grafton at Euston Hall they returned to Kensington. 'I liked some of the places very well,' Victoria recalled in her Journal. 'But I was much tired by the long journey and the great crowds we had to encounter . . .' The memory of these gruelling early 'tours' never left Victoria and probably accounts for the fact that she did not travel greatly through the British Isles.

September saw the royal party at Ramsgate again where they were joined by the Duchess's brother Leopold, King of the Belgians, and his young wife who was only seven years older than Victoria. 'What a happiness it was for me,' enthuses Victoria, 'to throw myself in the arms of that *dearest* of Uncles who has always been to me like a father, and whom I love so *very much!*' But still Victoria was feeling unwell and later in the month a medical remedy was sought. She was treated for a month and then seems to have thrown off the infection, whatever it may have been, a 'bilious fever', typhoid or septic tonsils, but not before she began to go bald and her cheeks became pinched, her chin sharp and, the seventeen-year-old girl told herself, her eyes those of an anxious old woman!

Meanwhile John Conroy was determined to become Victoria's private secretary. King William was over seventy, Victoria must soon become Queen and who better to look after her interests than her mother's confidant, a trusted friend of many years. Victoria, still weak and feeling ill, refused to discuss the matter. Conroy, seeing his chances slip away, insisted that she must promise to place herself unreservedly in his hands when she came to the throne, and he requested a written pledge to this effect. He prepared the necessary papers and, presenting them to her, said she must sign, and now. Victoria summoned all her strength and resisted Conroy. 'No,' she said, again and again. 'No, No,' and she did not sign. 'I resisted in spite of my illness,' she wrote some time afterwards. But it had been a terrifying ordeal for the girl whose growing suspicions and increasing worries about the relationship that existed between her mother and John Conroy seemed to be all too well-founded. It was undeniably a most powerful and strong hold that Conroy had over the Duchess of Kent, so strong, indeed, 'that it would once have been called witchcraft'.

Now Victoria was concerned that she should find full and complete health and she religiously followed the doctors' prescription: not to study for too long at a time; to stand at a desk rather than sit; to change position frequently; to take a warm bath twice a week; to use Indian clubs to improve her circulation; and to sleep in a ventilated room. Over the next month or so her health improved significantly, perhaps assisted by bracing walks in the areas of Finchley and Hampstead Heath.

In March 1836 the Saxe-Coburgs visited Windsor and, as ever, Victoria was in raptures: Ferdinand was tall and very good-looking with beautiful dark eyes and Augustus was also tall and very handsome, 'a dear good young man'. When Ferdinand left, ten days later, Victoria was writing, '. . . I love him *so* much, he is *so* excellent . . .' But within weeks there was another family visit. Uncle Leopold was bringing to England Victoria's cousins, Ernst and Albert, sons of the Duchess of Kent's eldest brother, Duke Ernest Saxe-Coburg-Gotha. Leopold made no secret of that fact that he was planning a match between one of them and Victoria who, at eighteen, was perhaps the greatest heiress in Europe. King William, however, did not look with undivided favour on the spreading influence of the house of Coburg and when his ministers suggested that the wishes of Victoria herself might lie elsewhere, he hastily invited the Prince of Orange to visit England with his two sons.

Victoria, however, was not amused by the Orange boys; 'they look heavy, dull and frightened and are not at all prepossessing,' she wrote. Her cousins Ernst and Albert, on the other hand, received kinder treatment in her Journal. Ernst was 'tall with dark hair and fine eyes . . .' while Albert was 'extremely handsome, his hair is about the same colour as mine, his eyes are large and blue, and he has a beautiful nose' . . . and so on and so on. Within days she was writing of her cousins: 'The more I see them . . . the more I love them . . .' Soon she and Albert were playing the piano and singing together and she was confiding to her Journal such phrases as 'I love Ernst and Albert more than

Ferdinand and Augustus . . . Dearest Albert . . . they are both very clever . . . particularly Albert . . . so very, very merry and gay and happy, like young people ought to be.'

Although there could be no question of a marriage or even engagement before Victoria's eighteenth birthday and perhaps not even then (if Conroy had his way), Uncle Leopold was only one of those who made no secret of the fact that he would welcome 'an understanding' between the couple, to safeguard Victoria against other, unwelcome, suitors. Victoria was not in love with Albert in 1836 but she 'approved' of him; 'He would do' very well, and she intimated as much to Uncle Leopold.

Conroy and the Duchess of Kent, aware that time was running out for them, again tried to influence Victoria who was now nearing her eighteenth birthday. Somehow, Conroy told himself, he must convince or force Victoria to accept that a young lady of eighteen could not and should not rule unaided, that he and her mother the Duchess of Kent were the most suitable and indeed the only persons capable of taking charge and she must ask for an extension of the period of regency. With this aim in view Prince Charles of Leiningen, the Duchess of Kent's son, was inveigled into seeing Leopold and endeavouring to convince him of Conroy's indispensability.

King Leopold I of the Belgians found himself in something of a quandary. He knew how he wished to guide Victoria but he also knew that he had to be careful to avoid any suggestion of being the cause of anything like a break between Victoria and her mother. In the climate of the period, motherhood and widowhood were sacred. In the end Leopold decided to send Baron Stockmar to support Princess Victoria during the crucial period following her reaching her majority and also, if at all possible, to explore all ways of reaching a compromise acceptable to the Duchess of Kent and John Conroy.

Baron Stockmar was a doctor and friend of the Coburgs, and as King Leopold's private secretary and political adviser he seems to have directed affairs of state without becoming himself involved. At one time he was so powerful that he was the only person who was permitted to enter and leave the homes of British royalty without notice and virtually as he wished. It was Stockmar who stood beside the young Victoria when she ascended the throne; it was he who changed Albert from an insipid and listless music lover to the suave opera addict with whom Victoria fell in love; and it was he who dealt with the problem of the Prime Minister, Lord Melbourne, and Baroness Lehzen exerting an undue influence on Victoria.

Before Stockmar's mission in May 1836 could be accomplished, the King of England offered Victoria an independent income of £10,000 a year and the opportunity of living elsewhere than at Kensington Palace if she so wished. In fact she was offered complete independence on reaching her eighteenth birthday. Conroy and the Duchess, thoroughly alarmed at this turn of events, hastily drafted a letter of reply to the King which they presented to Victoria to copy in her own hand and to sign. In vain she protested and tried to amend the letter; all her protestations were waved aside — she was under age, she must do as she was told, an answer had to be sent at once, and so on. Eventually, under continual pressure from both her mother and Conroy, she did as she was instructed, copying the letter that pointed out her 'youth and inexperience' and stating that she wished to remain as she was, in the care of her dear mother and requesting that any monies that might come to her on her achieving her majority should be given to her dear mother who would use them on her behalf . . .

King William was not deceived for a moment. As soon as he read the letter he said, 'Victoria has not written this letter'; indeed no one within the court circle had any doubt as to the origin of the letter and the fact that the Duchess and Conroy had every intention of continuing to control Victoria as long as they possibly could. Furthermore, the Duchess of Kent wrote to Lord Melbourne, the Prime Minister, suggesting that the country had every confidence in her and she was more than ready to publish the King's letter and show it as a deliberate attempt to separate a devoted mother from a frightened child who had, of her own free will, 'told the King that she desired nothing but to be left as heretofore with her Mother'. The Prime Minister felt it might be prudent to leave the Princess in her mother's care for the time being and he advised the King accordingly. (Lord Melbourne was later to assure Victoria that he had no idea of the bullying she was subjected to at Kensington Palace.) A sort of compromise was worked out and the Duchess of Kent was approached with an offer of splitting the £10,000 between her and her daughter, £6,000 to the Duchess and £4,000 to the Princess. This the Duchess of Kent immediately rejected.

While all this was going on Princess Victoria celebrated her birthday, on 24 May, and to cheering crowds she drove out with her mother, Marie von Klebelsberg (wife of the Prince of Leiningen), and dear Lehzen. Flowers or flags were in every window, bunting crisscrossed the streets, the parks and roadways were thronged with happy people cheering the borough's most distinguished resident. A blue silk banner stretched over the entrance to the palace itself with the single word, 'Victoria', and in the evening, driving to St James's Palace for her birthday ball, it was the same all over again, the courtyards and streets jammed solid with cheering people. Victoria was to write in her Journal that night: '. . . the anxiety of the people to see poor stupid me was very great; and I must say I was quite touched . . .'

Throughout the celebrations the Princess appeared 'very cool and collected' and quite grown-up but, as one observer put it, 'of no height'. The diminutiveness of Victoria was already the cause of comment and her own consciousness of it was to lead to the discreet use of steps, concealed raised platforms, and the employment of small people at court so that she would not appear shorter than those around her.

The world of intrigue and pressure that Stockmar encountered in May 1836 was far more powerful and involved than he had bargained for. Although Victoria still refused to promise Conroy any appointment on her succession to the throne, Stockmar noted that strain from the united forces of Conroy and the Duchess of Kent and Charles Leiningen was beginning to show. In welcoming her uncle Leopold's envoy, Victoria did not disguise the wounds caused by Conroy's 'impudent and insulting conduct', the damage that her natural affection and esteem for her mother had suffered through the Duchess's repeatedly allowing Conroy to insult Victoria in the presence of her mother and the disrespectful way that Conroy treated the Duchess in Victoria's presence. Reported Stockmar: he 'continues the system of intimidation with the genius of a madman, and the Duchess carries out all that she is instructed to do with admirable docility and perseverance . . .' while 'the Princess continues to refuse to give her mother any promise that she will make Conroy her confidential adviser'; but, remarked Stockmar, 'whether she will hold out, Heaven only knows, for they plague her, every hour and every day'.

Now the King lay dying and Conroy tried to get the Prime Minister, Lord Melbourne, to introduce a new Regency Bill; telling the much-respected politician Lord Liverpool that Victoria was mentally unstable and 'younger in intelligence than in years'; she would never be able to manage without a private secretary who knew how to control and guide her and who better than himself, John Conroy. But when he saw Victoria Lord Liverpool was told that apart from the many 'slights and incivilities' she had endured from Conroy, she knew things of him which 'rendered it totally impossible for her to place him in any confidential situation near her . . . things which she knew of herself without any other person informing her'. Still the pressure was kept up and Conroy is known to have encouraged the Duchess 'to bring matters to extremities and to force her daughter to do her will by unkindness and severity'. He even told the Duchess of Kent, in the presence of a witness, that if Victoria would not 'see reason', 'she must be coerced.'

Within a couple of days King William was dead and the news, as every schoolboy knows, was conveyed to Kensington by emissaries from Windsor, the carriage clattering into the quiet courtyard at five o'clock in the morning, awakening the sleeping Princess who appeared, a small child-like figure in a dressing-gown with her hair hanging loose over her shoulders, to learn that she was Queen.

Sometime during that busy day she ordered her bed to be moved out of her mother's room and that night, for the first night in her life, she slept alone, as she was probably to do for forty years after the death of Albert. The 'short, vulgar-looking child' now 'looked very well' and although 'without any pretension to beauty, the gracefulness gave her a very agreeable appearance . . .' 'She has great animal spirits,' wrote diarist Charles Greville, and she soon displayed them by making it very clear that she never wished to see or speak to Conroy again. The Duchess of Kent, consigned overnight to a place in the shadows from which she was never to emerge, was replaced by the King's widow, now the Queen Dowager, on whom Victoria bestowed her especial consideration and great tenderness. Already she seemed to be cutting herself off from her mother whose actions and weaknesses, both politically inclined and sexually stimulated, Victoria abhorred. Did she already experience too some mystical, magical, unmentionable elation and attraction to the recently bereaved Queen Adelaide; was the unrealized attractiveness of death, what may lie beyond and what is left behind, already manifesting itself?

In July 1837 Queen Victoria, as she now was, left Kensington Palace and its ghosts and moved into Buckingham Palace where she made a point of always seeing her ministers alone and she quickly came to look upon her first Prime Minister, William Lamb, second Viscount Melbourne, as a father figure. He was a cultivated and charming man, still strikingly handsome at fifty-eight, and it was not long before the close association between the Queen and her Prime Minister attracted attention; soon there were gibes about 'Mrs Melbourne' and the old suspicions about the Duchess of Kent and her confidential servant were revived and received a new airing. In her Journal the Queen wrote that he 'rode near me the whole time. The more I see of him and the more I know of him, the more I like and appreciate his fine and honest character. I have seen a great deal of him, every day, these last five weeks, and I have always found him in good humour, kind, good, and most agreeable . . . I am very fond of him.' Later she wrote, 'He has become so fatherly, and so affectionate and kind . . . that one must love him.' His marriage to the strange, eccentric and half-crazy Caroline Ponsonby only added romantic appeal to the glamour she already saw in him.

In October 1837, after 'the pleasantest summer I ever passed in my life', the Queen confided to her Journal, the court went to Brighton where Thomas Creevey, the renowned gossip, could hardly take his eyes off 'Vic', as he called her in his diary. 'She laughs in real earnest, opening her mouth as wide as it will go . . . she eats as heartily as she laughs, I think I may say she gobbles . . . She blushes and laughs at every instant . . . Her voice is perfect and so is the expression on her face when she means to say or do a pretty thing.'

When George IV, then Prince of Wales, first set about building his

Marine Pavilion the property commanded a full view of the sea, but as seaside holidays became fashionable the town grew quickly and soon the land between the Pavilion and the sea was covered with villas and small houses. 'I only see a little morsel of the sea from one window,' complained Victoria.

Ten years after that first visit, valuable furniture, decorations, porcelain, clocks and carpets were removed from the Pavilion to Buckingham Palace, Windsor Castle and Kensington Palace over a period of about three years. Some items were sold, even the plants and gardening implements being disposed of, and the place was locked up; but when the Government proposed to demolish the building it met opposition from the town of Brighton where there had always been curiosity concerning the Pavilion and what was left of the contents. In 1849, 27,500 people passed through the shell of the house in a single week and the borough suddenly realized they were sitting on a gold mine. A loan was arranged and the Royal Pavilion became the property of the town, and in 1850 restoration began.

Queen Victoria contributed several valuable chandeliers and paintings, and other members of the royal family followed suit. Some, including a descendant of the Duke of Wellington, helped with substantial donations over the succeeding years until today the Pavilion is close to what 'Prinny' intended it should be.

The Queen never liked Brighton Pavilion which she called 'a strange odd Chinese-looking thing, both inside and out'. Not even the tales of ghosts there could make the place appeal to her although she enjoyed hearing about the ghost of George IV haunting the long subterranean passage and the spectre of Martha Gunn, the Brighton Bather, in the Banqueting Room, and indeed the other ghosts of Brighton such as the phantom nun that haunts The Lanes, the Highwayman at the old coaching inn, The Battle of Waterloo, and haunted Preston Manor.

The coronation on 27 June 1838 had its difficult moments with Victoria asking the Sub-Dean at one stage, 'Pray tell me what I am to do . . .', the Archbishop of Canterbury crushing the ring on the wrong finger, to the Queen's anguished protests, the orb being passed to her too soon and it being so heavy that she nearly dropped it, and 82-year-old Lord Rolle falling and rolling down the steps of the throne. Towards the end of the service the Bishop of Bath and Wells inadvertently turned over two pages at once and prematurely informed the Queen that the ceremony was over . . .

Once the coronation was indeed over something of the extraordinary strain and pressure that the Queen had been under began to show itself in several ways. There were those who said the Queen was losing her prettiness, she looked 'bold' and had a discontented air and she was putting on weight. She admitted to feeling 'cross and low', she had all too frequent sick headaches and for the first time a nervous irritability began to show itself. At such times she would snap and shout at her maids, and sometimes, to her later horror, even find herself irritable with 'dear, kind Melbourne'.

By the autumn of 1838 she was suffering from periods of lethargy and depression and anxiety. She found herself worrying about her weight and her appearance, and her health in general including her eyesight. She worried too about being shy with those she did not know and about her lack of small talk and, perhaps most worrying for all concerned, she became extremely concerned about her youth, her ignorance in so many things and, she thought, her general unsuitability as Queen.

Some people thought that at the bottom of all this anxiety was the fear of losing Melbourne, for the Government of the day was by no means secure. Also at the back of her mind must have been the fact that soon she would be expected to marry Prince Albert and at present she was enjoying, in some ways, her independence too much to be in a hurry to marry anyone. Albert, she indicated, must await her pleasure. Even dear Uncle Leopold, when he began to bring politics into their private correspondence, found her cool towards him.

And always in the shadows lurked John Conroy who had come to hate the chubby, smooth-faced and confident little maiden whom he had once controlled but who now chose to ignore him. He never ceased to make mischief and openly sought revenge for the injustices he felt he had been forced to accept.

Victoria sought solace in the companionship of her beloved Lehzen (who hated Conroy as much as the Queen did) and in the company of her father figure Melbourne; she even went to the length of referring to these two in her Journal as her Mother and Father. Melbourne for his part was shrewd enough to comment at one stage: 'You have got some fixed fancies; Your Majesty has settled in your mind certain things.' Indeed she had.

During the course of the Hastings scandal, when Lady Flora Hastings was thought (especially by the Queen) to be pregnant by John Conroy, when in fact she was dying of cancer, the relationship between Victoria and her mother reached its lowest ebb. The Duchess of Kent sided with her lady-in-waiting Lady Flora when she blamed Baroness Lehzen for starting the whole sorry affair. Victoria became convinced that her mother had never really loved her and she hardly bothered to conceal the fact that she had not a particle of affection or respect for her mother, although she relented somewhat in later years.

Meanwhile the somewhat curious and, to certain people, alarmingly close contact between the nineteen-year-old Queen and the sixty-year-old Lord Melbourne continued. It is accepted by most authorities that Charles Greville was probably right when he observed: 'Melbourne . . . is everything to her. Her feelings which are sexual though she does not know it . . . are of a strength . . . to predominate in her mind with irresistible force.' And already those in the know were more than a little disturbed at the recurring exhibitions of the Queen's immaturity, her violent partisanship when pushed, her obstinacy and complete refusal to put constitutional matters before her private considerations.

During the festivities to celebrate her twentieth birthday she became, however mildly, enamoured of the Russian Grand Duke Alexander: she flirted with him and 'never enjoyed' herself more, adding in her Journal that when the Russian party left Britain's shores she 'felt so sad to take leave of this dear amicable young man, whom I really think (talking jokingly) I was a little in love with'.

Within a month that 'monster and demon incarnate' Sir John Conroy resigned his position with the Duchess of Kent and departed for Italy. His immediate cause for leaving is not altogether clear but was probably the result of a combination of reasons. He must have realised that the Queen would never forgive and forget (as her mother had advised her), and the Duchess of Kent, who not so long before had seemed a very bright star on which to hitch his wagon, was now a dejected, ignored and all but forgotten inhabitant of Kensington Palace. In addition there was the not inconsiderable matter of the management of the Duchess's financial affairs which, John Conroy knew all too well, would not bear investigation without some very awkward questions being addressed to him. And then again there was the Queen's curious and morbid interest in death and what may lie beyond death that Conroy had noticed with increasing concern and dismay for he was one of those people who had no time for ghosts and ghouls and things that go bump in the night and he was genuinely disturbed at the Queen's growing absorption in such matters.

Conroy's departure caused no great surprise and nothing really changed at court. Queen Victoria was indifferent to the news and reiterated that she simply could not get on with her mother; and then the serious illness of Lady Flora Hastings filled the papers and reminded the public of the Queen's harsh treatment of that lady-in-waiting, and Victoria, seeming puzzled and displeased, was hissed from the stands at Ascot.

When it became apparent that Lady Flora was indeed dying — only a fortnight earlier the Queen and Lord Melbourne had laughed at the idea — Victoria was overcome with remorse and went to see the dying woman. 'I found poor Lady Flora stretched on a couch looking as thin as anybody can be who is still alive; literally a skeleton, but the body very much swollen like a person who is with child; a searching look in her eyes, a look rather like a person who is dying . . . I said to her, I hoped to see her again when she was better, upon which she grasped my hand as if to say "I shall not see you again".'

A few days later Lady Flora was dead and the Queen recorded the event in her Journal: 'The poor thing died without a struggle and only just raised her hands and gave one gasp.' A post-morten revealed that Lady Flora had a tumour on the liver but her family and friends said she died of a broken heart and it was the Queen who had broken it. There were even a few minor demonstrations against Victoria and stones were thrown at the carriage she sent to Lady Flora's funeral. The rumours of scandal and rumblings of bad feeling continued for a while and then faded, but memories of such happenings are long and there is no doubt that the whole affair helped to destroy the popular image of a gay and innocent Queen.

Even the impending visit of the Coburg princes could not cheer up Victoria, for with the death of Lady Flora and its aftermath much of the fun seemed to go out of being Queen. She now had no great wish to see Albert, she told Melbourne; in fact the whole subject had become odious to her. She did not want to have to decide about marrying, adding that she would rather never marry at all! She even wrote to Uncle Leopold suggesting in a roundabout way that the whole visit be postponed indefinitely; did Albert realize that *no* engagement existed between them? And in any case she could make no final promise for the time being and any marriage could not take place for two or three years. Apart from her 'youth' and 'great repugnance' at the idea of any alteration in her present position, she told her uncle that there appeared to be no public anxiety for her marriage and she thought it prudent to await some such demonstration.

Uncle Leopold was wise enough to read between the lines and he pressed ahead with plans for the visit, confident that the young people would hit it off and all would be well. After all, Victoria would hear nothing but good about Albert from every side and she thought he was handsome; it might take a little time for the young people to get to know each other but Leopold had no doubt of the eventual outcome. He did not tell Victoria that Albert also was dreading the visit! Albert, a serious young man and very prim and proper, did not know what to think when he heard Victoria described as 'incredibly stubborn' and 'delighting in Court ceremonies and trivial formalities'. He already wished, wistfully, that she took an interest in nature and rather than enjoy sitting up at night and sleeping late into the day, he would have preferred someone who shared his passion of getting up at five in the morning and falling asleep over supper.

As Uncle Leopold had forseeen, everything went well once the couple met. The Queen stood at the top of the staircase at Windsor to greet him: 'It was with some emotion that I beheld Albert — who is beautiful.' Next day the Journal states, 'Albert really is quite charming and so excessively handsome, such beautiful blue eyes, exquisite nose, a beautiful figure, broad in the shoulders and a fine waist . . .' and so on. Five days after his arrival the Queen sent for Albert. 'He came to the Closet where I was alone, and after a few minutes I said to him that I thought he must be aware . . . that it would make me too happy if he would consent to what I wished (to marry me). We embraced each other, and he was so kind, so affectionate, I really felt it was the happiest and brightest moment of my life.'

When Albert arrived for the wedding, four months later, the Queen (as usual) got her own way and the engaged couple slept under the same roof; her mother's doubts about the propriety of doing so the Queen dismissed as 'foolish nonsense'. Furthermore, and out of character for a person who was fast becoming excessively super-stitious, the Queen defied tradition by seeing Albert on the wedding day, before the ceremony.

After the wedding in the Chapel Royal, St James's Palace, the young couple returned to Buckingham Palace, to the loud cheers of the large crowds, and after the wedding breakfast set off in a travelling coach with a small escort for Windsor — 'I and Albert alone which was so delightful.'

If otherwise all was not as it should have been that first evening, Victoria had no complaints. She had such a sick headache that she couldn't eat any dinner and was obliged to lie down on the sofa but, as she wrote in her Journal, 'never, never' had she spent such an evening.

'My dearest dearest dear Albert sat on a footstool by my side, and his excessive love and affection gave me feelings of heavenly love and happiness I never could have hoped to have felt before! To be called by names of tenderness I have never yet heard used to me before — was bliss beyond belief! Oh! this was the happiest day of my life . . .'

In the late summer of 1841 Lord Melbourne's government fell; the following year he suffered a stroke and from then on he aged rapidly. When he died six years later Queen Victoria dedicated twenty-four hours to his memory, conscientiously mourning her old friend although by this time she regretted her former intense affection for Melbourne, seeing now that she had worked herself up to what was, at the end, quite foolish.

With the departure of Lehzen at the Prince Consort's instigation, the calming presence of a husband and, in particular, the arrival of her first child in November 1840, relations between Victoria and her mother improved considerably. Finding a secure and honoured place in the royal circle, the Duchess relaxed and, to some eyes, recovered much of the cheerfulness and impression of being easy-going that Victoria's father had found so attractive when he married her.

On her mother's death in 1861 the Queen went through all her mother's papers and was, according to her Journal, unbearably moved to discover how very, very much she and her father had loved each other. And she found two little books with accounts of her, Victoria's, childhood 'and they showed such unbounded tenderness!' that Victoria was quite ashamed that on her wedding day she had publicly humiliated her mother by not embracing or kissing her but merely shaking her hand.

Alison Plowden in *The Young Victoria* (1981), has listed the 'several Victorias that were, in a changing world, presented to the public eye: Lehzen's Victoria, the withdrawn, enigmatic Princess; Melbourne's Victoria, the exuberant, headstrong little Queen; Albert's Victoria, the adoring, submissive wife; and finally England's Victoria, the formidable matriarch, grandmother of Europe and Regina Imperatrix who gave her name to an age.'

Victoria was showing herself to be a complex character, full of contradictions: shrewd yet sentimental; devious but direct and sharp-tongued; shy, quiet and composed but also at times hysterical; insecure, secretive yet at the same time loving, strong, alive to the possibility of spirit communication and, above all, terrifyingly regal when necessary.

CHAPTER THREE

PRINCE ALBERT – AN INFLUENCE IN LIFE AND DEATH

Albert of Saxe-Coburg-Gotha, Victoria's Prince Consort, who was the same age as herself, had several nicknames, most of which were appropriate.

'The Pauper Prince' may have been meant unkindly but it was true, Albert literally had no money at all. He was called 'Lovely Albert' for his looks — he was tall and handsome and it was not only Victoria who regarded him as 'beautiful'; he was described by many people as 'fine-looking' and 'fair'. General Sir George Higginson — with whom Hector Bolitho discussed this very subject on the General's hundredth birthday — described the seventeen-year-old Prince as 'the handsomest young man I have ever seen'.

Other people called Albert the 'German Professor' because the only time he seemed to be at ease and not rushing about on some business or other was when he was attending a lecture or studying or discussing some learned topic or some metaphysical problem. Never popular with the aristocracy or, for that matter, with the military, the latter referred to him as the 'Field Marshal who never went to war', which was true.

Perhaps a little sadly he was not infrequently the subject of ridicule in satirical magazines. He always seemed so very stiff and reserved, difficult to approach and even more difficult to get to know; one of his few relaxations seems to have been playing the piano, which he loved to do.

Before he left Coburg to marry Victoria, Albert had said, 'I shall never cease to be a true German.' And he never did.

Religion seems to have been almost instinctive in Prince Albert and Hector Bolitho tells us that 'all his actions, all through his life, were guided by a spirituality far beyond the formal piety in which he had been instructed'. Others, including Herr Florschütz, tutor to Albert and his brother Ernst, remark on the 'real and living faith' that gave meaning and colour to his life; he felt it was an inherent part of himself, 'engraved in his very nature'. The story of his whole life and perhaps especially his dying hours show that he believed in the immortality of the human spirit implicitly.

From Herr Florschütz's memoirs we learn that Albert's mother, the Duchess Luise (wife of Ernst I, Duke of Saxe-Coburg) was 'wanting in the essential qualifications of a mother'. Apparently she never concealed the fact that Albert, who was so like her in appearance, was her favourite.

It might well be thought that this partiality could have had a disastrous effect on the minds of Albert and Ernst had the family remained a unit, but in the event the Duke and Duchess were divorced in 1826 when Albert was not quite seven years old.

Albert has been described as illegitimate by some historians — he was already a year old when the first such accusations were made — but this seems unlikely. His parents were married in August 1817, in June 1818 Luise had her first son, Ernst and, in the summer of 1819, a second son, Albert. There still exist books and printed documents stating that the Duchess Luise, by her alleged infidelity, brought Semitic blood into the royal family. Max W. L. Voss, in his *England Als Erzicher* (1921), is in no doubt about the matter: 'Prince Albert of Coburg, the Prince Consort, is to be described without contradiction as a half Jew, so that, since his time, Jewish blood has been circulating in the veins of the English Royal Family, as well as in the veins of the Hohenzollerns.' Lytton Strachey, in his *Queen Victoria* (1921), refers to the divorce, saying, 'There were scandals: one of the Court Chamberlains, a charming and cultivated man, of Jewish extraction, was talked of . . .'

Documents in Coburg, which Bolitho examined in 1931, state that Luise was divorced for committing adultery with Lieutenant von Haustein, who was created Count Pölzig when Luise afterwards married him. She neither admitted nor denied the charges and made no accusations against her husband the Duke.

The Duchess, after a long and tragic illness, died of cancer at the early age of thirty-one. Albert never forgot her and one of his first presents to Victoria was a little pin his mother had given him.

Albert was never robust in health as a boy and as he grew up he was the victim of a delicate digestion; he always had trouble with his teeth and gums; he was always easily exhausted; and above all and perhaps most damaging, he 'worried perpetually' over unimportant details. As an adult he was often unwell and sometimes very ill; melancholia — the root of Prince Albert's troubles — overwhelmed him from time to time. Once, when the Prince had been so ill that the Queen had insisted on a full examination, she wrote in her Journal afterwards that the doctor 'admits that it is in the mind . . .'

Albert was described by more than one person as 'completely cowed' and living in perpetual dread of bringing on the dreaded but accepted (by the Prince) hereditary malady in the Queen, the madness that was thought to have afflicted her grandfather, King George III.

In fact Victoria's son Leopold, born 7 April 1853, did suffer from an hereditary illness, but this was haemophilia, that strange bleeding disease that is transmitted through either sex but usually affects only males. As the Prince Consort was free of the disease it must in some way have been passed on by the Queen, although there is apparently no record of any of her ancestors being afflicted with it. For months after Leopold's birth his mother worried about him, almost as though she had a premonition of what was to come, and the stress and worry caused her to become nervy and irritable with sudden bursts of violent temper which invariably hurt the ever-patient Albert. He made all sorts of attempts to deal with her outbursts and obvious distress but these well-meaning attempts only seemed to fan the flames of her near-hysteria. Their married life was not all blissfully happy although that is how Victoria chose to remember it after Albert had 'left her'.

Like Victoria, Albert could be extreme in his likes and dislikes. Victoria's faithful Lehzen he called 'a crazy, stupid intriguer, obsessed with the lust of power, who regards herself as a demi-God, and anyone who refuses to recognize her as such is a criminal . . .' 'Perfect' Albert could write this of someone who had devoted her life and given her unstinted love and service to Victoria for almost as long as the Queen could remember. Such unwarranted outbursts are often associated with usually quiet people who feel they are frustrated in some way; the diarist Greville invariably describes Albert as 'grumpy'.

When Prince Albert was elected Chancellor of Cambridge University in 1847 he had withstood the opposition of Lord Powys. Victoria never forgave Lord Powys for standing against her 'beloved angel' and she refused to speak to him later when they met. Indeed she would probably never have spoken to him ever again had he not managed to get word to her about his 'family legend'; soon afterwards he was received by the Queen and listened to with interest as he told how about a hundred years earlier a working woman had slept in the family castle in Wales and had reportedly seen a ghostly figure enter her room three times. When she eventually followed the phantom it led her to a secret room containing a box which, the old woman was certain, the ghostly form required her to despatch to the Earl, who was at the time in London. Having convinced the steward and his wife of the seriousness of the matter, the box was duly sent with all speed to the Earl in London. The contents of the box (thought to be lost) were of the utmost importance to the Earl while he was in London and when he returned home he made inquiries as to how the box came to be sent and he then sought out the old woman and saw to it that she never wanted for the rest of her life. The room where the old woman saw the ghost had long been known as the Haunted Room.

Hector Bolitho has pointed out that in 1848, 'as Prince Albert sat over his plans for the emancipation of the working classes, he might have listened to two voices from the ghosts of Windsor Castle: the voice of King John protesting "By god's teeth I will not grant them liberties which will make me a slave" and the voice of Richard II declaring, "What we approve shall be granted, and what we think improper refused. For think not we are to be ruled by our people. That has never been."'

By 1850 plans were well ahead for the Great Exhibition. This immense concept and the fairy-like charm of its interior fascinated the people of London and indeed of the world; and the visitors were so well-behaved that it is said afterwards 'not a flower was picked, not a picture smashed'. One wonders what would happen today in a vast glass-domed palace open to the public!

There were fourteen thousand exhibits from every part of the globe in the Great Exhibition of 1851, held in the enormous Crystal Palace, with its canopy of glass and steel built over and around the trees of Hyde Park and occupying a site of twenty-six acres; it was all Albert's conception but it was based on Paxton's gigantic conservatory at Chatsworth which Victoria visited with the Prince Consort. They had arrived there at dusk and were greeted with a sudden flourish of fireworks, but the horses were well trained and all was well. Today Chatsworth contains little of the house where Mary Queen of Scots was once confined, although a bedroom is known as 'Mary Queen of Scots' Bedroom' and the story goes that the room is a survival of the old house, being propped up by scaffolding when the former house was pulled down and incorporated into the new one. A staircase in the north-east corner would appear to be a genuine survival from those days. Sir William Cavendish began the house where Mary would be imprisoned for thirteen years but it was completed by the indefatigable builder of mansions, Bess of Hardwick, who achieved four husbands, numerous children and four mansions, Worksop, Bolsover, Hardwick and Oldcotes, in addition to Chatsworth. Victoria was fascinated to hear about the prophecy that Bess would not die as long as work was going on at one of her mansions and, interestingly enough, she died during a hard frost when her builders were unable to work on her new manor of Oldcotes.

Even at the Crystal Palace, that monument to the glorification of the new machine age, there were future associations with the occult, for two marble and ornate mantelpieces, probably of Italian origin, were included in the Exhibition and were later incorporated into rooms at Borley Rectory, built in 1863, and long known as 'the most haunted house in England' (see Harry Price's *The Most Haunted House in*

England', (1940). A few remnants of the unusual inlaid coloured mantelpiece that once graced the drawing room still exist — it seems likely that it was smashed when the house was finally demolished — but of the ornate mantelpiece that once stood in the dining room with a marble monk's head on either side, almost lifesize, nothing has ever been found. It would be interesting to know where it or parts of it finished up.

The Great Exhibition was a tremendous success, making a profit of a quarter of a million pounds which was used to begin the great cluster of museums at South Kensington. Albert was at last popular throughout the country, which was just as well for a few years later, in 1854, on the outbreak of the Crimean War, he had to put up with being branded 'the German lad' who 'was raving mad' — a pro-Russian traitor who was said to have been sent to the Tower!

After the Exhibition the Crystal Palace was taken to Sydenham and re-erected there. During the course of this work a railway line was laid from London Bridge, with a branch to the palace grounds, and rumour has it that a complete train and its occupants lie buried here as a result of a tunnel collapse. Needless to say, over the years there have been occasional reports of strange sights and sounds and experiences seemingly connected with the rumoured calamity.

In 1857 Albert was created Prince Consort and as the years passed he slaved more and more at his desk, often working from early morning until late evening. His stomach had always been weak — unlike Victoria, he was a wretched sailor — and on such occasions as when, earlier on, he and the Queen visited the French King, Prince Albert simply could not cope with the rich food provided. Even in America he found he had trouble with his stomach.

On 3 October 1860 Albert visited the White House in Washington where his grandfather, the Duke of Kent, had once taken tea with Mrs Washington. Albert wrote to Victoria that he was depressed to learn that dancing was forbidden at the White House (before long, Rutherford B. Hayes, wife of the nineteenth President and known as 'Lemonade Lucy', would forbid alcoholic drinks to be served) but Albert was much interested to learn of the several ghosts associated with the White House for he knew that Victoria would question him closely on the subject.

So he listened to the stories of the reported appearances of the ghost of William Henry Harrison, who died a month after taking office, roaming about the attic; the phantom Dolly Madison, wife of the fourth President, still seeming to tend her garden or appearing as she appeared at one of her celebrated parties; and of the shade of Abigail Adams, wife of the sixth President, moving silently through the long hall at dawn, wearing a cape and lace shawl, or in the East Room where the same figure had been seen.

Albert was not to know that Abraham Lincoln, who often held seances at the White House and was much interested in the possibility of spirit return, would himself return as a ghost to the same East Room where his body once lay in state and also to the magnificent Oval Room; or that a later Queen Wilhelmina of the Netherlands would see the ghost of this famous President. In fact no less than a dozen different ghostly forms would be reported at the White House.

In America, as elsewhere, especially in his later years, Albert was tortured with rheumatism and plagued with insomnia. Towards the end of 1860, as that 'grey winter' set in, he became more ill and more and more desolate. He could not sleep, his gums were swollen and the nerves in his cheeks were inflamed. Soon the Queen was watching him, anxious and afraid, remembering his remark that in a crisis he would have no great will to live.

Christmas came, the coldest for fifty years, and the New Year only brought more complaints from the suffering Prince: 'I am tired, I am tired . . . My sufferings are frightful,' he wrote in the secret pages of his diary and, four days later, to Stockmar: 'Sleepless nights and pain have pulled me down . . .'

March came. The Queen's mother was ill and in terrible pain and when she died the Prince Consort, affected by his wife's usual outpouring of exaggerated grief, sank deeper and deeper into gloom and despondency himself. He said to the Queen, and her heart turned cold at the words, 'I do not cling to life. You do; but I set no store by it . . . If I had a severe illness, I should give up at once.'

Albert, according to Disraeli, was the only person 'who ever attained the Ideal', and Disraeli was not the only person to voice such a sentiment. A descendant of Prince Albert, Queen Marie of Roumania, wrote in 1938: 'When death called, he gladly followed that call. It is lonely to be over-perfect and unrelentingly virtuous!'

The Queen, who was always physically robust, found it difficult to take seriously her husband's aches and pains and even as late as 30 November 1861, a fortnight before his death, she was to write to the Princess Royal ('Vicky', always the favourite) that Papa was 'as usual despairing as really only men are . . . when unwell . . . but is not inclined himself even to admit he is better'. At this time it did admittedly look as if the Prince had done no more than develop a very severe chill during a trip to Cambridge to see Bertie and bring him to task over a scandalous affair he was having with a young woman called Nellie Clifton. Probably only Prince Albert realized quite how ill he was. He wrote in his diary: 'Have scarcely closed my eyes at night for a fortnight . . . full of rheumatic pains and feel thoroughly unwell.' Before long he was saying he knew he was going to die.

After enduring some of the most terrible nights of her life (she would have said *by far the most* terrible) on the evening that Albert died,

Victoria, resting for a moment in an adjoining room, heard an unusual intake of breath and she rushed back into the sick room and leaned over him; he seemed to move his head. She asked him for *'ein kuss'* and his lips seemed to move; if they did it was the last movement he made on earth. 'Oh yes, this is death,' said the Queen quietly. 'I know it. I have seen this before.' She fell on the dead body and called it every endearing name . . .

Five days later the Queen was taken to Osborne, fast in the grip of what those of a later generation would call a nervous breakdown. It was perhaps well that the Queen was taken from haunted Windsor, its ghosts numbering among its members the pathetic shade of her own grandfather; a place, as Prince Philip said in 1984, having 'a very special atmosphere'.

Albert's death shattered Victoria completely. He had been her world and the light of her world; he had shown himself to be a thoughtful and loving husband, the dutiful, if initially reluctant, father of her children, and a great help, especially as time went on, in matters of state. He was an understanding 'father figure' during her moods of depression or sudden outbursts of temper, and his upright figure had always been there by her side during her public appearances. For twenty years they had rarely been apart and in every crisis, whether domestic or national, she had known she could count on his support. Now, suddenly and unfairly, it seemed to her, she was left with a vacant emptiness, a void so deep and bleak that the mere contemplation of it was more than she could bear. Little wonder that she wrote to Uncle Leopold, 'My life as a happy one is ended! The world has gone for me.'

For Queen Victoria death was always a fetish to be worshipped with all its accepted rites. Even as a girl she described the death of an aunt she hardly knew as an unforgettable loss, but then everything in her temperament came to the surface at such times and she would give full vent to emotional extremes — anything to relieve the burden of her exaggerated sorrow.

Her chief consolation in the years that followed Albert's death was to pray beside his tomb. Fortunately for her sanity she accepted personal survival and resurrection and believed that she and Albert would be reunited in the life to come. She also always retained the firm conviction that even after death Albert was ever near her, conscious of what was happening to her and to the loved ones he had left behind.

She found much comfort and relief in doing all she could to perpetuate the memory of 'dearest Albert', never forgetting that one day they would meet again. She personally chose the site at Frogmore, near her mother's grave, for the enormous mausoleum to house his body and eventually her own too, and she fervently hoped and prayed and longed for the day when her body would lie alongside his. As the years passed Frogmore became for her a place of retreat where she could go and spend hours gazing at his effigy; contemplating their past and future lives together; earnestly endeavouring to commune with his spirit. The keys to the tomb she kept on her person and she would let herself in and remain there for hours at a time.

In the years immediately after Albert's death her whole life, as she wrote to Leopold, was wrapped up in 'his wishes, his plans, his views about everything, they are to be my laws!' There could not be too many statues, or too many busts, or too many pictures of her 'beloved angel'. Soon the Albert Memorial bore witness to her determination that the country he had done so much for would never forget him; and the Albert Hall and the Victoria and Albert Museum were fashioned, as she saw it, exactly as he would have wished.

She often neglected affairs of state, preferring to sit in solitude and commune with Albert. When things piled up she said she could not deal with them, 'her heavy affliction, her isolated position without her dear husband, her weak health and shattered nerves the result of a broken heart', all this left her too weak and helpless to attend to such matters. At other times her wit came to her aid and once, when Lord Palmerston criticised her, she said he was impertinent and must be suffering from gout.

When Vicky, trying to cheer her up, confessed to pleasurable anticipation of her brother Bertie's approaching wedding, the Queen replied that for her the day would be worse than a funeral; how could she possibly be happy, she asked, 'when at every step' she would miss 'that one calm great being that led all . . .'

Year after year she refused to open Parliament in person, saying she failed to understand how the public could possibly wish to witness 'the spectacle of a poor, broken-hearted widow, nervous and shrinking, draped in deep mourning' take part in a 'show in which she used to be supported by her husband . . .' It was five years after Albert's death before she reluctantly performed the annual duty.

Invariably pessimistic whenever the opportunity arose, she now became dejected about the future of the British monarchy. By the time her two grandsons, Albert and George, were of an age to be learning, she came to the conclusion that they were dim and lethargic; had not the Rev. J. N. Dalton, their tutor for fourteen years, described one of them, Albert Victor, as 'incapable of being educated'. It was all very depressing. The Queen and Prince Albert had dreamed of founding a dynasty of paragons who would steer Britain to new and greater glories in the years ahead, but now Victoria, who never really had much faith or confidence in any of her heirs, became resigned to the fact that the British monarchy would not long survive her death.

In 1863 the Queen wrote, time and time again, of hearing what has been described as the ghost voice of Albert. In the vicinity of the mausoleum it seemed to say 'Germany, ever Germany . . .' and this at a testing time in world affairs when Queen Victoria, unlike many of her subjects, favoured neutrality with the result that German forces overran Denmark, an event that led inexorably to the First World War. Whether or not the ghost voice that the Queen said she heard was objective, there can be no doubt that Victoria believed she heard the voice of her dead Albert many, many times. Once, at least, she withdrew from a Privy Council to consult with the dead Albert and returned to announce that 'the Prince was hostile to any act of war by England'.

Lord Clarendon, for one, had no doubt about the invisible influence of the Prince Consort. He wrote, after one visit to Osborne: 'She acts as if he was in the next room, indeed it is difficult not to think that he was so, for everything was set out on his table, the blotting book open, pen upon it, even his watch going . . .'

The lessons and example of Victoria were not forgotten. When the eldest son of the Prince and Princess of Wales died in 1892 of pneumonia, raving, his mother Alix holding his hand, the room in which he died was left just as it had been when he was alive. Through many years that followed even the water in the jug was regularly changed and the soap renewed when it mouldered. Alix never again wore bright colours.

In 1879 Queen Victoria's son Arthur, Duke of Connaught, whom she always thought favoured Albert more than any of the others, married Princess Louise of Prussia. The wedding, notwithstanding, the recent death of the Princess Alice, was a grand affair, celebrated with considerable magnificence and marred only by the grumpy attitude of the bride's father, Prince Frederick Charles, who went out of his way to tell Victoria that he hoped he would never visit England again! But Victoria was in a good mood and she was not to be upset; she wore a court train for the first time since 1861, with a long white veil — and the Koh-i-Noor diamond. The British people breathed a sigh of relief and joy that court life had returned to normal and Britain had once more a visible Queen.

The fabulous Koh-i-Noor, the 'Mountain of Light' diamond which Disraeli acquired for his Queen, was presented to her on 1 May 1876, twenty-five years to the day after the opening of the Great Exhibition (a coincidence not missed by the superstitious Queen) and she was named *Indiae Imperatrix*, Empress of India. Victoria was delighted with the diamond and even more so when she learned something of its legendary history. While the diamond is not the largest or the most valuable, it is arguably the most beautiful and, of all existing jewels, it has the longest history in myth and legend and the most colourful in truth and fact.

The pre-history of the Koh-i-Noor begins in the oldest parts of

Indian literature, in records of sacred lore compiled fifteen hundred years before Christ. The story goes that the jewel passed through the hands of Krishna, the nephew of a king, who was athletic and wise and could satisfy an infinite number of lovers. The jewel, reputed to be an emblem of wealth and an amulet for protection and prosperity, originated in the Syamantaka and hung around the neck of the Sun God; it was said to bring good to the good and evil to the evil. The complete history of the diamond, the legend and the subsequent story of its travels, often leaving a trail of blood, intrigued Victoria and to her it did not seem fanciful to attribute the viciousness that surrounded the jewel to a supernatural quality in the jewel itself. Of all the jewels Victoria possessed, this was the one she treasured most. After all, was it not said to bring bad luck to any man who owned it but good luck to any woman? Its history undoubtedly pointed to some truth in the legend (see Stephen Howarth, *The Koh-i-Noor Diamond*, 1980). Today the Koh-i-Noor is mounted as the central point in the State Crown of Queen Elizabeth, the Queen Mother.

Once out of the gloom of Albert's death, and it took years for her to pass through that valley, Queen Victoria tried throughout the rest of her life to influence European policy and to manipulate the various monarchs in the way which she (and Albert) knew to be right, sometimes with and sometimes without her ministers or Uncle Leopold behind her; with, in fact, 'only the continuous voice of her dead husband to guide her', as one biographer has put it.

CHAPTER FOUR

BERTIE AND ALIX
– THE BLAMED AND THE BEAUTIFUL

Albert Edward, Prince and King, had, like his mother — and his wife — an intense interest in all aspects of the occult. He was very superstitious, believing fervently in fortunate and unfortunate periods and times, in events foretold by premonitions and so forth. Like his mother he would complain at great length about a broken mirror or, more often, the spilling of salt.

Count Louis Hamon, who was known as 'Cheiro', has written of this 'intense interest' in his *Confessions of a Modern Seer* (1937). His first interview with the eldest son of Queen Victoria was shrouded in secrecy. It was arranged by Lady Paget, an American heiress, and Cheiro was not told the name of the person he would meet or whose hands he would be asked to read.

Cheiro went to Lady Paget's house in Belgrave Square and was asked to sit behind some curtains that had been fixed up specially for the purpose and to read the hands of the gentleman who would sit behind the curtain, completely hidden. 'You are to be alone with the visitor,' Lady Paget explained. 'And you are to say frankly what you see without having any regard for his feelings.' Cheiro agreed to do his best and, left alone for a moment, he went to the curtains and arranged the available light so that he would be able to see the hands of his subject to the best possible advantage. He then seated himself and waited.

After a few moments he heard two people enter the room; he heard someone sit down facing him behind the curtains and he saw Lady Paget direct the subject's hands through the slits in the curtains; as soon as this had been done to everyone's satisfaction, she withdrew from the room.

Cheiro at once proceeded to examine the hands that were held out before him. After a moment he began to relate what he saw and what he could foresee. The man behind the curtains appeared to be keenly interested and once or twice asked pertinent questions, occasionally

71

withdrawing his hands to examine the marks that Cheiro saw and talked about. Cheiro soon saw that the hands were those of an interesting man who had an unusual career ahead of him. Soon, too, Cheiro saw and indicated certain important years for the subject when changes and events would take place which were beyond the subject's control.

Cheiro had reached the point where he was explaining the days and dates of importance to the subject, as revealed by the marks in the hands, when an unexpected incident occurred. Cheiro was saying that Tuesdays, Thursdays and Fridays were the most important days of the week for his subject, and that his important numbers were sixes and nines, and that the months representing these numbers, being 21 March to 20 April, 21 April to 20 May and 12 October to 20 November, had contained and would contain the most important events in his subject's life when he was startled to hear the deep and somewhat guttural voice comment: 'Strange, but that is remarkably true.' At that moment the subject allowed his hands to rest too heavily on the curtains; the fastening pins came loose, the curtains dropped and Cheiro found himself looking into the face of the Prince of Wales, as he then was.

Cheiro's looks betrayed his feelings of recognition and nervousness but in the kindest possible way the burly figure before him said, 'You have no need to be nervous. You have done splendidly. Proceed with this curious and interesting idea of numbers. Forget who I am and be as much at your ease as you were before the curtains so inopportunely fell.'

Composed and reassured by these gracious words Cheiro set to work and drew a diagram showing when the most momentous events of his subject's life would take place and how they fell into the revealed months and not into any other. His subject showed the greatest interest in what he was doing and eventually the Prince indicated the number 69, saying, 'As this is the only date when these two curious numbers first come together, which you say are the keynotes of my life, I suppose *that must be the end*?'

How far off the indicated date seemed at that time, yet with uncanny precision or perhaps with psychic awareness, he had picked out the right date, for King Edward, as he became, did indeed die in his 69th year.

Cheiro's system indicated April, the month in which the King was afflicted by his fatal illness, and the month of April has from time immemorial been represented by the figure 9. May, the month in which the King died, has similarly always been represented by the number 6. The addition of the two figures, 6 plus 9, equals 15; 1 plus 5 equals 6. The King died on 6 May, a Friday, which, in most ancient writings, is also symbolized by the number 6.

At the conclusion of the reading the distinguished visitor thanked Cheiro for his delineations saying he had been most accurate in dealing with past events, even if his prognostications had been of a gloomy nature. 'We will meet again,' he added and, as Cheiro took his departure, the Prince turned away, musingly murmuring, 'So sixty-nine will mean The End . . .'

In 1902 when his coronation was postponed due to his illness, Queen Alexandra sent an equerry to fetch Cheiro to Buckingham Palace to see her. There, addressing Cheiro in the simple manner and courteous way for which she was justly famous, she said, 'You so impressed His Majesty many years ago that he would not die before his 69th year, in his now serious condition I have sent for you to instil into his mind that his life is good for many years yet. As His Majesty is now only in his 61st year, you must impress on him that his present gloomy fears are not justified and that his coronation, which you predicted for August 1902, will take place as predicted by you.'

Cheiro promised to do his best and very quietly they entered the room in which the invalid King, looking pale and weak, was half sitting up in bed, propped there by many pillows. The Queen instructed the nurse to leave and motioned Cheiro to a chair by the side of the bed.

The King immediately recognized Cheiro — perhaps he knew that the Queen had sent for him. On a table beside the bed lay a sheet of paper, the same paper on which the King, when Prince of Wales, had jotted down the predictions and the figures that Cheiro had revealed to him at the home of Lady Paget; the number 69 was heavily underlined.

In a very weak voice the King welcomed Cheiro. 'I am very, very ill,' he said, trying to smile. 'Do you still believe I will reach my 69th year?' Immediately and with the utmost conviction, because that is what he felt, Cheiro replied, 'Your Majesty need have no fear. I know you will live till then. I am positively certain of it.' The obviously sincere assurance seemed to do the King good and he did manage a smile. 'Thank you,' he said. 'I hope you are right. I have many things to do before I pass away.'

Cheiro then used his undoubtedly strong willpower. Looking the King straight in the eyes, he said: 'Your Majesty will remember that I worked out many years ago that your coronation as King of England would take place in August 1902. We are now only at the end of June; this illness is only temporary, please believe me.'

'I am almost forced to do so,' the King replied, nodding. 'Every other date you gave me turned out correctly. I jotted them down on that paper. Tell me what date then in August would be the best one to fix for the coronation.'

'One of your number of nines, sir,' replied Cheiro. 'And I would suggest 9 August. The number 9 is your strongest "fadic" number. You were born on 9 November. From time immemorial in occult studies, November has been considered the House of the Nine, or the House of Mars *negative*; that is why your name will go down to posterity as Edward the Peacemaker. The month of August is called the Royal House of Leo the Lion; therefore 9 August would be the best date that you could possibly decide upon.' Fearing to tire the invalid and feeling that he had done all he could, Cheiro rose to go. The King smiled and said, 'Thank you for your visit. You have made me feel better.'

In his record of the incident Cheiro says, 'Call it hypnotism or anything you please but Queen Alexandra sent me a message the very next day to say that my words had cheered the King so much that he had slept well that night and already showed signs of improvement and orders had been given for the coronation to be fixed for 9 August.'

After his first meeting with Edward, Prince of Wales, Cheiro met the Prince again by accident one afternoon at the Berkeley Hotel when he was visiting the Princess of Montglyon who was also a friend of the Prince. The Princess was about to present Cheiro but the Prince recognized her companion and laughed. 'Why, this is the man who will not let me live past sixty-nine!' he exclaimed and the Princess rejoined: 'It is a good thing you are not the Kaiser. He would have had Cheiro executed for lèse-majesté!'

Shortly afterwards Cheiro was passing the Marlborough Club just as the Prince was leaving and the Prince, again recognizing him, said, 'I would like to have another chat with you about your theory of numbers. Come to the library where we will not be disturbed . . .' Together they entered Marlborough House and proceeded to the library where, over a cigar, the Prince asked Cheiro to work out the 'numbers' of several different unnamed people whose dates and places of birth he supplied. For the next two hours Cheiro did as he was bid and then he left. Afterwards Cheiro realized that the Prince had got him to work out the charts of the German Kaiser, the Tsar of Russia, the Queen and several members of the royal family.

The Prince was much interested in all Cheiro had to say about the ancient astrological theory that countries are ruled by planets and divisions of the zodiac and was fascinated to know that both England and Germany were under the same zodiacal sign, the House of Aries, and that as both were governed by the planet Mars, these nations were bound to fight for supremacy or be in active competition against each other, but that every effort should be made to form a strong alliance. The Prince became so interested that Cheiro had to work out for him the theory as it affected the principal nations of the world.

After his visit to Buckingham Palace when the King was so ill, Cheiro next met him at a reception in Paris at the British Embassy; and the last occasion when the two men met was just a few months before the King died. He was just about to join the royal train at Victoria station on his way to the South of France. When he saw Cheiro he stopped for a moment and said, 'Well, Cheiro, I'm still alive, as you see, and I have not reached that 69 number yet.' A few months later the King entered the fatal year; by the end of November telegrams told of the deterioration of the King's health. He returned to Buckingham Palace where the illness took its course and on Friday, 6 May 1910, in his sixty-ninth year, the first time that the 'fadic' numbers of 6 and 9 came together in his life, King Edward VII was 'gathered to his forefathers'.

Bertie, as he was known to the family, had been an affectionate child with considerable charm but to his parents he was a disappointment — although no one could deny that he was clever in certain ways. He was susceptible to and always willing to be charmed by the beauty of the fair sex; and he was not unaffected by the charm of certain men. During a state visit to France in 1855 Bertie, as well as his mother, were enchanted by Emperor Napoleon III and at least once the over-tutored and over-driven boy, when he was alone with the Emperor, declared that he would have liked to be his son!

Bertie was a poor scholar but instead of giving him help and encouragement and sympathy his parents poured scorn and abuse on his head. It could well have been, as Cecil Woodham-Smith has suggested, that his parents' minds were so haunted by the awful royal Dukes, the Queen's uncles, 'whose extravagance, dissipation and disreputability had brought the country to the verge of revolution', that their sole object, all they could think about as far as the growing Prince of Wales was concerned, was to do everything they possibly could to prevent any resemblance whatever to any of the royal Dukes. Time and time again the Queen prayed that Bertie would, in every respect possible, resemble and take after his father, the adored one. No reference was made or thought given, it seems, to the fact that the Prince Consort's father and brother Ernst were both as dissolute and unprincipled as any of the English royal Dukes.

It is an awful thing to have to record but by the time Bertie was no more than nine years old his mother was struggling to find something good to say about her eldest son. 'There is much good in him . . . he has such affectionate feelings . . . great truthfulness and great simplicity of character . . .' but the truth was that his lessons and his learning were a complete failure.

Soon the Queen, always aware of the occult and the unusual, suggested they should try phrenology and Prince Albert agreed that their son should be examined by an expert. Bertie was submitted to Dr George Combe for a professional inspection of his skull. Phrenology is the art of reading character and potential ability of a subject mainly from the size, shape and distribution of various bumps on the head, but also taking into account the shape of the skull. Phrenologists maintain that a person's character is revealed by the interaction of various organs of the brain located in specific positions; the size of these organs, or the bumps caused by them, revealing to the phrenologist a great deal about the brain power and activity of the person concerned.

Phrenology, which is still practised today, probably reached its greatest popularity during the nineteenth century when it had among its convinced supporters, Walt Whitman, Edgar Allan Poe, Alfred Russel Wallace, and Charles Darwin, but Dr Combe could not have been very helpful or hopeful as far as the Prince was concerned for we hear no more about phrenology.

The Prince Consort once described his son and heir as 'the most thorough and cunning lazybones' that he had ever met and the Queen took the strongest exception to his looks. She disliked his small head and large features, 'his nose and mouth are too enormous', she commented. His legs displeased her too for he was inclined to be knock-kneed. His loud voice drove her almost mad, she said, while his air of superiority, which it must be admitted was disliked by other people, infuriated her.

Certain it is that Bertie did not inherit his father's love of hard work and the Germanic pressures that his father and his tutors tried to force on him only made him more stubborn and determined to resist their wishes. All too often, as the pressures built up, there would be flushed cheeks, downcast eyes, a shuffling of feet followed by a screaming tantrum when anything to hand would be thrown, papers and books would be scattered, and anyone in reach would be liable to be kicked or punched.

In 1859, after three months cramming at Edinburgh, Bertie went up to Oxford; in 1861 he was transferred to Trinity College, Cambridge. At Christ's College at this time there was considerable talk of a ghost which might well have been just about the only topic the young Prince of Wales and his mother the Queen could discuss with a mutual interest and without losing their tempers.

The full story of the apparition, seen by many people, some without having the knowledge that it had been seen by others, is to be found in a curious little volume published by W. Heffer and Sons of Cambridge in 1923, *A College Mystery* by A. P. Baker, with five drawings of Christ's College by F. H. Round and subtitled 'The Story of the apparition in the Fellows' Garden at Christ's College, Cambridge'.

One of the Queen's first visitors after the death of Prince Albert was Colonel Francis Seymour (later Lord Hertford) and to him she revealed the thought that would haunt her for years: that the necessity for Albert to go to Cambridge to see the Prince of Wales over his affair with Nellie Clifton had killed him; that the cause of his death had been none other than his own son.

Bertie had been introduced to sex when he discovered Nellie Clifton in his bed following a ball at the Mansion House in Dublin on 12 September 1861. Nellie was a very experienced girl and Bertie had brought her back with him from Ireland to Windsor. The Queen recoiled in horror: 'Oh that boy — much as I pity him I never can or shall look at him without a shudder . . .' Bertie had never been allowed to be alone in a room with a girl — as far as his parents could prevent it — so his strong attraction to the opposite sex could have been largely provoked by his mother and father. Albert, the Prince Consort, had a horror of sex, probably because his rakish brother Ernst had contracted venereal disease when he had accompanied Albert on the trip to London which culminated in the engagement of the Queen and Prince Albert.

When the Prince Consort heard about the Nellie Clifton affair on 16 November he said, with some of the over-statement caught from Victoria perhaps, that it caused him 'the greatest pain I have yet felt in my life' (Philip Magus, *King Edward the Seventh*, 1964). Later that month he travelled to Cambridge, determined to sort things out with Bertie. He travelled to and from Madingley suffering a heavy cold on a wet day in late autumn. It was an act of sheer stupidity. He became worse and caught typhoid; then, instead of going to bed, he was allowed to wander about draughty Windsor Castle, relying on the singing of hymns to cure him. He grew weaker and weaker and still Victoria refused to call their eldest son. In the end, on her own initiative, Princess Alice sent a telegram to Cambridge on 13 December. Next day the Prince Consort was dead.

The Queen blamed the Prince of Wales, most unjustly, for his father's fatal illness. In fact the melancholy Prince Albert gave up the struggle himself and openly said he would never recover. With no will to live, he died.

For weeks after the death of his father Bertie could not enter his mother's room. If he did so she would glare at him with suppressed fury, followed by a spasm of terrifying grief. 'It quite irritates me to have him in the room,' she explained, more to herself than to anyone else.

One of the saddest aspects of the Queen's widowhood must be that she did not feel she could turn to her eldest son for support and consolation although he was only too anxious to help her in any way he could. His immoral actions had broken her angel's heart, had caused him to travel to Cambridge suffering the early effects of typhoid, and robbed him of any will to live. For years she could hardly bear to look at Bertie. Even on the rare occasions when he was allowed to take part at her side during state occasions she invariably reminded him that he was standing where his father rightfully should be.

It has been said that mother and son, after the Prince Consort's death, viewed life from completely different viewpoints and in some ways this was true yet, like his mother, Bertie was interested in mediums and seers.

In fact many of the court circle seem to have been interested in the subject of spiritualism. In the annals of the Ghost Club it is stated, for example, that the late Duke of Clarence and the Duke of Argyll were 'much interested in spiritualism'.

The Queen's paranoia that Bertie had caused the death of her beloved Albert resulted in her insisting he go on a five-month tour planned by the Prince Consort; it would conveniently absent Bertie from the country and the Queen would be able to ensure that the mantle of the noble Albert did not fall upon the unworthy Bertie, as of course it should have done.

Everyone hoped that on his return Bertie would be welcomed by his sorrowing mother and that the old dislike, bordering on hatred, would disappear. In the event the critical Queen found her son 'less coarse looking' and more serious in his outlook but, most importantly, she found him 'ready to do everything that I wish', according to Hans Roger Madal's *Christian IX* (1939). But such a state of affairs was not to continue. All too soon Bertie 'got on the Queen's nerves'. He insisted on arguing (she said) and this always gave her headaches. More to the point perhaps and unkindly, she became anxious about his performances as a husband and confided to King Leopold, 'I am *very* anxious for the result. I fear dear Alexandra is under a complete delusion' (Georgina Battiscombe, *Queen Alexandra*, 1969).

When Queen Victoria's eldest daughter Vicky, then only nineteen, first met Alexandra, with a view to sizing her up as a possible wife for her brother Bertie, she was captivated and said afterwards that she had never set eyes on a sweeter person. She sent a full and enthusiastic report to her mother — over eight hundred words — but added, somewhat mysteriously, that should the Queen think of this perfect creature as a wife for Bertie, it would be necessary for her first to be 'initiated'! Bertie, as we have seen, had by now been 'initiated' by Nellie Clifton and it was a changed young man who journeyed to Germany on the way to meet for the first time the sixteen-year-old Alexandra.

When the beautiful Alexandra arrived at Windsor Castle for her wedding to the Prince of Wales the Queen, after waiting as long as she could, eventually moved slowly down to greet her future daughter-in-law who looked, she wrote afterwards, 'like a rose'. But one way and another it was all too much for the bereaved Queen and after no more than a few moments chatting with her guests she retired to her room, 'desolate and sad'. Very soon there was a knock on her door and Alix peeped in. Already the Queen had cause to be grateful that Bertie should have chosen such an understanding girl.

Later the young people of both families gathered together; the first time they had all met, fourteen of them. Among the memorable incidents on that occasion it is recorded that there was an unpleasant and unnecessary remark to the effect that Alix was marrying Bertie because of his rank and money. Alix heard and quickly replied, 'You perhaps think that I like marrying your brother for his position but if he was a cowboy I should love him just the same and would marry no one else', which effectively silenced everyone on that subject. At the same gathering, and surely the first and probably the last time such a feat was accomplished in the stately rooms of Windsor Castle, the lithe young Alix turned a cartwheel! She did the same thing some years later at Sandringham, explaining that 'speed was the secret of propriety!'

With his marriage to Alix in March 1863 Bertie became free of the ties with which his mother had always bound him to her. He now had two establishments of his own — Marlborough House in the Mall and Sandringham Hall in Norfolk — a beautiful young wife who within months of the marriage gave birth to their first child, and the opportunity to dance and revel away to his heart's content for most nights of the week. Such activity did not suit Alexandra, however, who was used to plain food, early bed, outdoor exercise and little excitement.

Queen Victoria soon noticed that Alix looked unwell and within six months of her marriage she had become, according to David Duff (*Alexandra, Princess and Queen*, 1980) 'little more than a skeleton and the deafness which was soon to afflict her seriously was daily becoming more obvious'.

Queen Victoria worried and worried about Bertie and Alix: 'I fear she will never be what she would be had she a clever, sensible and well-informed husband, instead of a very weak and terribly frivolous one . . . Oh! what will become of the poor country when I die! . . .'

What some people regarded as ill omens attended the Princess Alix's first official drive through London when she arrived for her wedding. A horse carrying an officer of the Blues caught a foreleg in the wheel of her carriage and to the surprise of everyone the Princess quickly jumped down, seized the hoof and released it. Another horse and rider fell near her and had a lucky escape from injury. A young mother, thrust forward by the pressure of the throng behind her, threw her baby into one of the carriages to save it from being crushed; and a boy was pulled to safety just in time from under the wheels of the Princess's carriage. There was yet another omen for some observers: Alix kept Bertie waiting for more than ten minutes at the chancel steps and when she did eventually arrive there were distinct signs that she had been crying.

The Prince and Princess boarded at Paddington the special train that took them to Slough, then the nearest station to Windsor, where the widowed Queen awaited them. She is said to have been pleased and gratified at the tumultuous reception given to her son and his bride to be, but that is not the impression given in her Journal where she wrote: '. . . the people are very anxious it should be known that it is meant out of love and affection to us both . . . when I married, I had only reigned two years and dearest Albert was not known and could not be, though everyone had heard the highest praise of his character and talents. Still, no one knew or dreamt of his becoming such a wonderful great man. There was great rejoicing at my marriage, but on this occasion, as on that of my dreadful loss, there are outbursts of depth of feeling, which are most touching and gratifying, testifying to the appreciation of *our* domestic life of twenty-two years, and all my beloved did . . .'

Queen Victoria visited Sandringham only once or twice in the eight years after Alix's marriage and then only, as in 1871, because Bertie's illness made her presence imperative. It is not easy to pinpoint the reason for the Queen's ostracism of Sandringham but it is a fact that throughout her long reign she virtually ignored East Anglia. Perhaps she could not forgive even the part of England that she felt had contributed to the death of 'dearest Albert'. When in April 1889 she did make a visit (her first visit for eighteen years) her hosts went out of their way to entertain her. In front of an audience of three hundred people in the ballroom at Sandringham, Henry Irving and Ellen Terry thrilled and intrigued the Queen with a performance of *The Bells*, a tense melodrama in which the murderer, played by Irving, imagines he hears the bells of the horses in the sledge in which sat the man he had murdered. Next morning the Queen left Sandringham with few regrets.

One wonders whether, knowing of her interest in such matters, Sir Henry Irving mentioned to the Queen that his hands had been 'read' by the famous Cheiro, or that the Count had also read the hands of another walker of the boards who would play a big part in the emotional life of her son Bertie — Lillie Langtry. Ten years after that visit to Sandringham Cheiro was in Lillie Langtry's suite of rooms at the Carlton Hotel on her brithday when a gift arrived for her from King Edward VII.

Lillie Langtry was to say that Cheiro's predictions of her future influenced all her dealings, because she was so impressed by the extraordinary precision with which he read her past. After she became Lady de Bathe, Lillie wrote to Cheiro to say how accurate had been his predictions ten years earlier; in major events as well as minor details he was equally true in all he had said. In gratitude she presented Cheiro with an autographed photograph which he always treasured, coming as it did from a person whose 'wonderful charm of manner and kindliness of heart made those who really knew her so devoted to her'.

Lillie Langtry was the daughter of the Dean of Jersey; she was painted by Sir John Millais as 'The Jersey Lily' and her entrance into London society and presentation to Queen Victoria caused a 'furore' on account of her exceptional beauty. By this time she had already met Edward, Prince of Wales, Disraeli, Gladstone and most of the celebrities of the day. She must have told the Queen about her great admiration for Cheiro — if she did not mention her admiration for Bertie!

Interestingly enough, Sandringham now harbours not only the ghostly presence of George V, who died there, but also of Alexandra. As one of her biographers has it, 'her presence can still be felt at Sandringham, where she was always happiest . . .' (David Duff, *Alexandra, Princess and Queen*, 1980).

Bertie, who was referred to by his mother when she was displeased as 'You-know-who', was a lesson to everyone. He was undoubtedly starved of love, understanding, sympathy and encouragement, all of which, in common with everyone, he needed, and the deprivation of them caused him to become something of a poseur and a dilettante; he could be rude and was often regarded as very unpleasant. In many ways his life seemed fated with misfortune: even the woman who was his wet nurse, Mary Ann Brough, murdered her own six children.

Bertie was subject to the most frightful outbursts of temper, a trait he inherited from his mother, but while the Queen was slow to anger and slow to forget, Bertie blazed up into a fury and then the storm abated as quickly as it had arisen.

Bertie was unfortunate too in that he was taught no sense of discipline, he did not have a reasoning mind or even a strong constitution. Work was a bore to him and he was much more interested in fancy waistcoats, the cheapest kind of novelette and the pleasures of drinking, smoking and associating with women, all of which he did very well. Sadly, Bertie was held entirely to blame for his failings whereas of course the causes were genetic. His mother's grandfather George III had died of porphyria, her uncle George IV was a physical wreck, William IV was eccentric and had long been regarded as 'unwell'; while on the paternal side there was haemophilia, tuberculosis and syphilis. Bertie's father had been a weak child who suffered terribly from nightmares and he aged prematurely: by the time Albert was twenty-five he was plagued by rheumatism and constipation; by the time he was forty he was in effect an old man and the victim of periodic depression, the muscles twitching in his face. Bertie had little to look forward to as far as heredity was concerned, but his one great stroke of good luck was the choice of his wife.

Alexandra was beautiful in appearance and also inwardly; she was always thoughtful of others, she did an enormous amount of charity work and she was loved by everyone who met her. Much of the change in Queen Victoria from a sad-faced and hard woman, more and more inclined to be a recluse, into a respected and benevolent sovereign, sprinkling gifts wherever she travelled and throwing coins to beggars from a purse kept full for the purpose; smiling and receiving smiles in return, emerging from an embittered woman into one of the best-loved queens of England — much of the reason for all this is to be found in the sweet and quiet person of Alexandra, who met adversity and misfortunes with love and kindness and understanding.

As Patron of the Barnardo Homes, for example, Queen Alexandra did a great deal of good work and when Dr Barnardo died in 1905 she expressed the hope that his work would be continued 'as an everlasting tribute to his memory'. The public rallied by starting a National Memorial Fund and from all parts of the world money poured in. Soon all Dr Barnardo's debts of some £250,000 were cleared and, more importantly, his work continued. Today Queen Elizabeth the Queen Mother is Patron and Princess Margaret is President of the Barnardo Homes, but if Queen Alexandra had not shown an enthusiastic interest in the Society at a time of great difficulty it is more than likely that there would have been no Barnardo Homes today.

Queen Alexandra also showed a sympathetic interest in the horribly deformed Elephant Man, then being looked after at the London Hospital where Sir Wilfred Grenfell, 'Grenfell of Labrador', was working for his finals as a doctor.

The pathetic creature who won Alix's sympathy was an extremely sensitive person himself and he was always terribly aware of his terrifying appearance; he had been billed as 'the Elephant Man' in a cheap side-show when he was seen by some of the hospital students and he had been rescued by Sir Frederick Treves. The disease 'leontiasis' caused an enormous over-development of bone and skin on one side, and his head and face were so deformed as really to resemble a big animal's head with a trunk. After visiting him Queen Alexandra sent him an autographed photograph of herself which he always kept in his room (known somewhat unkindly as the Elephant House) and one could not help but think, seeing them together, of Beauty and the Beast.

Queen Victoria would have found a kindred spirit in Grenfell who was utterly convinced that the dead still 'live' and exercise an influence over mankind; he was fascinated by superstitions and was an authority on the lore and legends of Labrador. He was also a member of the exclusive Ghost Club, founded in 1862.

Not long before Bertie, then Edward VII, died, Alexandra invited a London medium to Windsor and unknown to the King a seance with a dozen sitters was held in one of the castle anterooms. One of the remarkable messages received on that occasion foretold the early death of the King in the house where he was born; and the outbreak of a great war that would take place within a few years. This was 1909.

The following year Queen Alexandra was on holiday in Corfu when she was told that Edward was unwell. Despite being assured that he was in no danger, she hurried home and arrived at Buckingham Palace in time to see him breathe his last; and she lived to see the outbreak and conclusion of the First World War. She died in 1925.

Lady Warwick always maintained that after his death Bertie communicated with her. Once at Warwick Castle she heard the voice of her old friend the King talking in German and when Mrs Etta Wreidt, the American medium, visited the castle, Lady Warwick sat with her and heard King Edward's voice on many occasions.

Queen Alexandra herself was no stranger to ghosts. Once, in her dressing room at Windsor Castle, she saw 'a tall woman in a black and white dress' standing at the doorway. There was no explanation. Queen Alexandra also attended at least one seance with John C. Sloan, the Glasgow medium, when she obtained apparent communication with her dead husband. Sir William Barrett, one of the early members of the Ghost Club, was also present.

Queen Victoria may have died in the arms of the Kaiser but the last word she spoke coherently was 'Bertie', the name of her son who was by her side. If it was a conscious act, it was a gracious one and her eldest son never forgot that his name was the last word on the lips of one of the greatest queens England has ever seen; a queen and a mother who, whatever the difficulties, shared with her son and his wife and with many of her family and friends an undying conviction that death was not the end and that the dead could be seen long after they had passed on, and sometimes, it seemed, it was possible to make contact with the dear departed and to obtain comfort and advice from them.

CHAPTER FIVE

DISRAELI AND GLADSTONE
– THE LOVED AND THE UNLOVED

During the year 1845 Queen Victoria met both Gladstone and Disraeli for the first time but neither man made sufficient impression on her to warrant a mention in her Journal at the time, although Mrs Gladstone, the Queen thought, had great charm while Mrs Disraeli, she decided, was a most singular person.

Both men were to play a considerable part in the Queen's future and both were deeply interested in evidence of an afterlife and the whole realm of the occult.

Gladstone enjoyed Queen Victoria's high regard until Disraeli's influence became supreme and then she looked upon Gladstone as a 'violent, mischievous and dangerous' politician. Gladstone, in turn hated Disraeli, so much so that when he came to compile a tribute on the death of Lord Beaconsfield, which he was to read to Parliament, he confided to his diary that the very thought of what he was doing brought on an attack of diarrhoea! Nevertheless the Queen was much impressed which was, in part at least, the purpose of the exercise.

Gladstone in his prime was one of the most striking figures ever to have graced the House of Commons; a man with superb health and astonishing powers of work — it was said he could do in four hours what took another man sixteen hours. He was a disciplined man with fine manners, a voice of incomparable flexibility and strength and, to many people, he seemed to breathe 'an ampler ether, a diviner air' — once, at Blackheath, he spoke for two hours in the open to many thousands of people and completely conquered an audience that at first was disposed to be unsympathetic and disorderly.

Interestingly enough, Gladstone and the medium Robert James Lees were friends; Lees, according to his family, helped Gladstone write *The Impregnable Rock of Holy Scripture*. There are many references to Gladstone in the annals of psychical research. He was, apparently, impressed with his sittings with slate-writing medium William

Eglinton, one of the psychic celebrities of the day, who, as Harry Price has put it, 'may have produced genuine phenomena; he certainly cheated on many occasions' (*Fifty Years of Psychical Research*, 1939). Gladstone showed his serious interest in the scientific study of such phenomena by becoming a member of the Society for Psychical Research, research which he considered to be 'the most important work which is being done in the world — by far the most important'.

It was during the time he was Prime Minister that Gladstone sat with William Eglinton at a house in Grosvenor Square. Eglinton said afterwards that during the course of discussion before the seance Gladstone had indicated that he 'was already convinced that there were subtle forces with which our puny mind could not deal and which he could not comprehend'. The much respected statesman told the medium and others present that he held 'the attitude, therefore, not of a scoffer, but of a student who had no reason to doubt the genuineness of his pretensions'. His experiences in thought reading, he added, 'were sufficient to show that there were forces in nature which were not generally recognised'.

This particular seance comprised three other sitters, in addition to Gladstone, and as they took their places round an oval table one of them produced two ordinary school slates while Eglinton brought forth his own lockable double slate.

Eglinton described the sitting in the following manner: 'We began by asking Mr Gladstone to write a question upon one of the school slates. He did so, and the slate was held by me beneath the table with the question upon the under side so that I could not see it, the other side being pressed closely against the under side of the table. Presently the writing began . . . Did Mr Gladstone hear the writing? he did — and his face was a study: His intense look of amazement would have been amusing to those who have had experience of such phenomena, and was intensified when the slate was brought up and the few words which had been written were declared by him to be a pertinent reply to his question. The reply was "In the year 1857" and on the slate being turned over, it was found that his question had been, "Which year do you remember to have been more dry than the present one?" After that, Mr Gladstone took the locked slate into a corner of the room, and on the inside of it he wrote a question, which of course none of us saw. Then, locking the slate, and retaining the key, the slate was handed to one of the ladies and myself, and we both held it in the sight of all. While in this position, the writing was heard going on upon the close surfaces, and upon the slate being opened, it was found that the question had been, "Is the Pope ill or well?" which had been answered in red pencil by the words, "He is ill in mind, but not in body".' The questions, as Nandor Fodor has pointed out in his book *These Mysterious People* (1934), were purposely trivial at this stage,

Gladstone wishing to determine whether it was possible to obtain any writing in the circumstances he wished to impose.

'Of the subsequent experiments,' Eglinton stated, 'I can only say that they were perfectly successful; that some of the communications were written upon the sitters' own slates when held under the table; that several messages were given, not only between these two slates, but also within the locked slate, in full view of all present; and some of the questions were put in Spanish, others in French and others again in Greek; all were satisfactorily answered in the same languages.' Eglinton, says Nandor Fodor, knew a little French, but no Spanish or Greek. Moreover, asserts Eglinton, 'the written questions were in every case unknown to me; and the pertinent answers, as I have said, were written between slates fully exposed to view . . . the writing being distinctly heard while in actual progress. Mr Gladstone had the fullest opportunity of observation and I have no doubt whatever that his keen, penetrating eyes, as he carefully watched all that was going on, assured him that everything was genuine . . . I may mention the evident interest he took in the messages themselves, which he would scarcely have done if he had any suspicion whatever of the bona fides of the experiments. From first to last he made a careful record of all the questions and all the replies.'

William Eglinton was also a remarkable materialization medium, if we are to believe contemporary reports. At all events it has been established that he never gave a seance in his own rooms and he readily complied with all conditions of control; often the sleeves of his shirt would be sewn to his knees or behind his back but still convincing phenomena of materialization occurred. One witness reported: '. . . All this time his breathing became increasingly laboured and deep, then, standing in full view, by a quick movement of his fingers, he gently drew forth, apparently from under his morning coat, a dingy white-looking substance. He drew it from himself at right angles and allowed it to fall down at his left side. As it reached the ground it increased in volume and covered his left leg from the knee downwards. The mass of white material on the ground increased in bulk and commenced to pulsate, move up and down and sway from side to side. Its height increased and shortly afterwards it quickly grew into a form of full stature, completely enveloped in white material. The upper part of this the medium then drew back and displayed the bearded face of a full-length materialized form, considerably taller than himself. During all this time a link of white material was maintained between it and the medium, but this was now severed or became invisible and the spirit form walked round the circle and shook hands with the various sitters. The enveloping white material was now seen to be a flowing robe, fastened round the waist with a girdle. After a few minutes the medium, still in trance, drew forth more of the white material and stretched it out towards the spirit form which eagerly grasped it. Finally the medium became weak, staggered, and was supported by the nearest sitter whereupon the spirit form approached and seemed to assist the medium back into the cabinet . . .'

Such descriptions of apparent spirit manifestation were not uncommon but when they took place outside the restriction of a medium's seance room with its special cabinet, that was something different, and this does seem to have occurred during the mediumship of William Eglinton. Small wonder that Gladstone was impressed.

The experience of a Dr Nichols at Malvern with William Eglinton seems to be almost unique in the annals of psychical research. He stated that 'Mr Eglinton lay on a garden bench in plain sight. We saw the bodies of four "visitors" form themselves from a cloud of white vapour and then walk about, robed all in purest white, upon the lawn where no deception was possible. One of them walked right round us, as we sat in our chairs on the grass, talking as familiarly as any friend . . . one took my hat from my head, put it on his own, and walked off with it to where the medium was lying; then he came back and put it on my head again; then walked across the lawn and up a gravel path to the foot of the balcony and conversed with Mrs Nichols. After a brief chat he returned to the medium and gradually faded from sight . . .'

William Eglinton visited Russia and was received by Alexander III; later, after his marriage, he retired from mediumship and became the editor and chief proprietor of such magazines as the *British Export Gazette*, the *British South African Export Gazette*, the *New Age* and *Tatler*. Queen Victoria could have listened for ever to W. E. Gladstone telling her about such marvels and such mediumship. He was inclined to talk rather a lot and there seem to have been occasions when the Queen curbed his flow of words with a crisp comment — she once lamented that he spoke to her 'as if I was a public meeting . . .' — but on psychic matters she could never hear too much.

It is no exaggeration to say that by all accounts Gladstone, a moral and sincere man, should have become a royal favourite. Certainly Prince Albert admired his good character and conduct at all times and this may have played its part in 'Willie' Gladstone sometimes being chosen to accompany Bertie when he went abroad, for Bertie could be wayward. There were other reasons why Gladstone should have been a favourite; he was ten and a half years older than the Queen; his four children played with the royal children at Windsor; she liked Mrs Gladstone; W. E. Gladstone's sister had married the eldest son of the Queen's beloved Lady Lyttelton; and indeed the Queen did eventually manage to write favourably of Gladstone in her Journal: '. . . he is very agreeable, so quiet and intellectual, with such a knowledge of all subjects and such a *good* man . . .' but still when he died, no expression of royal regret ever appeared in the *Court Circular*. 'I am sorry for Mrs

Gladstone,' said the Queen. 'As for him, I never liked him and I will say nothing about him.' The Prince of Wales, in a rare demonstration of independence, was among the pall-bearers at Gladstone's funeral and he kissed Mrs Gladstone's hand.

In spite of everything, even his 'goodness' which ought to have commended him to her, the Queen never really got on well with Gladstone; she was never comfortable with him; she found his quirks of conscience hard to understand and it is obvious from her interminable Journal that he remained a major source of irritation and even distress to her.

After Disraeli's resignation she tried all ways to avoid having Gladstone as her Prime Minister. She said she could never give him her confidence and even threatened an abdication but in the end she had to give way. Even so she was always saying how ill he looked and she listened with glee to reports of possible splits within the Cabinet; she even resorted to corresponding with the Opposition on Government matters.

She clashed bitterly with Gladstone on many aspects of foreign affairs but in particular over Egypt where, in the Sudan, a fanatical religious leader, the Mahdi, almost wiped out an Egyptian army commanded by a British officer in the pay of the Egyptians. Victoria favoured swift and vigorous action but Gladstone said no. Instead it was decided to evacuate the scattered garrisons still remaining in the Sudan and their choice of the man to carry out this difficult manoeuvre was Colonel Charles Gordon.

Gordon had proved himself a brilliant soldier but he was the last man to be entrusted with arranging a withdrawal. Once in Khartoum he began delaying tactics and asked for reinforcements. Again and again the Queen urged that additional troops be sent before it was too late. Her urgency was justified. Khartoum fell just as the relieving force was approaching the town. Victoria was appalled and went as far as to despatch an uncoded telegraph message saying 'to think that all of this might have been prevented and many precious lives saved by earlier action is too frightful . . .' Gladstone was furious and attempted to administer a remonstration to his sovereign for her 'unconstitutional revelation of her personal opinion' but he was defeated in Parliament and the general election that followed made it clear that the public, like the Queen, blamed Gladstone for Gordon's death.

In the archives of the Ghost Club there are records of General Gordon's psychic experiences — an alleged communication from the dead General describing his death in great detail and an amusing incident related by Ghost Club president, Alaric Alexander Watts, author and founder of the *United Services Gazette*, at a meeting in 1899. Apparently Gordon was in the habit of using the Bible for guidance and during the course of discussion with Sir Samuel Baker as to whether he should accept the mission to Khartoum, he took his Bible from his pocket and, opening it at random, found his eyes fell on the words 'Smite the Amalekites hip and thigh', whereupon he turned to Sir Samuel and said: 'Well, I suppose I shall have to accept!'

Gladstone, while he was living at No. 10 Downing Street, repeatedly saw the ghostly Pink Lady that has long haunted the residence of Britain's Prime Ministers. When Mrs Harold Wilson was being interviewed in September 1985 she revealed that when she and her husband were living at the house a cleaner saw a lady dressed in pink on the stairs, a figure that suddenly disappeared, and her husband saw the same unidentified figure of a lady dressed in pink on the stairway. Disraeli too, always psychically perceptive and possessing an almost supernatural intuition, was well aware of the Pink Lady apparition in the 'lone rambling house' as he called No. 10. Queen Victoria would have been very interested and there is reason to suppose that she made inquiries into the matter.

Gladstone was interested in all aspects of psychic activity and he once sent one of his famous postcards to Count Louis Hamon, the seer and palmist who was known as 'Cheiro', inviting him to Hawarden Castle, having heard about his apparent powers from explorer Henry Morton Stanley (later Sir Henry Stanley).

It was a hot August day when Cheiro arrived at Hawarden Castle, to be met by Mrs Gladstone who informed him that her husband had the previous day addressed the Horticultural Society of Chester (his last public speech) and was so fatigued that she could not allow him to be disturbed on any pretext.

Cheiro said how sorry he was to hear of Mr Gladstone's indisposition and was about to leave when the former Prime Minister appeared at the door of his study and insisted on seeing his visitor saying, a little sadly, 'I may never be better than I am today.'

As soon as Cheiro was comfortably seated in the book-lined study Gladstone pointed to one of Cheiro's books that he had been reading and said, 'I have been told that you are the son of Count de Hamon? Your father had the same love of higher mathematics that I have. We corresponded many times on difficult problems — here is one which he worked out a few years ago, and which has interested me many times since.'

As he spoke he unrolled several sheets of paper which were covered in calculations and algebraical figures in the hand of Cheiro's father. 'Is your father still living?' Gladstone asked. No, Gladstone was told and, in answer to the next question, no, Cheiro had not inherited the same love of figures and mathematics; his calculations only related to the occult.

At Gladstone's request Cheiro explained the theories associated with the study of the hands, showing the statesman some impressions of hands that exhibited heredity and other signs. He then attempted to show Gladstone that man, like everything else in life, had his number as well as his place in the universe and that if this number could be determined, the years that corresponded to the number could also be determined, either for good or for evil, as the case might be.

Cheiro went on to tell Gladstone about his researches and theories, describing the different vibrations in each tone of music and illustrating what he was saying with a simple instrument that he had with him which showed that 'each vibration produced different forms in matter, and that the same vibration repeated dozens or hundreds of times, always created a distinct figure of its own that never varied in its basic principles, that such tones or vibrations had their distinct number — and so on through the scale of creation up to man who, as the image of the universe, vibrated in exact accordance with the vibrations of those planets which, as the instruments of God, called the universe into being'.

Cheiro invited Gladstone to test the 'Thought Machine' for himself, which he did and then called some of the servants into the room and quietly and thoughtfully tested it with them, one after another.

When they were again alone Cheiro asked to be allowed to take a chart of the movements of the needle when operated upon by the great statesman's will and he later wrote that of the thousands of examples he possessed, Gladstone's stand out as the most remarkable for will-force and concentration, 'as shown by the length of time he was able to make the needle remain at certain points'.

Afterwards Cheiro took impressions of Gladstone's hands for his collection and accepted an autographed and dated photograph of the Prime Minister. Cheiro did not disclose that Gladstone's Line of Life showed that he was very near the end of his mortal life. The date on the photograph is 3 August 1897. Within nine months Gladstone was dead.

When Disraeli first became Chancellor of the Exchequer the Queen was much intrigued by his 'curious notes' on parliamentary debates. She even copied some of them into her Journal: 'They are just like his novels,' she wrote. 'Highly coloured . . .' But she was amused and interested and, to the astonishment of many, she invited Mr and Mrs Disraeli to dinner. '*She* is very vulgar,' the Queen wrote afterwards, but 'he is most singular . . .' Every author's favourite literary anecdote is the one about the lady who asked Disraeli whether he had read *Middlemarch*. 'Madam,' he replied, 'when I want to read a book, I write one.'

Before long Disraeli was boasting to Lord Esher about the way he handled 'the Faery', as he had named the Queen: 'I never deny; I never contradict; I sometimes forget'. But it was their mutual dislike of Gladstone that drew them together. Victoria once told Sir Henry

Ponsonby that Gladstone had 'caused' the Russian war and she considered his conduct to have been nothing more than 'one series of violent, passionate invective against and abuse of Lord Beaconsfield (as Disraeli had by then been created).

In the summer of 1868 Disraeli went to Balmoral where his friendship with the Queen seems to have been cemented. Certainly on his return home he was showered with gifts from her: two volumes of Scottish views, a box of family photographs, a portrait of the Prince Consort and a Scottish shawl for his wife. When he gave her a set of his novels she reciprocated with a copy of her *Leaves from the Journal . . .* and during the course of a chat with the Queen afterwards, Disraeli used the much-quoted phrase, 'We authors, Ma'am', which 'pleased her greatly'.

It may have been during this journey to Balmoral that a curious incident is said to have occurred that had its echoes many years later when a man visited the Natural History museum in South Kensington and made inquiries about the moth that had saved the life of Queen Victoria. No one seemed to know what the man was talking about and he related the following story, according to Barry Herbert's *Railway Ghosts* (1985).

During the course of a railway journey to Scotland the Queen was accompanied by Disraeli and suddenly, as darkness fell, the train came to a stop. The Queen asked Disraeli what had happened and, anxious as ever to serve her, he set out to discover the cause.

When he reached the engine and inquired on behalf of the Queen the cause for the delay Disraeli was told by the engine driver that he had stopped the train because he thought he had seen a figure dancing on the line ahead. The observant Disraeli looked at the train's headlights and discovered that a large moth, probably attracted by the light, had become attached to the headlamp, flickering on the glass, causing its shadow to be projected ahead onto the line and perhaps resembling a dancing figure. Disraeli removed the moth and returned to the Queen to show her what had happened.

The incident had resulted in the Queen's train being delayed and the engine driver sought to make up some of the lost time but was soon forced to stop the train again when he came to a signal box showing a red light. There he learned that a tree had fallen across the track further up the line. The visitor to the Natural History Museum suggested that the moth, having caused the royal train to be delayed, had perhaps saved the Queen's life.

Soon Disraeli was writing to Queen Victoria letters that were as near love letters as he dared make them; she was sending him Valentines and in a public demonstration of friendship she lunched with Disraeli at his home at Hughenden. Disraeli was also friendly with Lady Ely who was generally considered to be psychic; she was certainly very interested in psychic matters and had joined the Queen and Prince Albert in table-turning sessions at Osborne House and elsewhere. Friendship it may have started out as between Disraeli and the Queen but surely it was more than that by the time that Disraeli had occasion to complain to Lady Bradford, among others, about the fact that 'The Faery writes every day and telegraphs every hour . . .' Their conspiracy, during the 'terrible time' of the secret treaty forced upon Turkey by the Russians in 1878, was described by the Russian Ambassador as 'this conspiracy of a half-mad woman with a political clown'.

Gladstone and Disraeli were not the only influential people in England to be unpopular of course; there were several attempts on the life of the Queen herself but only two of them seem to have had vague political overtones, the others being activated by unbalanced or inadequate individuals who either failed to load or cock their guns properly or whose purpose seems to have been to threaten rather than harm.

The first was in June 1840 and two years later, in 1842, there were two similar attempts and a further one in 1849 when a retired lieutenant of the 10th Hussars, apparently unhinged, struck the Queen violently over the head with a stick. That night, undeterred and as obstinate as ever, she appeared at the Royal Opera House and was loudly cheered.

By 1871, however, the monarchy in general and the Queen in particular were more unpopular than they had ever been but public opinion changed almost overnight when it was revealed that the Prince of Wales was suffering from typhoid. Following his seemingly miraculous recovery he and the Queen attended a public service of thanksgiving at St Paul's Cathedral and received a tremendous ovation and demonstration of loyalty.

Two days later the Queen was threatened by a weak-minded youth who pointed a pistol at her but the pistol was found to be unloaded and John Brown quickly seized the youth; however by now the Queen seemed to be prepared to play her expected part in the life of the nation and much of her former popularity returned, helped to some extent by Disraeli obtaining his second term of office.

In the years that followed, Disraeli, no doubt grateful to the Faery for having created his 'odd little wife', Mary-Anne, Viscountess Beaconsfield, flattered her and fussed about her until she came to look forward more and more to his visits.

Disraeli's gift for entertaining Victoria would not have been confined to anecdotes about Parliamentary debates and the like. One story that he would have relished in telling to the Queen who would have 'much enjoyed' hearing it would stem from his great success at the Berlin Congress in 1878. After playing his ace card, and winning the trick and the game, he had strolled down the Unter den Linden and past the massive buildings of the Old Imperial Palace, reputedly haunted for several hundred years by the most famous of all European ghosts: the 'White Lady of Berlin'.

Begun in 1538 the palace was one of Berlin's most prized architectural monuments for about four centuries. At one time it housed an Iron Maiden, the instrument of supreme torture, in the Tower of the Green Hat, where the cruel Frederick, first King of the Prussians, is said to have pierced and crushed many innocent people. The well-authenticated ghost does not appear to be one of these victims, however, although there were those who maintained that the White Lady was a model for the Iron Maiden, a beautiful woman who apparently reappeared many times after her death to warn descendants of King Frederick of their approaching deaths.

Others believed that she was a ghost of an early Hohenzollern, Margrave Albert, who murdered two of her own children, and so the ghost was sometimes known as the White Lady of the Hohenzollerns. The ghostly White Lady was first reported in 1619 and was immediately associated with a royal death. Subsequently she is said to have been seen by, among others, King Frederick William II in 1792, by Prince Louis of Prussia in 1806, and by Napoleon Bonaparte when he was staying at the Old Palace. An immediate search revealed no intruder although a painting of the White Lady is said to have fallen to the floor — there exists a report of this episode written by Napoleon's bodyguard Marshal Ney.

What neither Disraeli nor Queen Victoria would have known was that the White Lady would also be seen by her grandson Kaiser Wilhelm II in June 1914 and that the ominous figure would be reported yet again in April 1945 as Berlin burned. After the Second World War the Old Palace, severely damaged but not impossible to repair, was razed and every trace of its existence obliterated to make way for the bare desolation of the present Marx-Engels-Platz, a great open expanse, the Red Square of Berlin; and still there are occasional reports of a mysterious White Lady being glimpsed where once stood the great Imperial Palace . . .

It has been suggested that Disraeli made Victoria feel important as a woman and she certainly came to feel that she could relax in his company; something, as a widow, she could not do in the company of any man, with the exception of John Brown.

'Much has been made of the romantic passages between them, a plump widow in her fifties and the elderly eccentric,' Dorothy Marshall says in her *Life and Times of Victoria* (1972). And not without just cause, one cannot help thinking. He would kiss her hands, murmuring, 'I plight my troth to the kindest of Mistresses.' The Queen understandably enjoyed such unusual attentions and just how much she enjoyed it and how much truth there was in the rumours that were rife at the time we shall probably never know. After the death of his wife, Disraeli was a lonely old man and we have it on record that he found the Faery 'exhausting'.

Towards the end of his life Disraeli wrote to Lady Ely, who we know shared his interest in psychic matters and who knew of the closeness between the Queen and himself: 'I love the Queen — perhaps the only person in this world left to me that I do love . . . it worries me and disquiets me, when there is a cloud between us . . .'

When he finished writing his last book, *Endymion*, he wrote to the Queen, praying that he might be allowed to send a copy to one 'who is the Sovereign not only of my person, but of my heart'. His last letter to her said, 'At present I am prostrate, though devoted . . .'

After his death Queen Victoria referred to him as 'one of the kindest, truest and best friends and wisest counsellors' she had ever had; but Victoria was always inclined to over-enthuse.

Rumours of romantic involvement were not confined to Disraeli and John Brown. When Disraeli succeeded in obtaining for Queen Victoria one of her heart's desires, the title Empress of India, she immediately imported an Indian flavour into her court. A Durbar Room was installed at Osborne and, John Brown having died in 1883, she employed an Indian, Abdul Karim, the Munshi, as her personal servant. Very quickly the airs which he adopted brought him almost as much dislike and unpopularity as John Brown had become accustomed to. This only made the Queen defend him with her customary stubbornness and there began again talk of a romantic liaison. Although the Queen was by now fifty-seven, there are those who believe that Karim was her last lover. He remained in her service, bombastic and swaggering, until her death in 1901.

Disraeli was in London during his last illness and his rooms at Curzon Street were fragrant with flowers sent to him from Windsor. One day he turned to his secretary and said, 'I had rather live, but I am not afraid to die' — the sentiments of almost any believer in spiritualism and the continuance of life after death. He died on 19 April 1881, 'without suffering, quite calmly, as if in sleep'. A few days later the Queen received a note from his secretary saying, 'There lies, and will ever lie, close to that faithful heart, the photograph of the Queen he loved.'

It is clear that Disraeli was only too well aware of the Queen's interests and beliefs in life after death as viewed by spiritualists. When he was on his deathbed he was asked whether he would like the Queen to be invited to come and see him. 'No, better not,' he replied. 'She'll only ask me to take a message to Albert . . .'

The Queen's wreath for Disraeli comprised primroses, that long-lasting flower that symbolized the romance that had existed between the Queen and her faithful subject. The Queen also sent a huge memorial tablet to Hughenden — to the amazement of many people, not a few of whom felt that she rather overdid things, for the words read: 'Placed by his grateful Sovereign and Friend, Victoria R.I.'

Benjamin Disraeli, that 'undoubtedly mysterious personality', as the *Encyclopaedia Britannica* has it, loved beautiful Hughenden Manor, his home for more than thirty years, and much of the house and grounds remain as they were during his lifetime, the study in particular still retaining the armchair made especially for him, his ormolu inkstand, the black-edged notepaper that he always used after his wife's death and a number of his books.

After his death Queen Victoria visited Hughenden and spent some time alone in the room that 'Dizzy' called his 'workshop', communing with his spirit and perhaps providing the atmosphere necessary for repeated spectral appearances of the dead owner, for there have been many occasions when the unmistakable form of Disraeli has been seen in several parts of the house. One writer says that his ghost has been seen with papers in his hand in the vicinity of a staircase; another relates a witness 'distinctly' seeing the form standing near a portrait of Beaconsfield. 'I thought it was someone dressed up as Disraeli,' she said. 'He appeared to be quite normal; I smiled and he vanished.' During the course of a visit to Hughenden by a party of Ghost Club members one of them saw the ghostly Disraeli in his study, looking completely natural and unaware of her presence; she looked away to warn other members who were approaching the room, and when she looked back the seemingly solid form had completely disappeared.

CHAPTER SIX

ROBERT JAMES LEES
– MEDIUM AND MENTOR

As a result of her 'closest investigation' of the story that John Brown was the Queen's medium through whom she is said to have made contact with the dead Prince Albert, Elizabeth Longford in her biography *Victoria R.I.* (1964) pours scorn on the whole story related by Miss Eva Lees, the daughter of medium Robert James Lees, and does her best to destroy any idea that Queen Victoria was a spiritualist or was even interested in the subject. But much of what she says is, I feel, open to criticism and indeed she has to admit a great deal but seeks to tuck it away where it might not be noticed.

For example Lady Longford admits that the Queen knew and approved of a book entitled *Our Life After Death*; the Queen believed in the possibility of intercourse between the other world and those still in this world; she wrote in her Journal, after recording that Princess Feodora had been talking just before she died about a beloved child who had predeceased her, 'Surely at the approach of death the veil is raised and such pure spirits are allowed to see a glimpse of those dear ones waiting for them'; she and Prince Albert were sufficiently interested in the practice of spiritualism to attempt table-turning at least once, and probably on many occasions; she was intrigued by stories told to her from personal experience by Napoleon III about the medium D. D. Home; she wrote to the Princess Royal about feeling near the 'unseen world'; and there exists a record of at least one psychic experience that she always remembered. What seems to have been overlooked by many writers is the fact that so much of the writings of Queen Victoria has been repressed or destroyed that it is the biggest wonder in the world that *anything* remains. Perhaps we should take a cold look at the stories of Queen Victoria and her interest in mediumship; a detached look that has long been crying out for exploration.

Stories of Queen Victoria's interest in and indeed involvement in the practical side of spiritualism have been published for over a hundred years and one might argue that if it were all false it would have been categorically denied or disproved long ago. That it has not been denied or disproved perhaps suggests that it is impossible to do so.

One author has no doubt that Queen Victoria had little concern that her interest in spiritualism and similar matters should become public knowledge and 'she talked about them' (E. E. P. Tisdall, *Queen Victoria's Private Life*, 1962). Stories of R. J. Lees and his involvement with Queen Victoria have appeared periodically ever since the death of Lees in 1931, most recently in Tony Orzen's book *When Dead Kings Speak* (1985). What is perhaps significant is that the accounts are consistent in substance and in detail wherever they are to be found.

Robert James Lees was born in 1849. He was psychic for as long as he could remember and before he was three years old he spoke of seeing a ghostly kilted figure beside his bed. Up to this time the little boy Lees had been frightened of the dark and had to have a candle alight in his room at night. After seeing the ghost Scotsman he said, 'You can take the candle and leave me alone', and he was never given a nightlight afterwards.

Lees was not a professional medium but rather a man of more or less independent and private means, something of a scholar and a philanthropist. As we have seen, he helped Gladstone write a scriptural tract. Lees was a very religious man; and it was his arm, it is said, on whom the ailing Disraeli leaned when he took his last walk in a London park.

When Robert Lees was seven (he was the third in a large family) his parents moved into a larger house nearby which was relatively cheap on account of the fact that it was reputed to be haunted. One night as the young Lees sat up with his father watching for the ghost, around one o'clock the lad suddenly went white and fell to the floor unconscious. He was put to bed and only recovered consciousness three hours later. When they inquired as to why he had collapsed, he replied that he had seen a boy about his own age walking down the stairs; when the ghost boy was four steps from the bottom he had lifted his head and blood had poured from his gashed throat. The shock had caused young Robert Lees to lose consciousness.

The next night he and his father sat again and young Lees saw the same figure but this time it continued on down the stairs, passed through the kitchen and disappeared behind a door leading to the cellar. When the cellar floor was examined and eventually dug up, the skeleton of a boy aged about eight years was discovered. Police checked the records and discovered that a man and a woman had lived in the house with a young boy. The couple claimed that the boy had gone missing; and they said they were so heartbroken that they left England and went to live in America. What young Robert Lees had experienced seemed to suggest that in fact the boy had been murdered and his body buried in the cellar. Lees grew up aware that he was a medium and, it is claimed, was the first medium to make contact with the spirit of the dead Prince Albert.

When spiritualism became popular in Britain the Lees family, naturally enough, tried their hand at table-turning and believed that they made repeated contact with the dead. Soon after the Prince Consort died the Lees family were preparing to hold one of their table-turning sessions when Robert asked whether he could join in.

During this session Robert suddenly felt very sleepy and in spite of being shouted at and physically shaken, he dropped off into a deep sleep. Afterwards he had no recollection of having said anything or of what had happened but his parents told him that apparently he was the reincarnation of their first baby boy who had died when he was only twelve hours old.

The Lees parents discussed what had happened with their Bible class leader, Aaron Franklin, and he attended the next seance when Robert again went into trance. Franklin was impressed and contacted the editor of one of the first spiritualist newspapers, *The Spiritual Magazine*, who joined the sitters at the following seance. This time when Robert again went into trance the alleged spirit voice of the Prince Consort came through. The editor, understandably, lost no time in printing an account of the seance, and he sent a copy to the Queen.

A week later, according to Miss Eva Lees, Robert James Lees's daughter (who only spoke of the matter after the death of her father in 1931), the editor and Franklin turned up for another seance accompanied by two strangers. At this sitting the entranced Robert greeted the strangers by name and welcomed them, for he said he knew they came from the lady concerned respecting the information that had come through at the last seance. The strangers then admitted that they had been sent by royal command to ascertain whether it really was the Prince Consort communicating from beyond the grave. Would the medium, they asked, write a message and sign it with the communicator's private and pet name that was used between the Prince and the person he wished to send a message to; the Queen's name was never mentioned.

The Prince Consort apparently came through and gave a personal message, a pet name was written down, a name known only to the Queen, the note was sealed and handed to the two people present. Then Robert rose and shook hands with the two strangers using 'the highest Masonic sign in England' to prove that they and the communicator belonged to the same Masonic lodge. The royal emissaries then hurried back to the Queen.

Soon a message came to say that the Queen would like to see Robert Lees who was then about fourteen years of age. After a seance at

Windsor the Queen was satisfied that she had been in contact with her beloved Albert and she suggested appointing Robert J. Lees as her Resident Medium. Robert's family were agreeable but during the course of a further seance the boy's spirit guide said that the boy had other work to do but at Balmoral there was a youngster, named John Brown, through whom the Queen would be able to communicate with the Prince Consort. Only under exceptional circumstances, for example if the Prince Consort could not get through, should the young Robert be sent for.

'When we saw a carriage and pair and the two gentlemen occasionally arrive,' Miss Lees said, 'we knew where he was going and what he was going for but nothing was ever said about the matter outside the family until after his death.'

This state of affairs continued, claimed Miss Lees, for the rest of Queen Victoria's life and she sent for Robert Lees shortly before she died. Grateful for his services to her over the years the Queen asked him whether there was anything she could do for him. Lees explained that he regarded what he did as work for God and that He would look after him. The Queen then said that she was going to the Isle of Wight 'and I shall never come back. I hope God will reward you.' She then kissed Lees's hand and Lees told her: 'If I have done for my Queen what my God wishes me to do there's nothing more to be said.'

Doubt has been cast by some writers on the idea that Queen Victoria could possibly kiss the hand of Lees but if she could kiss the hand of Mr Gladstone (which she did) it is surely no less likely that she would kiss the hand of Lees who was not someone whom she assuredly disliked as she did Gladstone, but someone who to her open mind had done a considerable service for her over many years without payment, by making original and repeated contact with her dearest Albert.

By way of tangible evidence for her story Miss Lees had in her possession six envelopes bearing the royal cipher which she said had contained letters from Queen Victoria and other royal personages, including Queen Alexandra. She also had a copy of her father's first book *Through the Mists* (published in 1898) bound in crimson morocco with the royal cipher stamped in gold on the cover, which she said was a gift from Queen Victoria. She claimed that this was one of six specially-bound copies of the book that the Queen had ordered; she had presented the other copies to members of the royal family. Miss Lees maintained that her father was summoned by Queen Victoria on six occasions and that each time the Queen had communicated through him with the spirit of the Prince Consort. Miss Lees also maintained that her father received a pension from the Privy Purse for his services but I am informed that there is no official record of this pension.

It has been suggested that the envelopes, which it is not disputed do bear the royal cipher and did originate from the Palace, could have been obtained by other means than that claimed by Miss Lees; anyone writing to the Palace might get a reply in an envelope bearing the royal cipher. It might be thought that this could have been the explanation for one envelope being preserved, perhaps two, but *six*?

The alleged gift copy of *Through the Mists* is not exactly the same as Victorian bound volumes in the Royal Archives. These are all bound in fine-grained calf whereas the Lees copy of *Through the Mists* is bound in a coarse-grain morocco. Furthermore the royal cipher on the Lees copy is not identical with the available blocks used by the royal binder, lacking as it does a diamond point between each word of the Garter motto, which all bindings in the Royal Library are said to carry. Obviously there could be many explanations for these slight discrepancies and it may well be that the likelihood is that the envelopes and the volume are genuine.

However there are some puzzling aspects about the Lees story. Elizabeth Longford says Prince Albert had no secret pet-name, but if he had a *secret* pet-name how would this author or anyone else know? The same author says Prince Albert was not a Freemason and one of Queen Victoria's letters mentions that he disliked Freemasonry. Could it be, one wonders, that the method of shaking hands which the entranced Lees apparently conducted with the royal envoys was thought by the Lees family to be a Freemason's handshake but was in fact a particular type of handshake or individual grip that the emissaries recognized as having been used by the Prince Consort? Certainly there seems to have been no mention of Freemasonry, other than verbally from Miss Eva Lees. The various dates — Robert Lees's birth date, his seances at which the Prince Consort allegedly communicated, the arrival of John Brown from Balmoral — all tie in fairly well with the long and involved story related by Miss Lees.

Fred Archer in his book *Ghost Writer* (1966) states 'a biographer has written that "conviction had grown unshakeable among many near the Queen that Her Majesty, John Brown and the spirit of Albert formed some mystic kind of triangle"'. As early as 1864 it seems to have been common knowledge and *not refuted* that Queen Victoria was a spiritualist, and a member of the royal household is mentioned in connection with the Queen and Prince Albert reading books that suggested the Prince was preparing her for contact with the spirit world. It is further stated, on the authority of a person attached to the court, that it was generally understood that 'Her Majesty holds constant communication with the spirit of Prince Albert'. These reports were never challenged and indeed there are numerous first-hand reports to suggest that the statement was factual. Lord Clevendon has not merely mentioned but dwelt in some depth on the Queen's 'eerie behaviour and beliefs' and, long after the Prince was dead, the Queen continually referred to the Prince's opinions as though he were in the next room and believed that 'his eye is constantly upon Her, that he watches Her and that in fact she never ceases to be in communion with his spirit . . .' Clevendon was described by the Queen in her Journal as 'an able, sensible and impartial man'.

There is another — admittedly somewhat tenuous — connection between the medium Robert J. Lees and Queen Victoria in the unlikely character of Jack the Ripper, the perpetrator of a series of shocking murders which took place in the Whitechapel district of the East End of London in 1888. Officially the crimes have never been solved and the identity of the murderer has not been established although a number of writers have theorized on the case and come up with various answers. A strong contestant seems to be Montague John Druitt, a failed barrister; but other suggested candidates include a vengeful midwife; a Jewish slaughterman; poisoner Thomas Neill Cream; wife murderer George Chapman, a deranged surgeon who died in South America; and even James Kenneth Stephen, the tutor of Prince Eddy, Queen Victoria's grandson, among others.

An intriguing solution to the case has long been claimed by spiritualists. The medium Robert Lees maintained that one day, during the period of the Ripper murders, he saw during the course of a clairvoyant vision a man who wore a dark suit of Scotch tweed and a woman walking down a mean-looking street. They entered a narrow courtyard and Lees was able to read the nameplate on the wall and, through a lighted window of a nearby public house, he saw a clock and noted the time, 12.40 a.m. He then saw that the woman was drunk and offered little resistance as the man put a hand over the woman's mouth, drew a knife, cut her throat and then inflicted some terrible injuries on the body with gashes and slashes from his knife.

Lees was so impressed by what he had seen that he went to Scotland Yard and reported the matter but no one seemed to be interested in his story. The following night a woman was indeed murdered at the place and approximate time that he had foreseen! On another occasion Lees was said to have had a further clairvoyant vision in which another murder was committed and in this instance the victim's ears were cut off. Again the medium went to Scotland Yard and this time, in view of what had happened after his previous visit, he was treated more seriously, especially when it was revealed that a card, signed 'Jack the Ripper', had just been delivered containing a threat to cut off the ears of his next victim.

Before what is usually regarded as the last of the Ripper murders, Lees is said to have had another psychic vision and again he hastened to Scotland yard and gave the authorities all the details *before* the discovery of the body. Lees, it is claimed, accompanied the police to the scene of the crime and agreed to use his powers to try and trace the murderer.

Apparently picking up the trail at the scene of the murder, he led the police, 'almost like a blood-hound', across London and to the home of a much-respected West End physician. Although the police were sceptical, they questioned the physician's wife at length and discovered that everything pointed to the physician being a split personality, sometimes the considerate and celebrated doctor and at other times a cruel and sadistic murderer. After a number of discreet inquiries had been made the doctor was committed to a private asylum at Islington and his identity was never made public.

There have been some variations of the story: in one Lees recognizes the murderer on a London bus and, after following him home, is able to point out his house to the police. Some versions of the story have the physician practising from premises in Harley Street and having aristocratic connections. There are also variations in the time, date and locations of the murders witnessed in the visions. A diary said to have belonged to Robert Lees and now preserved at Stanstead Hall in Essex is generally considered to have been interfered with and to be unreliable as evidence; I was informed of this by Brigadier R. C. Firebrace some thirty years ago and the personal perusal of the object leads me to agree.

Fred Archer, for sixteen years editor of the spiritualist weekly *Psychic News* and author of such volumes as *Ghost Writer* (1966), *Ghosts, Witches and Murder* (1972), and *Ghost Detectives* (1970), states in the latter volume that although he never knew Robert James Lees (who was sworn to secrecy on the matter), he was acquainted with his son, Claude Lees, and he knew his daughter Miss Eva Lees for many years. The Lees family, according to Fred Archer, were always reluctant to talk about the more sensational aspects of their father's work but Archer says he had access to Robert Lees's own account (left to be opened after his death) and, familiar with nearly all the published theories concerning the Jack the Ripper murders, he believes the Lees story to be the most persuasive.

He admits to some discrepancies with the generally accepted facts of the murders, especially over the time 12.40 that is included in Lees's account of his first vision which is said to have taken place in the autumn of 1888, soon after the first of the Ripper murders. But the six murders usually attributed to Jack the Ripper took place on 7 August 1888 at 3.00 a.m., 31 August at 3.30 a.m., 8 September about 4.00 a.m., 30 September at 12.45 a.m., and on the same date another at 1.35 a.m., and 9 November early in the morning. Archer suggests that either the bar-room clock was wrong or Lees misread the time and that it would be unwise to question the validity of the main story due to such errors which depend on memory. Archer makes the point that someone making up such a story would surely ensure that the details fitted the facts. Lees was eighty-one when he died and by then forty-three years had elapsed since the Ripper murders. Furthermore Archer points out that this solution does rest on the word of a named person who allegedly played a principal part in bringing the Ripper to book — if the story is accepted; all the other theories are just that, theories, and no definite named witness speaks with Lees's authority. Fred Archer is also persuasive in his argument that any plausible theory must account for the surgical skill demonstrated by the murderer; the scope of his operations being confined to the East End of London; his ability to lull the suspicions of his victims; and the abrupt cessation of the crimes.

With reasonable answers to all these points Archer maintains that the Lees story is the most plausible. Surgical skill seems to be evident: *The Times* had no doubt about that and neither did *The Lancet* or most of the doctors, coroners and the divisional surgeon who examined the bodies. It must seem likely that the Ripper had anatomical knowledge and skill. The East End was probably chosen because it was as far as possible in the metropolis from the usual locale of the murderer: the West End. Several students of the case have come to the conclusion that the Ripper belonged to the 'upper class' and not many such men in such surroundings would pass unnoticed, but a doctor would. Not many of the 'unfortunate' women who became victims would go with such a man at such an hour of the night into dark corners of the locality but they would if they thought they were in the company of a doctor. And Lees's story suggests why the murders stopped so suddenly.

There is another account from a completely different source that seems to corroborate Lees's story. Dr Harold Dearden, a well-known writer and criminologist, related that in a dug-out on the Somme one day in November 1918 he and a companion were celebrating, as best they could in the circumstances, the fortieth birthday of Dearden's friend who chanced to remark that his tenth birthday had also been ruined — by Jack the Ripper!

He explained that his father, a widower, ran a private mental asylum on the outskirts of London and as a tenth birthday treat for his son he had promised him a visit to a theatre. At the last moment the outing was cancelled because of the arrival of a new patient. The boy had glimpsed the arrival of the patient who had spoilt his birthday treat, a man surrounded by well-dressed attendants. Before he was old enough to ask any relevant questions his father died and he was living abroad with an uncle. There were three things however that he had gleaned: the patient was the son of one of his father's oldest friends and it must seem likely that the friends of such a man would belong to his own class and that many would be medical colleagues. Secondly the patient was ambidextrous and, according to the opinion of the majority of expert witnesses, so was Jack the Ripper. Thirdly the boy's tenth birthday fell on 9 November 1888; the Ripper's last murder took place the night before and he was never heard of again.

One other theory of the identity of the Ripper must have caused consternation at the palace for it was suggested that the culprit was none other than Prince Albert Edward (Eddy), Duke of Clarence, eldest son of the Prince and Princess of Wales! Another theory said he was merely involved in the terrible series of murders; he did not commit them. The idea was that the Ripper murders had been organized by a group, mainly Freemasons, led by the then Prime Minister, Lord Salisbury (who was *not* a Freemason) to protect the Duke from blackmail by prostitutes over an illegitimate daughter. This, it was said, was all done with the knowledge and connivance of Queen Victoria and the Queen's surgeon, Sir William Gull. The whole story may have originated from Joseph Sickert (the natural son of the painter Walter Sickert) who convinced the late Stephen Knight of the truth of the story. As a result Knight wrote *Jack the Ripper — The Final Solution* in 1976, but in June 1978 Joseph Sickert said he had made up the story as far as Jack the Ripper was concerned.

There are just a few points of interest to raise before leaving the claims of Robert Lees with regard to the Jack the Ripper mystery. It was with some interest that I read in the *Journal* of the Society for Psychical Research in 1949 (not long after I joined that organization) an examination of this alleged psychic solution by Donald J. West, then Research Officer and later a President of the Society. When I came to write the present book I wrote to Dr West (with whom I once investigated a reputedly haunted house in Bedfordshire) and he has been good enough to supply me with a copy of his notes concerning an interview that he had with Miss Eva Lees in November 1948.

These notes state that Miss Lees, an elderly but well-preserved lady who gave her age as seventy, was voluble in the extreme and talked incessantly for over two hours, relating what to her interviewer were 'the most fantastic stories concerning her father's mediumship'. She stated that spirits regularly materialized in his study and spoke to him naturally like real people; sometimes she had been in the study at the time and had also seen these spectral forms.

Miss Lees claimed to have in her possession a great mass of papers and diaries but she was not prepared to hand these over to 'sensation hunters'. Her father, she claimed, was an intensely spiritual man (and this is borne out by his writings) but he had at one time been a member of the Society for Psychical Research and by psychic means he believed he had obtained the contents of the Myers so-called posthumous letter. F. W. H. Myers, a prominent founder member of the S.P.R., passionately anxious to establish evidence that conscious human personality survives bodily death, left a sealed letter in the care of Sir Oliver Lodge in the hope that he (Myers) would be able to transmit the contents after death through a medium. Lees and his friend Dr Abraham Wallace (an early member of the Ghost Club) planned to present the spirit message to a meeting of the Society when both the Myers envelope and Lees's spirit message would be opened and compared before the S.P.R. audience. Sir Oliver Lodge saw both Lees and Wallace and discussed the matter with them. He was sceptical and was against their plan, saying 'he didn't want to risk being made a fool of'. Lees was so angry that he tore up the spirit message and left the Society.

Another story related by Miss Lees had her father reporting, in response to spirit voices, the whereabouts of a notorious Irish revolutionary, Dr Gallagher of the Fenians, to Sir John Anderson at Scotland Yard. Sir John knew Lees and went to the address in Villiers Street and arrested Gallagher. 'But,' added Miss Lees, 'it's no use trying to check up on this because father's name was never connected with the affair.'

In his notes Donald West refers to the strange coincidence that for one reason or another circumstances always conspired ingeniously to make verification of Miss Lees's stories impossible. He adds that her stories were so numerous and so unlikely that he felt they were probably hysterical fantasies and he found her inconsistent on some points, as when at one moment she would say her father was not in touch with John Brown and the next she would speak of their association. She also referred to permits to visit royal places which her father had been given, personally issued by Disraeli and Gladstone, and Dr West makes the point that he feels these gentlemen would hardly have been concerned with such permits. One cannot help wondering, however, whether the Queen might, if Lees's stories were true, have insisted on confidentiality to the extent that no one knew about the passes other than her great confidants.

It should be acknowledged that the first published account of Lees and his alleged tracking down of Jack the Ripper appeared in the Chicago issue of the *Sunday Times and Herald* dated 28 April 1895; ostensibly it originated from a friend of Lees to whom he had told the story. Over the years virtually the same story was published in the *Daily Express* (9 and 10 March 1931), and *Le Matin* (21 and 22 March 1931), *Cavalcade* (13 and 20 December 1947), *Fate* (May 1949), and elsewhere; it also appeared in book form in *Crime and the Supernatural* by E. T. Woodhall (1935) and subsequently in many books, including Fred Archer's *Ghost Writer* (1966).

E. T. Woodhall, a former Scotland Yard detective, stated in his book that although he had no actual proof of the story, during his years at the Yard it was recounted to him on several occasions and personally he had not 'the slightest doubt' that it was true.

On the other hand Donald West made inquiries at Scotland Yard and was told (17 March 1949) by the Secretary: 'I am directed by the Commissioner to inform you that, according to the records in this office, there is no foundation for the newspaper stories that the murderer was known to the Police, and traced through the aid of a medium. I am to add that there is no record of the person named James Lees.' Presumably they were referring to Robert James Lees.

Other inquiries at Scotland Yard and elsewhere have failed to elicit any corroboration of the Lees story but ex-Inspector Woodhall's account mentions a private file in the Home Office which is said to bear witness to the truth of the Lees story. Inquiries here brought forth a reply which stated, 'I am directed by the Secretary of State . . . to say that there is no reference in the records of the Department to the statement said to have been left by a medium named Lees and no such file as you mention appears to exist.' Those familiar with the problems of making unwelcome inquiries at such establishments as Scotland Yard and the Home Office will recognize the signs of a possible cover-up. I might also add that Scotland Yard keeps close tabs on what its officers and ex-officers publish and it seems inconceivable that ex-Inspector Woodhall's original account would not have been officially approved at the time.

At any rate, Robert Lees was by all accounts a spiritual, deeply religious and dependable man, much respected and with, as far as we know, an unblemished reputation. If the story of his involvement in the Jack the Ripper crimes is factual, as seems likely, it must be probable that his story of involvement with Queen Victoria is equally truthful in essence. It might also explain to some extent the Queen's great interest in the Ripper crimes and their solution.

One somewhat puzzling aspect about Queen Victoria and her interest in spiritualism concerns a finely embossed gold presentation watch which I have seen and examined. Engraved, 'Presented by Her Majesty to Miss Georgiana Eagle for her Meritorious and Extraordinary Clairvoyance produced at Osborn House, Isle of Wight, July 15th, 1846', it would appear that this presentation was made fifteen years before the death of the Prince Consort. Queen Victoria is said to have agreed to the watch being given to W. T. Stead, the famous journalist and spiritualist, since Georgiana Eagle died before it could be presented to her, and the Queen requested that Stead present it to the medium he considered most deserving. Stead, after consultation with Sir William Crookes and Alfred Russel Wallace, decided it should go to Mrs Etta Wriedt, the American direct-voice medium. Ten years after the death of the Queen she, Queen Victoria, is reported to have spoken in London through the mediumship of Etta Wriedt and the second inscription on the watch commemorates this, reading: 'Presented by W. T. Stead to Mrs Etta

Wriedt through whose mediumship Queen Victoria's direct voice was heard in London in July 1911.'

Towards the end of her life Mrs Wriedt decided that the watch should be returned to Britain and she asked the then Canadian Prime Minister, Mackenzie King, who often attended her seances, if he would undertake to deliver it. The Canadian Premier, a convinced spiritualist, passed the watch to the Duchess of Hamilton and she presented it to the College of Psychic Studies (formerly the London Spiritualist Alliance and then the College of Psychic Science) and there it remained until stolen in 1963.

Several questions arise as to the authenticity of this relic and at least one of Queen Victoria's biographers rejects the watch as fraudulent. The date 1846 suggests that Queen Victoria was deeply involved in spiritualistic practices before such activity was widely popular in this country but my inquiries indicate that this could well have been so. The date was six years after Queen Victoria and Prince Albert were married; already they had twice visited the Château d'Eu and knew all about Louis Philippe's fascination with the occult and they had certainly met many other men and women of standing who were attracted to the possibility of communication with the dead.

Other doubts arise from the fact that Osborne is incorrectly spelt and that the watch was originally inscribed to Miss Georgiana Eagle. 'Who was "Georgiana Eagle"?' asks one critic. While it may be true that her name is not to be found in spiritualist or royal records, it is also true that there are and always have been many sensitives, clairvoyants and mediums who do not seek publicity and who practise solely in private. It would not be in the least unlikely that such a person could give 'meritorious and extraordinary clairvoyance' to Queen Victoria without there being any special or royal writing to record the fact. This has certainly happened since Victoria's day and there is every reason to think that it happened in her day.

The incorrect spelling of 'Osborne' is odd and at first sight one is inclined to think that Queen Victoria would never have let such a mistake pass but we must consider the event in its context. Presuming that the clairvoyance sessions with the Queen were clandestine and unrecorded officially (as they surely would have been), the preparation of the inscribed gold watch would have been undertaken equally quietly. It could well have been that the Queen gave the necessary instructions for the inscription and the watch was then despatched without further inspection by her. After all, it would seem that Georgiana Eagle was ill (she is said to have died before she received the watch) so it could well have been the case that the Queen asked for the inscription to be completed without delay and the watch despatched with all speed. Similar stringent conditions of secrecy could have resulted in the slight difference in the usual royal binding as reported in the Lees special presentation copy of his book.

Criticism has also been made of the idea that the Queen would turn to Stead for advice about who was most worthy of the watch. He was associated with the *Pall Mall Gazette* (*not* one of the Queen's favourite periodicals!) and neither Stead's daughter nor his biographer Joseph Baylen are said to accept this version of the story. But perhaps there is no question of the Queen approaching Stead. After the death of Georgiana Eagle there is no evidence that the watch was returned to Queen Victoria, which seems an unlikely course to take; more likely surely that those dealing with the estate of Miss Georgiana Eagle would pass the watch to some prominent spiritualist such as W. T. Stead for him to pass on to a suitable recipient. Since he was personally much impressed by the mediumship of Etta Wriedt, as were many others, what more natural than that she, after he had consulted other suitable friends, should become the recipient? It is perhaps odd that the affair does not seem to have found its way into any of Stead's writings but there could be many reasons for that and it is no valid basis for rejecting the whole story.

What cannot be disputed, it seems, is that the prominent American medium Mrs Etta Wriedt did accept the watch and that it eventually found its way to the College of Psychic Studies where it was exhibited for many years.

CHAPTER SEVEN

JOHN BROWN
– AN ENIGMATIC INFLUENCE

Soon after her first holiday in Scotland with Prince Albert the Queen mentions in her Journal the Highlanders who had helped to look after her at Balmoral and the list includes a certain 'young John Brown'. By the time this young man had become a little older, the Queen, in her wisdom, could or would never see anything wrong in him.

One of the natives of the village of Crathie who watched the new mock-Gothic Balmoral Castle rising upon its ancient foundations could well have been the powerful, red-whiskered and probably drink-sodden John Brown, then in his twenties, for when the castle was being built the Queen had already, on the recommendation of her husband, accepted Brown as her outdoor personal attendant.

After the traumatic death of Albert and the Queen's flight to isolation in the Isle of Wight, it is said she did not smile again until some years later when she looked out of her window and saw John Brown with her favourite pony.

There is some mystery about how John Brown came to be summoned to Osborne in the first place. Some say it was the Queen's idea, which seems unlikely given the state she was then in; others that her advisers though the sight of a loyal Scottish servant and her favourite Highland pony might bring her out of herself; still others say it was in response to psychic messages or a message from a psychic; others again say the idea came from her favourite, Alice, Grand Duchess of Hesse and the Rhine, always a thoughtful and dutiful daughter.

At all events, that bright March morning in 1864 the Queen looked down to the frosty lawns and saw John Brown in his kilt leading 'dear little Lochnagar' harnessed to her own tiny pony cart. She probably looked from the pony to the cart and then to the Highlander leading it and thought to herself: had not Albert himself chosen Brown as her normal outdoor servant? That being so, she would have decided that his presence at Osborne must be a sign.

In 1864 Queen Victoria was at an awkward age; often she was seen to be near to tears and, consciously or unconsciously, she was in desperate need of a man in her life. Various well-meaning people tried to help Victoria in her deep sadness but when her daughter Vicky had, quietly and tactfully, suggested to her that it was time for gloom and mourning to be put aside, the Queen replied sharply that it was all very well for her to talk; she had a man in her bed while all the Queen had to clasp was her husband's nightshirt or an old red dressing-gown. And when a gentleman of the cloth told her that she should regard herself as a bride of Christ, the Queen dismissed such an idea as 'twaddle'. But in John Brown she was to find, it seems, everything she had been looking for although he was by no means universally popular.

Bertie, to mention only one, could not abide John Brown and could never understand his mother's blatant relationship with the low and often foul-mouthed gillie. Bertie, of course, was a snob at heart whereas his mother could always make herself at ease with the lower classes.

Before long Brown does seem to have become more than a personal servant and the Queen and he went for long and solitary walks and rides together. John Brown was, by all accounts, a kindly man and he was sorry for the Queen wallowing in her widowhood. He had a fierce appearance and he frequently smelt of drink and stale sweat but oddly enough this unwholesome aspect of Brown does not seem to have worried the Queen (of course she was always good at closing her eyes to things she did not wish to see) and soon everyone at Osborne found themselves forced to keep on the right side of the strange man who had the Queen's ear at all times; why, they asked themselves time and time again, why on earth had he been brought from Scotland to 'please' the Queen?

It is possible that her reaction to Albert's death and what it did to her meant that most of her family found it more difficult to look up to her, and the Queen, aware of this, turned to her servants, to whom she was still a majestic and all-inspiring figure. Certainly within a matter of months the young widow had fallen completely under the spell of John Brown; she hung on his every word and was quoting him in familiar terms in letters to her friends and family. All this may have been just what she needed but it caused considerable public concern.

What is interesting to realize, at this distance of time, is that the new and formidable hold that Brown had over the Queen led her to a new and heightened awareness of psychic activity and, she believed, to a new closeness with her departed Albert. She certainly had sittings and seances with John Brown acting as medium and although practically all the records of such seances have 'disappeared' it is known that King George VI discovered one such record and spent a long time reading it.

Prince Albert had, we are told, picked John Brown to serve the Queen but in his wildest nightmares he could not have dreamed that within a few short years it would be widely believed that the Queen and John Brown were lovers and that to many people John Brown seemed to rule Britain as much as Queen Victoria.

When Prince Albert died, John Brown had already been the Queen's 'particular' gillie for nearly three years. There is no doubt that he proved himself useful in his duties close to the Queen; he was already a familiar help on 'expeditions' as long as he was not too 'bashful' (the Queen's word for tipsy). He had first been seen by the Queen in the south of England when he made a brief visit to the Second International Exhibition in June 1862 with Grant, the chief gillie, and other servants and attendants — and already the Queen admired the 'cut of his jib'. She always had an eye for a manly figure and at that early date she does seem to have seen something exceptional in the somewhat strange Scot; and she was of course well aware of his reputed psychic ability. Yet there was something more about the rough, handsome, strong, silent and dour Highlander that struck a chord deep inside the Queen; he appealed overwhelmingly to her and she found herself overlooking his rough ways and brusque manner as he attended to her comforts. Indeed she found more and more pleasure in his presence as he became more and more familiar in his ways.

Within a couple of months of Brown's arriving at Osborne the Queen was referring to him in her Journal as 'the good soul', and by February 1865 she had decided he would be with her permanently. Besides such mundane duties as looking after her pony, he would 'make himself useful in other ways besides . . .' Furthermore he was to be called 'The Queen's Highland Servant' and it was to be understood by everyone that he was just that; that he would take orders from no one but the Queen herself. Thereafter he attended her not only out of doors but also indoors and sometimes behind locked doors, hardly ever leaving her side and never taking holidays or days off. The Queen promised him a cottage at Balmoral if he married and a few years later, in 1876, he got his cottage although he was still, as far as is known, unmarried. By that time his salary had risen in five years from £120 to £400 plus £70 for clothes, and the Queen was writing: 'You will see in this the greatest anxiety to show more and more what you are to me and as time goes on this will be more and more seen and known.'

A reputable magazine of the day, *Tinsley's Magazine*, published an alleged account of an American visitor to England describing the 'loose manner in which Englishmen think of and speak about women . . . Soon after my arrival in England,' the writer went on, 'at a table where all the company were gentlemen of rank or position, there were constant references to and jokes about "Mrs Brown" . . . I lost the point of all the witty sayings, and should have remained in blissful ignorance throughout the dinner had not my host kindly informed me that "Mrs Brown" was an English synonym for the Queen . . . I have been told that the Queen was not allowed to hold a review in Hyde Park, because Lord Derby and the Duke of Cambridge objected to John Brown's presence; that the Prince of Wales remonstrated with his mother over a cartoon depicting Brown in charge of the crown and the throne; that the Queen was insane and John Brown was her keeper; that the Queen was a spiritualist and John Brown was her medium — in a word, a hundred stories, each more absurd than the other, and all vouched for by men of considerable station and authority.'

The title 'Mrs Brown' seems to have stemmed from a privately printed pamphlet entitled 'Mrs John Brown' which circulated widely among the upper class and their servants. Whoever wrote the pamphlet possessed information about aspects of palace life that were not common knowledge and it was not reasonably possible to dismiss the pamphlet as wholly inaccurate and complete nonsense.

It declared that the Queen and Mr Brown were married at a secret ceremony at which the Duchess of Roxburghe, the Queen's Mistress of the Robes, was the only woman present. Although no one had the audacity to broach the Duchess on the subject direct, she was viewed thereafter by many people in a different light and she did seem to move in a shaded area that left everyone wondering.

The son of Sir Henry Ponsonby has related that years after the Queen was dead and the Duchess was very elderly, a young nephew ventured to ask her if she really had been present at such a marriage. The Duchess is said to have laughed and protested that she had never heard the story before and for all those years she had been totally unaware of being regarded as notorious!

Although there is no evidence that there ever was such a secret marriage, it has to be said that there was little to prevent the Queen entering into a morganatic marriage with John Brown if, as some people have thought, she was drawn to him by some profound and irresistible attraction or if, as others suspected, she connected Brown in some spiritual way with her dead Albert. If this were so, it was argued, her conscience might have urged her to marry Brown rather than continue an otherwise emotional attachment, upon which, as E. E. P. Tisdall has put it, 'the ghost of the Beloved One would be more likely to frown'.

There is no doubt that many people near the Queen thought that she felt there was a mystic bond between Brown and Prince Albert. Indeed something in her mind did bind the three of them together for it was not unusual for the Queen, when she was troubled or worried on some particular point, to look towards one of the many busts of the Prince and, after concentrating there for a moment, to turn her gaze on John Brown where it would linger for a minute before she made her reply.

There are even said to have been watchers (again according to E. E. P. Tisdall) 'who experienced a slight chill, an uncanniness in the air, when they saw this'.

Soon after Brown became her permanent and personal servant the Queen was writing that it was a 'real comfort . . . for he is devoted to me, so simple, so intelligent, *so unlike* an *ordinary* servant' (the Queen's italics). She would write in great detail about how he came to her room, how everything was always right, how devoted he was, how attached, how clever; his only object and interest being to be of service to her and 'and God knows how much I want to be taken care of', which sounds like a cry from the heart. The Queen, in turn, seemed to have Brown's welfare always in the forefront of her mind; she hardly seemed to think of anyone or anything else. Small wonder that the world outside the court became intrigued and speculated as to what was happening or had happened.

By the end of 1866 Brown was evidently feeling the burden of all he did. The Queen wrote to the wife of Sir Thomas Biddulph, her Master of the Household: 'my poor Brown has so much to do . . . he is often *so tired* from being constantly on his legs that he goes to bed with swollen feet and can't sleep from fatigue!'

Things went from bad to worse from the court's point of view. With the publication of the article in *Tinsley's Magazine* and the appearance of other articles and pamphlets a wider public read the malicious rumours that were widely circulating in elite circles; and although the journalist writing in *Tinsley's* added a footnote to the effect that the article was silly nonsense (doubtless to safeguard himself), the Queen continued to provide evidence of her undoubted infatuation with John Brown. Victoria's response to all this was interesting and possibly enlightening. Writing to Lord Charles Fitzroy she said the Queen would 'quietly and firmly continue to do what she thought and knew to be right'.

The opinions of those who knew the Queen, according to Hector Bolitho, was that the relationship between the Queen and John Brown was wholly innocent but that it would have been expedient if she had moderated it. Her reply to this would no doubt have been the reply she made to the minister who once used the word 'expedient': 'that is was a word she never wished to hear again nor to understand'.

By now, John Brown was faultless in every last little thing, just as Albert had once been right in all he did. When Brown complained, for example, that royal smokers (meaning Bertie and his companions) kept him (John Brown) up too late, the Queen immediately asked her equerry to make it known that 'for the sake of the servants' the smoking room should be closed by midnight.

Queen Victoria was in fact violently opposed to smoking and very sensitive to smoking having taken place. She would not allow it at

Balmoral or at Osborne, if she knew about it, apart perhaps from a small empty room somewhere across a courtyard. It is said that if a person had been smoking when he or she wrote a letter to the Queen, she could detect the fact when she received the letter. Yet Brown was known to smoke his pipe in his bedroom which, after he had become her personal servant, was invariably close to the Queen's apartments; and still there are those who refuse to accept that John Brown was anything more to the Queen than a servant. The argument that Brown must have had some extraordinary and possibly supernatural hold over the Queen has been put forward by those who claimed to have seen the Highland gillie actually smoking his pipe in the Queen's presence. For this to have happened, they say, some very exceptional circumstance must have been present.

The Queen's advisers and her family tried to persuade her to dispense with Brown's services but the Queen, nothing if not obstinate, refused. Although the general disquiet at the affair gradually subsided, Brown's overriding presence and loud and rude comments in any company caused embarrassment to everyone but the Queen and John Brown. Soon there were open comments about the laxity of the servants' supervision but nothing seemed to be capable of assailing John Brown.

Very few people could understand the Queen's extraordinary devotion to her personal attendant and her unreasonable bias in favour of everything Scottish except in the context of her having married him, or at least taken him as her lover. At the same time it cannot be denied that Brown brought about a welcome change in the Queen's emotional life. During those awful days and weeks and months of bereavement when she would not leave her rooms at Osborne and ministers and those close to the Queen began to fear for her reason, it was Brown alone who managed to talk quietly with her and gain her complete confidence. Brown it was who brought her jars of jam from Scotland and who gave her a present of a dozen eggcups which were used for breakfast every Sunday morning that she was at Balmoral, the use of one of which became a fetish for the Queen; the time came when she would not use any other eggcup, anywhere. In his eyes Victoria was a woman, not a Queen, and he treated her accordingly, which was just the medicine she needed at just the right time.

In 1866, five years after the death of Prince Albert, the Queen was still writing about her duty to preserve her health 'and very shattered nerves (every day more and more shattered) from becoming seriously worse'. By now some of her familiar father figures had gone: Baron Stockmar died in 1863 and her dear Uncle Leopold in 1865. In her need to feel safe and secure, so that her nerves could relax, she depended more and more on her servant John Brown and on her Prime Minister Disraeli.

Queen Victoria was always whole-hearted and boundless in her enthusiasm once it had been aroused. When she gave her affection and trust she did it without stinting and often without thinking twice about the consequences. As John Brown came to play an increasingly important part in her life, members of the royal household found themselves forced to communicate with her through John Brown. Not unnaturally, this was resented by the other servants and even more so by the Queen's children, resulting in long and bitter quarrels. The Prince of Wales, in particular, disliked Brown, the man who regularly entered the Queen's room without knocking, who sat down familiarly in her armchair, who nightly escorted her to her bedchamber, who swore repeatedly, who referred to her as 'Her *Mad*-jestie', and who even issued orders himself.

The time came when the Queen's advisers, who wanted Brown dismissed, went in a body to express their concern about the relationship and her infrequent public appearances and to give their advice. The Queen told them that John Brown was necessary to her comfort and her safety. Whether or not this was so her obstinate loyalty would have ensured that she stood by him. In short, as Dorothy Marshall puts it in her *Life and Times of Victoria* (1972), she would appear in public when she felt able, and Brown would stay. Her family, ministers and servants retreated defeated.

As her closeness to John Brown increased so the Queen became less and less involved with other people. For example, Bertie would not accord Brown the special treatment and status at Sandringham that the Queen insisted upon, so she did not visit Sandringham, for she would not go anywhere without Brown.

There can surely be no doubt in anyone's mind but that the Queen loved John Brown. Can anyone read *Further Leaves from Our Life in the Highlands* and come to any other conclusion? He is the hero of the book; it is full of the most trivial incidents concerning him.

During the course of a night in March 1883, John Brown died. It so happened that the Queen herself was ill with painful rheumatic attacks following a fall down some stairs at Windsor earlier in the month and at first no one dared to inform her of Brown's death. Eventually, however, her son Prince Leopold, Duke of Albany, agreed to undertake the task. When he had spoken an awful silence came over the Queen and, as one writer has put it, 'only the tears trickling in rivers down her cheeks betrayed that she was not a wax effigy'.

Eighteen and a half years of strange nearness and devotion had ended, a nearness and devotion that was of inestimable value and necessity to the lonely sovereign. As soon as she had recovered from the initial shock of his death she poured out her sorrow in announcements and letters to all and sundry. John Brown had been her 'best and truest friend — as I was his'; she filled half a column of the Court

Circular with praises for him and his services to her; he was, she said, the one servant who in all the years he had been with her 'had not absented himself from duty for a single day'. 'To Her Majesty the loss is irreparable, and the death of this truly devoted and faithful servant has been a grievous shock to the Queen.' A gold Devoted Service medal and a silver Faithful Service medal, both given by the Queen to John Brown, were auctioned for thousands of pounds at Sotheby's in 1984.

A memorial seat was erected at Osborne and a statue set up at Balmoral to celebrate the virtues of one who was 'not only a servant but a real friend'. To her grandson Prince George of York she wrote, 'I have lost my dearest friend who no one in the world can ever replace . . .' There is evidence that some of the notes that passed between the Queen and John Brown were far more extreme and 'interesting' than this example of her feelings would suggest. E. E. P. Tisdall, the author of *Queen Victoria's Private Life* who first became intrigued by the 'strange affair of John Brown' in the early days of the Second World War, has revealed that he put an advertisement in a national newspaper appealing to anyone with personal memories or family records about 'Queen Victoria's John Brown' to communicate with him. A number of interesting replies rewarded his resourcefulness but it was the contents of one large envelope which thoroughly startled him and everyone else to whom he showed them.

Inside the envelope was a note typed on an oddment of paper, unsigned and with no address, only a telephone number, and two photostated copies of a letter with deep black mourning borders. This letter had a printed Osborne House address, it bore the royal monogram of Queen Victoria, and it was handwritten, the words, 'Burn this' heavily underlined. It was quite obvious that the original from which the photocopy had been taken had been torn into little pieces and carefully restored for reproducing. The handwriting appeared to be Queen Victoria's and there were many of those familiar underlinings with which the Queen used to emphasize words in every letter she ever wrote.

The accompanying typed note stated that the sender had a near relative who had once held a post of some authority at Osborne during the 1870s, and he had received the letter as a curiosity from one of the royal footmen with whom he had been friendly. This footman, it was stated, frequently carried messages between the Queen and John Brown; usually they were routine orders and requests concerning household matters but the footman noticed that on occasions, as soon as he had read the note, Brown quickly tore it into small pieces and dropped it into a wastepaper basket. One day the opportunity occurred for the footman to retrieve such an apparently confidential note and having done so he painstakingly pieced the scraps together. The photocopied letter was the result.

116

Tisdall says the letter was not addressed to anybody and it was not signed. The first few sentences were clearly addressed to someone with whom the writer was fairly intimate, a person who made 'arrangements' for the writer; and the message went on to state that 'Helena' (presumably Princess Helena) and her children would be needing the bathing machine that afternoon and requested the person to whom the note was intended to make the necessary arrangements — but then there occurred a sentence so completely out of context that it took one's breath away: 'Oh, forgive me if I offend, but you are so dear to me, so adored, that I cannot bear to live without you.' Tisdall says he hurriedly read on, wondering what on earth was coming next but, to his surprise, there was nothing more of a personal nature, only something about a 'visit to my Scottish capital'. The message ended with the words 'your own loving one' and nothing else.

Tisdall suggests that the letter, if genuine, revealed a lovers' quarrel and he feels that only someone under considerable strain would jump headlong from the practical to the emotional and as suddenly back again, as the writer had done. It is known that the Queen and John Brown sometimes had violent arguments and it is not difficult to imagine that during such a confrontation Brown, perhaps laced with whisky, might stamp out of the room saying he had finished with royal service. Tisdall considers too the possibility that the letter was a practical joke, concocted by someone familiar with the royal handwriting and having access to the correct headed notepaper but, he sensibly argues, if it was an invention surely something more shocking would have been produced, something more crude that would have prompted a snigger in the servants' quarters — and there was no question of financial gain from the anonymous correspondent who answered Tisdall's advertisement. The author rang the telephone number given and asked for an address to which he could return the letter. He was told, 'It doesn't matter, they're only copies; keep them if you think they may come in useful' and the line went dead.

During the war Tisdall and his family moved to Devon and while sorting his papers there in 1946 he came across the letter and the note again. He showed them to a number of people and then returned them to the buff envelope in which they had arrived. Fourteen years later he again sorted through his papers as he prepared to leave Devon for London and he threw out and destroyed many of the accumulated mass of correspondence. He felt certain that he had not destroyed the Osborne letter but he never found it again.

After John Brown died, Tennyson called on the Queen to offer his condolences and later composed an inscription for the statue of John Brown that was erected at Balmoral, a powerful likeness that caused violent reactions from a number of people. Lady Errol, who abhorred graven images, likened it to Nebuchadnezzar's image of the idol Bel;

Bertie seethed quietly and bided his time, and as soon as he became King he smashed many of the busts and images of John Brown with his own hands. The one at Balmoral he eventually succeeded in having banished to a much less conspicuous site than where it had been erected; indeed it is only with some difficulty that it can now be found. Mementoes and photographs of the hated John Brown were destroyed and his apartment at Windsor Castle, which was his on his elevation to 'Esquirehood', was converted into a billiard room — all on the orders of Bertie, by then King Edward VII.

But all this was in the future; immediately following Brown's death the Queen's Journal is sprinkled with references to how much she missed him and his 'good strong arm . . .' Within a month of his death she set about having a biography prepared of her favourite gillie, an idea that caused consternation and arguments. Discussions rumbled on and on as the Queen worked on another edition of her *Leaves from a Journal*, which was eventually published in 1884 under the title *More Leaves from a Journal of Our Life in the Highlands* with many a fulsome tribute to John Brown. Years later Max Beerbohm, the witty young caricaturist and writer, embellished his copy of the latter volume with a mock inscription in what appeared to be the Queen's hand and characteristic of her beliefs and feelings: 'For Mr Beerbohm, the never-sufficiently-to-be-studied writer whom Albert looks down on affectionately, I am sure . . .'

In February 1884, eleven months after John Brown's death, Sir Henry Ponsonby received from the Queen a manuscript together with a note that was in the nature of being a direction to him that she was engaged on a 'little memoir' of John Brown, her object being to show that Brown was a 'great deal more' than a devoted servant. A few days later Ponsonby sent a lengthy letter to the Queen saying, among other things, that he doubted whether 'this record of Your Majesty's innermost and most secret feelings' should be published. In the event, publication of the John Brown memoirs was 'postponed'. Eventually, according to Sir Arthur Ponsonby, Sir Henry's biographer, the manuscript was destroyed. Many people thought then and many think now that what Ponsonby destroyed were records of Brown's spiritualistic seances with Queen Victoria. Other people, who should know, suspect that these records still exist, closely guarded in the 'unavailable' royal archives.

Lionel Logue, a distinguished speech therapist who cured King George VI's stammer and a man of unimpeachable honour, has revealed that the King told him that he had found and read with the greatest interest one of Brown's diaries describing many seances and communications, a diary that had evidently escaped the Ponsonby fire. The Royal Librarian at Windsor tells me that he has no knowledge of this diary.

Whether or not John Brown was a medium it must seem likely on the available evidence that the Queen regarded him as a link between herself and the dead Albert. Brown could easily have pretended to receive such messages for the Queen; he may even have allowed her, in her unbalanced state, to think that he was a kind of reincarnation of her lost Albert. What is interesting is that the Queen was interested in spiritualism at a very early date, long before she met Brown, and that the John Brown scandal had little, if anything, to do with her regard for him as a medium.

According to Sue Bredbury, writing in *Weekend Extra*, 'the kilted figure of John Brown, Queen Victoria's confidant, is often seen to this day stalking the corridors and entrance hall at Balmoral'. *Psychic News* published a piece in November 1978 stating that ten years previously the present Queen was reported to have seen the ghostly form of John Brown at Balmoral; while the ghost of Queen Victoria, it seems, appears periodically in the grounds of Osborne House.

CHAPTER EIGHT

GHOSTS AND HAUNTED HOUSES – A CONTINUAL INTEREST

Any reading of almost any life of Queen Victoria reveals, to a quite remarkable degree, the number of visits she paid as a youngster to places and houses that had legends and ghost stories associated with them. It must seem likely, given her undoubted interest in psychic matters, that later on she sought out such places where she would be likely to hear ghost stories with an historical background, which she never tired of hearing. Although as Queen Victoria she can never be said to have travelled extensively throughout the British Isles, she did stay at many places that had the reputation of being haunted, including The Anchor — now The Royal Anchor — at Liphook where a road is still named after her. She was at The Anchor as a little girl with her mother and again later as a married woman with Albert.

Other visitors to The Anchor when it was an important posting house include the redoubtable Blücher, the Prussian field marshal and Prince of Wahlstadt; Queen Anne, King William IV, Lord Nelson, the Duke of Wellington, Queen Elizabeth I, King James I and King Charles II; tradition even has it that King Edward II visited the inn in 1310. It is not, however, an illustrious historical ghost that allegedly haunts the inn but the ghost of a highwayman, Captain Jacques, who once plied his trade in the area around Liphook.

The story goes that eventually the dishonourable Captain was cornered in Room No. 6 by Excisemen who shot him down as he tried to hide in a secret passageway behind the fireplace. Over the years many visitors occupying Room 6, without knowing the story, have reported hearing and seeing things they could not explain in the quiet of the night.

It is known that Victoria had the happiest childhood memories of a house at Esher. 'Claremont,' she was to write, 'remains as the brightest epoch of my otherwise rather melancholy childhood — to listen to some music in the hall when there were dinner guests — and to go and see dear old Louis!' This was Mrs Louisa Louis, Princess Charlotte's devoted dresser and friend, and later housekeeper at Claremont.

Leopold never seemed to recover from the death of Charlotte. When he was nearly seventy he was writing to his niece Victoria: 'Saw the ruins of this happy home, and the destruction, at one blow, of every hope and happiness. Never had this feeling of happiness, which blessed my short married life, returned.' After Charlotte's death all her possessions remained as she had left them, the watch just where she had placed it on the mantelpiece, the coat and hat where she had thrown them over a screen when she came in for the last time.

Leopold lived on for years at Claremont, drawing the $50,000 a year that was granted to him on his marriage, and he made only occasional visits to the Continent. On one of these, however, he thought he detected an extraordinary likeness to Charlotte in Karoline Bauer, a cousin of his faithful Stockmar, and he suggested a morganatic marriage. Whether this took place or not we do not know for certain but Leopold brought Karoline and her mother back to England with him and settled them in a house near Claremont where he was in the habit of taking dinner with them. Once, in Leopold's absence, Karoline came upon Victoria walking in the grounds.

Claremont was a place of memories: Leopold sitting with a bust of his dead wife at his elbow; the exiled Louis Philippe, who also died there, and his active interest in spiritualism; and the ever-present spectre of Charlotte. The 'sweet stillness of Claremont' enchanted Victoria and she spent the first ten birthdays of her reign there; and then there were the ghosts.

There can be little doubt that Victoria saw the ghost of old Louis after Charlotte's death. The Queen has described the much-loved servant 'standing in my room of an evening, dressed in her best, holding herself so erect, as she always did and making the low dignified curtsy so peculiar to herself'.

Buckingham Palace, originally Buckingham House and built by John Sheffield, first Duke of Buckingham in 1705, was erected on the site of a priory where a monk is supposed to have died in the punishment cell and to have haunted the place thereafter; subsequently the same ghost was reportedly seen in the vicinity of Buckingham Palace. When she moved into Buckingham Palace, Queen Victoria was told about the phantom monk and that it was reputed to appear on Christmas Day, or thereabouts, in irons on the broad terrace overlooking the gardens at the rear of the property.

Recent events have shown that entry by unlawful persons to Buckingham Palace is not too difficult and it seems that it has always been so. In December 1838 'the boy Cotton' was apprehended in the Palace having spent no less than a year there, inhabiting various domestic offices and servants' quarters and living on excellent food which he

121

talked of for the rest of his life. He was twelve years old and frequently concealed himself in chimneys. Unlike a later intruder, he never attempted to penetrate the state apartments or the royal boudoir but he did open a sealed letter addressed to Queen Victoria and help himself to a few small articles. He was apprehended while trying to leave the Palace by the equerries' gate.

A later ghost at Buckingham Palace — not seen during Victoria's time — is that of a private secretary to King Edward VII who committed suicide after being cited in a divorce action. His ghost was seen in 1939, sitting at a desk in a first-floor office, apparently searching through the drawers. The desk was the one he had used when he had worked for the King.

Nearby St James's Palace, where Victoria and Albert were married and where the Queen held her court until the death of the Prince Consort, was originally a hospital; indeed the chapel where the royal couple were married is supposed to be the same building that was used when the building was a hospital for fourteen leprous women. An inner courtyard still contains fourteen stones bearing crosses, worn but still visible, which are said to be the graves of the fourteen unfortunate 'maidens that were lepers' who apparently rest undisturbed in that place of memories.

Charles II was born at St James's Palace, and so was James II, Queen Anne, and George IV, and it was here that Charles I spent his last days before his execution when he walked across St James's Park to the scaffold in Whitehall.

When George I resided at St James's Palace he had with him Mlle Schulemberg, Duchess of Kendal, his German mistress, and Miss Brett, his English mistress; the two women used to quarrel continually. George II was also at the Palace with his mistress, Mrs Howard, afterwards Countess of Suffolk, and she had the same apartments as those once occupied by the Duchess of Kendal. The Countess used to say she could hear the ghostly quarrelling voices of Schulemberg and Brett.

Queen Caroline, wife of George II, died here, as did his daughter Caroline; and in the days of Charles II it was the residence of his mistress Hortense Mancini, Duchess of Mazarin, who shared with Queen Victoria an interest in apparitions and the possibility — or probability — of immortality. When the Duchess of Mazarin resided at St James's, there was also in residence Madame de Beauclair, the mistress of Charles's brother and successor, James II.

Both ladies, living in retirement, were allotted handsome suites of apartments in the palace and they became great friends. On more than one occasion they discussed the immortality of the soul, the evidence for apparitions and the possibility of returning to earth after death. They gave each other a solemn undertaking that whoever should die first would return, if it were possible, to show herself to her friend. This promise was reaffirmed in the presence of witnesses when the Duchess of Mazarin lay dying.

Some years later Madame de Beauclair stated that she had no faith in an afterlife, for she considered the fact that her friend had not returned to her as proof of its non-existence.

A few months later Madame de Beauclair sent an urgent message to a friend with whom she had discussed the matter of life after death, entreating her to come at once if she wanted to see her alive. The lady concerned was unwell, and hesitated and was about to send her excuses when a still more urgent message arrived, accompanied by a casket of jewellery, imploring her to come at once.

Hurrying to St James's Palace she was surprised to find Madame de Beauclair seemingly in the best of health and still more surprised when her friend told her that she had been visited by her dead companion, the Duchess of Mazarin, and knew that she would soon be dead herself. The ghost of the Duchess had apparently walked round the bed of Madame de Beauclair, 'swimming rather than walking', and had stopped beside an Indian chest and, 'with her usual sweetness', said, 'Between the hours of twelve and one tonight you will be with me.' Having made this grim prophecy the apparition vanished.

The midnight hour was in fact close at hand and, even as the clock began to strike the hour, Madame de Beauclair exclaimed suddenly, 'Oh, I am sick at heart!' and about thirty minutes later she was dead.

Queen Victoria twice visited the Chateau d'Eu in Normandy as the guest of Louis Philippe, 'The Citizen King' as he liked to be called. In fact Queen Victoria's first visit in 1843 was the first time she had crossed the Channel and the first time an English sovereign had visited a French sovereign since Henry VIII and Francis I met in 1520 at the Field of the Cloth of Gold. Louis Philippe was much interested in all aspects of the occult and Victoria and Albert greatly enjoyed listening to his various stories and experiences. Among a number of eccentricities, he cherished some curious superstitions which interested Victoria who was also very superstitious. Louis Philippe was very afraid of cats, sharing with Lord Roberts, among others, an almost painful aversion to their presence. He also hated green, which is generally considered to be an unlucky colour, and everyone close to him made sure they never wore it.

Today the Chateau d'Eu, I am informed by the Curator, Martine Bailleux-Delbecq, is a Museum (created in 1973) dedicated to Louis Philippe and displayed there are a number of reminders of the two visits made by Queen Victoria in September 1843 and October 1845. There are pictures, including one showing the arrival of Victoria in the courtyard of what was once the summer palace of King Louis Philippe, engravings, letters, a theatre programme, particulars of the concerts arranged for Victoria, and a detailed plan of the Queen's engagements. In closing his charming letter to me M. Bailleux-Deblecq says:

> I think you should come here and see the trees of the Park
> and the Forest which your Queen liked very much . . .
> unfortunately, we have not yet met a ghost on the staircase of
> the Palace, but I think a small part of the soul of Queen Victoria
> is floating in the air here. . . .

King Louis Philippe lost his throne in 1848, because of 'licentiousness at Court', as Prince Albert had a habit of pointing out to anyone whom he felt might benefit from the knowledge. Victoria was never over-fond of the greedy Louis Philippe but she was interested in his quite remarkable knowledge of the Chaldean system of predicting future events by using numbers.

After losing his throne the Duke of Orleans (the title the King reverted to) entertained Cheiro to dinner on his yacht where for several hours they discussed the 'hidden wisdom' of Cabala (or Kabbalah), the obscure 'true knowledge' and magical doctrine that is basically a philosophical system which believes that the ultimate spirit somehow 'fell' through ten 'planes' to the human level in which we find ourselves, which is supposed to be the lowest of the ten. However, a kind of ladder, known as the 'Tree of Life', stretched upwards through the ten planes and students of the Cabala believe that man can, theoretically, clamber upwards through these reservoirs of power, eventually developing an ultimate serenity.

The Duke was fascinated by the way lives, according to Cheiro, were ruled by numbers and he referred to himself as 'fated'. He had in his possession a remarkable chart of the lives of his ancestors, drawn up in 1656. It held out no hope of a restoration of the French monarchy and Cheiro pointed out that it would seem that the Duke would not reach fifty-seven years of age. His eventual death confirmed this.

During the course of the 1843 visit to the Continent, Victoria also visited Bruges, Ghent, Brussels and Antwerp. In Bruges she must have heard some of the many ancient legends associated with the Saye Halle, the Mysterious Vault, the Rue Queue de Vache, the Baudouin of the Iron Arm, the Street of the Blind Ass, and the story of the famous Bruges swans. She would also have heard about the sacred relic of the Holy Blood that solidifies and liquifies; she may even have visited the Church of the Holy Blood and seen the curious phial said to contain some of the blood of Jesus Christ, as I did during a visit some years ago.

At Bruges she would have delighted in such tales and especially perhaps in the legend of the so-called Inquisition House in the Place du

Three of the most influential people in Victoria's life: Her mother, who kept Victoria tightly under control for as long as she was able to do so; Lord Melbourne *(bottom left)*, on whom she lent for valuable advice in the early years of her reign; and Sir John Conroy *(bottom right)*, whom Victoria never forgave for what she deemed indiscretions and manipulations.

Woolbrook Cottage, Sidmouth, in 1819. Here Queen Victoria's father died and the infant Princess nearly lost her life. Today the Royal Glen Hotel is, in many ways, little changed.

The nursery window at Woolbrook Cottage (now Roya Glen Hotel), Sidmouth. Through this window a shot narrowly missed killing the infant Princess Victoria in 1819. The actual pane was the top one, now marked with coloure glass.

(top left) Cheiro — Count Louis Hamon, the seer and palmist who greatly impressed Edward VII, Queen Alexandra, King Leopold of Belgium, the Tsar of Russia, Gladstone, Lillie Langtry, Sarah Bernhardt and many other well-known people. A signed portrait in the possession of the author.

(top right) Alphonso XIII, King of Spain, fascinated Queen Victoria with his strange reputation. He was regarded by his own people as a *jettatore* and possessed of the evil eye. A signed portrait in the possession of the author.

(bottom left) Sir William Crookes, prominent psychic investigator, President of the Society for Psychical Research, Chairman of the Ghost Club, Fellow of the Royal Society; knighted by Queen Victoria in 1897 and awarded the Order of Merit in 1910.

Queen Victoria's marriage to Prince Albert was the joining of two minds with a similar outlook on the spirit world.

Albert and Victoria — as she like to be pictured by her subjects: a submissive, dutiful and loving wife, although their life together was not always like that. Albert, a weak and doom-laden man, and his physically strong young wife frequently tried their hands at table-turning and spent innumerable hours discussing the 'after life'.

The strange 'monks fireplace', originally exhibited at Prince Albert's 1851 Great Exhibition, and here shown in the dining-room at Borley Rectory, long known as 'the most haunted house in England'. Notice the print of Victoria and Albert over the fireplace.

Robert James Lees (1849-1931) whom Queen Victoria wished to appoint as her 'Resident Medium'. He is reported to have given many sittings to the Queen, and through him Prince Albert manifested to the widowed Queen's satisfaction.

John Brown. Many maintain that he was Queen Victoria's trusted medium. The monarch once called him 'God's own gift'.

Queen Victoria — an official portrait taken at the time of her Diamond Jubilee, Spring 1897.

Disraeli's study at Hughenden Manor. After his death Queen Victoria spent some time here alone and 'sensed' the apparition of her favourite statesman; other people too have seen Disraeli's form in this room in recent years. The Queen and her Prime Ministers often discussed the reality of psychic phenomena.

Queen Victoria's bedroom at Osborne House. Notice the portraits of Albert (one over his side of the bed) and a photograph of his coffin amid other mournful accessories.

Théâtre. In later years it was to become a cinema and a café but years ago it was a very gloomy and ancient black house with an ominous reputation. During alterations workmen discovered the foundations of a previous building and subterranean passages.

One passage was blocked by a large and elaborately carved door and when this was broken down it is said that a once magnificent hall was revealed, its walls still retaining traces of Spanish leather decorated with solid gold. In the centre of the hall there was a long table with carved and gilded chairs arranged all round it, and sitting at the head of the table were the long-dead remains of a man and woman clothed in what were once rich fifteenth-century costumes.

At the far end of the hall there was another richly carved door and when this too was broken down it revealed the skeleton of a man in armour standing at the entrance of a corridor. Few of the people who years later laughed and enjoyed themselves in the premises above knew anything about the tragic happenings that once took place in the hidden apartment below. After the discovery of the gruesome remains, there were, it was said, occasional phantom appearances of the unidentified couple in fifteenth-century costume and of the ghost of a man in armour, all in the immediate neighbourhood.

Victoria would shiver with delight at such stories, especially in this instance when she would have been told that it seems certain that the hall that was uncovered was either the scene of trials of the Inquisition or a secret meeting place of the Knights Templar. Certainly many a rich citizen and fair maid and many a gay knight disappeared mysteriously in the days of the Inquisition; a touch on the shoulder from a soldier and they would pass within the dread walls, never to be seen again.

In 1844, when a planned visit by the Queen to Ireland was cancelled due to political disturbances, Lord and Lady Glenlyan put Blair Atholl Castle at the royal party's disposal and the subsequent holiday that Victoria and Albert enjoyed in Scotland was one that convinced the Queen that she must find a house there. 'Scotland has made a favourable impression upon us both,' she wrote; not least, she might have added, because of the wealth of 'occult' associations she encountered wherever she travelled in that beautiful land.

Just a few miles south-east of Blair Atholl Castle, for instance, was the impressive Pass of Killiecrankie where in 1689, on 27 July, the Battle of Killiecrankie took place when William III's troops under General Mackay were routed by three thousand Highlanders under John Graham of Cleverhouse, Viscount Dundee, for James II.

The battle was fought on the hillside above the main road a mile north of the pass through which King William's men advanced to engage the Jacobites and shortly afterwards returned in retreat as they fled from the torrent of bare-footed red coats and tartans that swept down the valley. And each 27 July, Victoria would have been told, a red glow hangs over the scene of the conflict; a phantom light that many people can see in the valley through which the Highlanders charged. The mysterious glow is thought by local people to have its origin in a vision seen by Vicount Dundee on the eve of the battle.

As he slept, 'Bonnie Dundee' saw a man whose head poured with blood standing at his bedside, bidding him to get up and follow where he led. Dundee awoke but, seeing no one, interpreted the vision as a dream and returned to sleep. But again he was awakened by the same voice and the same figure; this time the form pointed to its bloody head and seemed to implore Dundee to rise and follow where he led. Now Dundee did get up and ascertained from the guard that no one had entered the tent. Satisfied, he once more returned to his bed but for a third time the same form appeared to him, bidding him arise and follow. The figure pointed towards the plain of Killiecrankie, seeming to indicate that he would meet Dundee there.

Dundee got up, dressed and discussed the strange vision with a Highland chief who agreed never to speak of the matter if the coming battle should prove successful for the Highlanders.

On the day of the battle Dundee was reluctant to descend from the high ground. Perhaps he had a premonition of his own death or maybe he wished to wait until darkness before coming to close quarters with the enemy, so that his troops could find shelter in the mountains if they were routed. At all events it was sunset, red and glowing, before he gave the order to charge. Within minutes King William's forces were defeated and beginning to flee when, almost as if by accident, a fatal shot struck Dundee in the side.

In 1844 Queen Victoria and the Prince Consort also visited Chiswick House where they are both said to have experienced the overwhelming odour of food being cooked, a smell that had been reported there for a number of years although the kitchens that were once situated in the north wing had not existed for many years; the same 'paranormal' smells have been reported there in recent years.

The old Jacobean Chiswick House has now quite disappeared, pulled down in the eighteenth century by Richard Boyle, third Earl of Burlington (after he had altered Burlington House, now the Royal Academy). On the site he built the present Palladian villa which drew from one critic the comment: 'too small to live in and too large to hang on a watchchain'. Among notable visitors here were the Tsar Nicholas and the Prince of Wales, later Edward VII, who lived here during his family's childhood.

When Victoria and Albert visited Chiswick House they were fascinated by such stories as those involving Frances, Countess of Somerset, a staunch believer in witchcraft and spells who procured love philtres to bring to her bed King James I's favourite Robert Carr,

Viscount Rochester. Frances had also obtained from a Norwich fortune-teller a charm to ensure that she would conceive a child. This seems to have worked and she did indeed bear a child, Lady Anne Carr, while imprisoned in the Tower for the murder of Sir Thomas Overbury.

The old Jacobean house changed hands rapidly, perhaps because of the evil memories left behind by the Countess of Somerset who died there 'in misery and disgrace'. After Richard Boyle had pulled down the old house and built the present villa, more as an art gallery than anything else, it was inherited by his daughter Charlotte who married the fourth Duke of Devonshire. Their daughter-in-law added two wings, in one of which Charles James Fox was to die in 1806. Another statesman, George Canning, breathed his last in one of the wings in 1827. At one period the property became a private lunatic asylum and some of the ghostly activity there has been accredited to this period. Victoria and Albert seem to have found all the stories they heard about Chiswick House 'most amusing'.

In 1845 the Queen paid an informal visit to the Duke of Wellington at Stratfield Saye. The Grand Duke had been present at Victoria's birth; he had been in no doubts about the Duchess of Kent, Victoria's mother, and the hated John Conroy being lovers; the Queen wrote in her Journal that the Duke was 'the best friend we have'. Not everyone liked Stratfield Saye and Victoria herself was not over-enthusiastic but she found the house 'convenient', presumably referring in her own fashion to the blue-patterned china water closets which the Duke had installed in every room, an almost unheard-of 'comfort' in those days.

On 8 September 1846 Queen Victoria and Prince Albert drove from Fowey to the ruined castle of Restormel. Here a strange custom was once observed, a 'mock prince' being chosen from among the free-holders of Lostwithiel and paraded through the streets decked in full regalia. He was led to the parish church with great ceremony and then taken to a previously selected house for a banquet. Afterwards the 'prince' reverted to his normal standing in the town. It is thought that the odd ritual was a folk memory of the days when a real prince was resident at Restormel Castle, at a time when Lostwithiel was an important town in Cornwall.

Queen Victoria was much interested in this former custom and also in the possibility of ghostly happenings in the vicinity of Restormel where many people have remarked upon a distinct and disturbing atmosphere. During the course of this visit to Cornwall the Queen and her husband went down an iron mine where she found 'something unearthly' about the cavern-like place with its flickering lights.

Three years later, in 1849, Queen Victoria became the first British sovereign ever to set foot in Cork where she soon heard that there were a number of ghosts and hauntings and superstitions associated with this, one of the most charming cities in Ireland. Just five miles away was the square keep of Blarney Castle with its famous Blarney Stone which is in fact the sill of one of the machicolated battlements. The power of eloquence can be obtained, it has long been thought, by those who succeed in kissing the stone. The Queen did not attempt the difficult manoeuvre to reach the stone, which is situated about twenty feet from the summit, but she was interested to learn that the term 'blarney' dates from the days of Elizabeth I who used it in referring to evasive answers that she met from the castle owner at that time.

From Cork the royal party went to Dublin where they stayed at Dublin Castle. Dublin is full of ghosts: dead people returning to their spouses; mummified bodies walking in St Michael's church, which is unique for its vault containing naturally mummified remains; nocturnal noises that cannot be explained; unidentified ghosts of 'beautiful ladies' and 'tall men'; an 'old woman whose pale eyes seem to glow maliciously'. In particular the Queen was interested in the remarkable story that involved a painting that hung for many years at Tyrone House, Dublin.

A manuscript account of the 'Tyrone Ghost Story', firmly accepted by successive generations, is preserved at Curraghmore House in Co. Waterford, the seat of the Marquess of Waterford. It was written by the Lady Elizabeth Cobb, granddaughter of the Lady Beresford to whom Lord Tyrone is said to have appeared after his death.

John le Poer, Lord Decies, succeeded as Lord Tyrone in 1690 and he is the ghost of the story. This Lord Tyrone made a serious pact with Nicola Hamilton, the daughter of Hugh, Lord Glenawley (who married Sir Tristram Beresford in 1687), that whichever of them died first would — if possible — appear to the other with the object of proving life after death.

In October 1693 Sir Tristram and Lady Beresford were visiting the latter's sister, Lady MacGill, at Gill Hall. One morning Sir Tristram rose early, leaving Lady Beresford asleep, and went for a walk before breakfast. On his return his wife joined him and their hostess but she seemed agitated and embarrasssed. Her husband asked after her health and questioned her as to what had happened to her wrist which he and others present had noticed was tied up with black ribbon. Lady Beresford implored her husband and the others present not to question her, either then or later, about the reason she wore the ribbon, adding, 'You will never see me without it.'

After breakfast she was anxious to know whether the post had arrived. It had not and Sir Tristram asked her whether she was expecting any particular letter that day. She replied that she expected to hear of Lord Tyrone's death, which she felt certain had taken place on the previous Tuesday. Sir Tristram concluded that his wife must have had a vivid dream and said so, adding that he had never considered her to be a 'superstitious' person but perhaps he should now revise his opinion!

Within minutes a servant brought in the post including one envelope sealed with black wax. 'As I expected,' exclaimed Lady Beresford, 'he is dead.' The letter was from Lord Tyrone's steward to inform them that his master had died in Dublin on Tuesday, 14 October, at 4 p.m.

Sir Tristram consoled his wife, distraught at the news and yet somehow relieved and easier now that her uncertainty had become fact. She then told her husband that she was with child, adding that she would have a son. A boy was born the following July. Sir Tristram survived the birth by only a few years.

Lady Beresford continued to reside, with her young family, at their home in Co. Derry. She seldom went out and had few friends, with the exception of a Mr and Mrs Jackson of Coleraine. Mr Jackson was a leading local citizen and, through his mother, related to Sir Tristram. Mrs Jackson was descended from Sir Adam Lofters, and a relation of theirs, Richard Gorges, married Lady Beresford some three years later, in 1704.

They had a son and two daughters before her husband's wild and dissolute conduct forced Lady Beresford to seek a separation, which she obtained. Four years later General Gorges expressed repeated regret for his misdeeds. On the strength of solemn promises for the future, Lady Beresford agreed to his return and she became the mother of another boy. A month after the birth of this infant, on the occasion of Lady Beresford's birthday, she sent for her eldest son, Sir Marcus Beresford, then twenty years old, and her married daughter Lady Riverton. She also invited Dr King, Archbishop of Dublin (an old friend), and the elderly clergyman who had christened her and who had always maintained a kindly interest in her life.

During the course of conversation with the clergyman Lady Beresford remarked that she was forty-eight that day, whereupon her old friend said no, she was forty-seven. He went on to say that Lady Beresford's mother had a discussion with him once about her daughter's age and he had consulted the registry; so he could say with complete certainty that she was forty-seven that day. This news brought consternation to Lady Beresford who told her friend that what he had said was in effect a death warrant. She implored him to leave her for she was convinced that she did not have long to live and had a number of things to settle before she died.

When her son and daughter were in her presence Lady Beresford told them that she had something of great importance to communicate before she died. She reminded her children of the friendship and affection that existed in their early life between Lord Tyrone and herself. She revealed the pact they had made that whichever of the two died

129

first should, if possible, appear to the other as proof of life after death. One night, Lady Beresford said, many years after this, she was sleeping with the children's father at Gill Hall when she suddenly found herself awake and saw Lord Tyrone sitting on her side of the bed. Lord Tyrone told her that he had died the previous Tuesday at four o'clock and said he had been permitted to appear to assure her of the truth of life after death. He was further allowed to inform her that she was with child and would produce a son who would marry an heiress, that Sir Tristram would not live long and that she would re-marry and die from the effects of child-bearing in her forty-seventh year.

Lady Beresford begged Lord Tyrone for some convincing sign or proof of his presence so that in the morning she would know that it had not been a dream; whereupon Lord Tyrone hooked up the bed hangings in an unusual manner through an iron hook and wrote his signature in her pocket book. But still she was not satisfied and, after she had asked for still more substantial proof, he placed his hand, which was as cold as marble, on her wrist for a moment and immediately the sinews shrank and the nerves withered at the touch. Warning her never to let anyone see the mark, Lord Tyrone vanished. In the morning, after Sir Tristram had gone for an early walk, Lady Beresford arose and with great difficulty succeeded in unhooking the bed curtains. She bound up her wrist with black ribbon and went down to breakfast, quite certain that Lord Tyrone was indeed dead and had visited her that night. She stated that under the impression she had passed her forty-seventh birthday she had consented to a reconciliation with her husband but now she knew she was only forty-seven that day, she was certain she was about to die. She instructed her two children, after her death, to unbind the black ribbon and look at her wrist before she was put in her coffin.

An hour later Lady Beresford was dead and, after everyone had left the bedroom, her son and daughter untied the black ribbon and found their mother's wrist to be exactly as she had described it; the nerves withered and the sinews shrunk. She was buried by her clergyman friend in the Cathedral of St Patrick, Dublin, in the Earl of Cork's tomb, where she lies to this day.

Lady Beresford's son Sir Marcus later married Lord Tyrone's daughter and both he and his sister always swore to the truth of the story for the rest of their lives. Lady Elizabeth Cobb, granddaughter of Lady Beresford, preserved both the ribbon and the notebook with the signature of a ghost for many years at her home in Bath.

The black tape which Lady Beresford had worn on all occasions and at all times, even at court, has been repeatedly vouched for by witnesses, and the painting at Tyrone House clearly showed a black ribbon visible on one wrist. This painting, however, disappeared in a peculiar manner. It hung, with other family portraits, in the main drawing room at Tyrone House and when Henry, Marquis of Waterford, sold the family's town residence to the Government, he arranged for Mr Watkins, a well-known dealer in pictures, to collect the paintings and *objets d'art* for removal to Curraghmore. Mr Watkins was interested in the legend and saw to it that this particular picture was carefully packed for transportation. When the consignment was received at Curraghmore, however, the picture had disappeared and in spite of considerable exertions and inquiries on the part of Mr Watkins and the Tyrone family, it has not been located to this day.

Queen Victoria always loved the story of the Tyrone ghost and would relate it to 'disbelievers'.

During the course of a visit to the Paris Exhibition in 1855 the Queen went to Versailles for an impressive display of fireworks which included a piece representing Windsor Castle. She was not to know that forty-six years later two much-respected ladies would walk into one of the most remarkable psychic 'adventures' every recounted. One, Miss Anne Moberly was the daughter of Dr George Moberly, headmaster of Winchester College and Bishop of Salisbury; she herself was Principal of St Hugh's College, Oxford. Her friend Miss Eleanor Jourdain was the daughter of the Rev. Francis Jourdain, Vicar of Ashbourne, Derbyshire. Miss Jourdain became head of a large girls' school at Watford, an M.A. at Oxford and a Doctor of the University of Paris, and she succeeded Miss Moberly as Principal of St Hugh's.

These two ladies, whose standard of learning and respect for truth must count for something, had looked over the Palace of Versailles one hot August afternoon in 1901 and they were on their way to have a look at the Petit Trianon, the little retreat which Louis XVI presented to his ill-fated Queen, Marie Antoinette, when as they walked together they apparently encountered figure upon figure and object upon object that unaccountably arose from an unfamiliar past. They conducted considerable and lengthy research into their experiences and eventually published the results in a volume entitled simply *An Adventure* (first published in 1911 and subsequently reprinted in many editions with additional matter); it is a remarkable personal psychical experience that has never been satisfactorily explained.

During the course of Queen Victoria's visit to Paris in 1855 she was taken, in a thunderstorm, to the tomb of Napoleon I, lit by torchlight, and there she made her fourteen-year-old son kneel down with her and say prayers for her great-grandfather's bitterest foe — and a man whom she knew had been psychic. The Emperor claimed to have had no less than four visits from France's 'national' ghost, known as the Vermillion Phantom, who is said to put in an appearance at critical times in the history of France.

Whenever she was in Edinburgh, be it in 1860 reviewing 22,000 volunteers with 200,000 civilians looking on from the surrounding

131

hills, or in pouring rain in 1871 for the Scottish Volunteer Review when John Brown had no hesitation in snatching umbrellas from startled onlookers for the protection of the Queen, it is likely that Victoria was thinking of the several ghost stories she had heard about Edinburgh Castle, including a headless drummer boy . . .

In 1882 the long-widowed Queen visited Netley Hospital, the large military establishment near Southampton, which accommodated a thousand patients during most of its history and in the Second World War managed to take in double that number. The Queen seemed pleased with the hospital, apart from a shortage of chairs. She had laid the foundation stone on 19 May 1856, saying as she did so that she had sanctioned the naming of the building the *Royal* Victoria Hospital and she was glad to think that her 'poor brave soldiers will be more comfortably lodged' than she was herself. In fact throughout its history Netley seems to have been a 'difficult, depressing and unsatisfactory hospital' as C. Woodham-Smith says in his biography of Florence Nightingale who was the first person to criticize the Indian-style building. Be that as it may, while at Netley in 1882 the Queen heard all about the well-authenticated hospital ghost.

The building had long been reputed to be haunted by a nurse from the early days of the Crimean War, who committed suicide by throwing herself from an upstairs window after discovering that by mistake she had administered a fatal overdose of drugs to a patient.

The ghost of the repentant nurse was always seen in one particular corridor and officials and staff at the hospital, a clergyman, visitors and patients have all reported seeing the same figure, although such stories were suppressed for many years because whenever the ghost was seen, a death seemed to take place in the hospital. A service of exorcism was held but it seemed to have no effect.

The apparition was reported to be particularly active when the building was being demolished and one witness stated: 'The figure was dressed in an old-style nurses' uniform of greyish-blue with a white cap and was about twenty-five feet away from me when I saw it. She walked slowly away, making no sound and disappeared down a passage that led to the chapel.'

One night an orderly saw 'the grey lady' pass a ward where a patient died the following morning; he claimed to know nothing of the ghost that was said to haunt the hospital until he saw it. A night staff telephone operator, employed at the hospital for twenty-seven years, also claimed to have seen the ghost; he said that he heard the rustle of her dress as she passed and there was a perfumed scent in the air after she had disappeared.

Variations of the legend suggest that the ghost was a nursing sister who fell in love with a patient and, after finding him in the arms of another nurse, poisoned him and then committed suicide; or that the patient died and the nurse jumped from a window because of a broken heart; or that it was the ghost of Florence Nightingale herself, who was mainly responsible for the building of the hospital, and that her frequent appearances during its last years were aimed at preventing its demolition.

During her Golden Jubilee celebrations the Queen attended a garden party at Hatfield, the home of Lord Salisbury, where a phantom coach drawn by four horses is supposed to race up the drive, through the main doors of the house and disappear into the stairway, presumably travelling where it once travelled before the building of that portion of the house or when there was a different use for that part of the house which dates back to 1497. The other ghost at Hatfield House, never identified, is a heavily veiled woman who, so runs the legend, was caught trying to get a message to some notable resident of this noble house.

In 1894 the old Queen visited White Lodge in Richmond Park to see her two-day-old great-grandson Prince Edward, George (for England), Andrew (for Scotland), Patrick (for Ireland), David (for Wales), the later Prince of Wales and Edward VIII. Queen Victoria drove over from Windsor to be greeted by great crowds at Richmond where she saw what was left of the old Palace of Richmond, haunted by the ghost of Elizabeth I who died there, and into Richmond Park with its several stories of ghosts and strange happenings; and then back to Windsor with its ghostly footsteps in the Deanery, the woman in grey, and the ghost of Henry VIII in the Cloisters.

Surely it is significant that all the houses the Queen knew best — Osborne, Balmoral, Windsor Castle, Buckingham Palace, even Kensington Palace where she spent her formative years — all had, during her day, and still have today, a well-established reputation for being haunted.

CHAPTER NINE

THE QUEEN'S FRIENDS AND ACQUAINTANCES – AND THEIR INTERESTS

Just as it might be regarded as astonishing how many allegedly haunted houses Queen Victoria visited, lived in and had personal knowledge of, so it is equally surprising how many of her friends and acquaintances shared her interest in ghosts and other 'occult' subjects.

In June 1837 the English colony in New York celebrated Princess Victoria's birthday with a banquet, not knowing that the King was already dead and that she was Queen. The chief speech was made by no less a patriot and hero than Captain Marryat, author of such books as *Mr Midshipman Easy*, who said, prophetically, 'I could serve a Queen with even greater zeal and fidelity than I could a King . . .' Captain Marryat, a brave and honest man, was perhaps the last person one would think of who might be interested in ghosts but, like Queen Victoria, he was fascinated by the subject and visited many haunted houses including Raynham Hall in Norfolk where he apparently encountered a ghost and fired a revolver at it. The bullet, Marryat always swore, went through the figure — presumably the famous Brown Lady of Raynham Hall. The figure disappeared and directly behind where it had appeared a bullet was found embedded in a door.

At an early meeting of the Ghost Club Member Charles Edward Cassel spoke of an interview at Balmoral in 1882 between Queen Victoria and Stainton Moses, one of the founders of the Ghost Club in 1862 and also of the Society for Psychical Research in 1882. The interview was at the request of the Queen.

W. Stainton Moses was the son of the headmaster of Donnington Grammar School. He was educated at Bedford College and at Oxford where he took his M.A. and was ordained a minister of the Church of England by Bishop Wilberforce. He had little interest or faith in spiritualistic phenomena until about 1872, when he attended his first seance. The experience apparently converted him to a belief in 'discarnate spirits' and before long he developed psychic powers himself. It was said that he shared D. D. Home's power of levitation and that 'spirit lights' appeared in his presence. He was an untiring propagandist for the spiritualist cause. When talking to Queen Victoria he would have described the mediumship of Mrs Leonore Piper who was considered to be 'probably the greatest mental medium'; Moses conducted a whole series of experiments with Mrs Piper. He wrote under the pseudonym 'M.A. Oxon'.

In 1857 Emperor Napoleon III and Empress Eugénie of France were invited by Queen Victoria to Osborne. On arrival they were first taken to Carisbrooke Castle where there were many tales of ghosts and ghouls, mostly invented during the seventeenth and eighteenth centuries to keep people away from the place where a lot of smuggling went on; but Victoria, as ever, enjoyed the stories and so did Napoleon who shared Victoria's interest in the 'occult'. A highly cultured man who wrote a number of influential books, dealing principally with his political views and fostering the Napoleonic legend, he was always interested in paranormal activity.

On his visit Napoleon related to Queen Victoria and Prince Albert some of his experiences with the celebrated medium Daniel Dunglas Home and in her Journal Victoria goes as far as to state, 'he told us some certainly extraordinary things', as indeed Napoleon III could for he had personal experience of Home's remarkable powers.

In the spring of that year the Emperor and Empress attended a seance at which massive pieces of furniture, which it would have taken half a dozen people to lift, rocked violently, untouched by human hand, and armchairs flew from one end of the room to the other as if driven by a hurricane: such were the stories and the wonders that Napoleon and Eugénie related, and Victoria, in particular, could not hear enough about this man Home.

D. D. Home, perhaps the most colourful and greatest of all physical mediums, was born near Edinburgh in 1833. There is, incidentally, nothing odd in the fact that the Queen in her Journal refers to him as Hume for his father's name was Humes and D.D. called himself Hume for years and always insisted that such was the correct pronunciation of his surname. His mediumship, according to his biographer, was to some extent congenital and hereditary, and at the early age of four years he could spontaneously describe far-off happenings, usually of a dismal nature, as though they were taking place before his eyes.

All his life D. D. Home was the centre of inexplicable happenings and had he been a charlatan, interest in his person and his performances, as Harry Price has pointed out, would have petered out long since. Raps and movement of a table apparently took place while Home was being questioned in the office of a police official in Rome. Home became a Roman Catholic but he was expelled from the Church as a sorcerer.

The wonders that D. D. Home is credited with include levitation, and it is claimed that in the presence of witnesses he once floated out of one window and into another at Ashley House in Victoria Street, London; that on occasions, and sometimes in the presence of witnesses whose intellectual standing cannot be questioned, he was capable of becoming physically elongated; he certainly handled glowing hot embers with his bare hands and lit gas-jets in an apparently inexplicable manner; and of course he was the conveyor of countless messages, seemingly originating in the afterlife, that were accepted as proof of such by the recipients.

D. D. Home frequently performed in daylight; he was never exposed as a fraud and the vindictive Robert Browning's savage poem, *Mr Sludge, the Medium*, probably intended to show up Home, was written because Browning was jealous of the attention paid by Home to his wife Elizabeth Barrett Browning, and also because Home's reputed homosexual tendencies disgusted Browning who did not, of course, publish his mischievous doggerel until after the death of his wife. Elizabeth Browning, no mean judge of character and nobody's fool, completely accepted the 'phenomena' as 'too numerous not to be recognized as facts'. What she saw she accepted as genuine and she believed there was no question whatever of Home being consciously responsible for 'anything seen and heard on that occasion'. Queen Victoria got on well with Mrs Elizabeth Browning.

At a meeting of the Ghost Club in 1899 it was revealed by Member Sir William Crookes (who had been knighted in 1897) that Home had had only one seance with Robert Browning and that when Sir William met Browning the poet said nothing to suggest that he had detected fraud. If Browning had detected Home cheating in any way Sir William was confident that the poet would have told him of it.

On another occasion (1903) Sir William Crookes revealed at the Ghost Club that he had himself conducted experiments with D. D. Home, including the use of a spring balance, the 'spirit' having to move the balance at a word from the experimenter. Once, as Sir William had walked round the table to adjust something, Home interjected, 'You have walked through the "spirit" and disintegrated him!' Whatever had happened it took some little time to restore matters so that the experiments could proceed!

Napoleon was a fairly good amateur magician himself yet, he was able to tell Victoria, raps in the vicinity of D. D. Home answered questions which he put *mentally*. The Empress told of her robe being pulled by unseen hands and of her clasping her dead father's hand, which 'seemed to be gloved in silk'. The Emperor related how a table repeatedly moved towards him and of knocks on his hand from a distance.

Home never sought to make money from his exhibitions and he

gave numerous seances in England and throughout Europe which were attended by many well-known people including crowned heads and national leaders. Home was in fact the world's most famous medium whose phenomena were endorsed by eminent scientists of the day. Victoria was bowled over by the marvel of it all. With such extraordinary events feeding her long-standing interest, little wonder that she sought out stories of ghosts and hauntings and strange happenings wherever she went.

Andrew Lang, a one-time President of the Society for Psychical Research, quotes Adrian de Montalembert, almoner to Francis I, as early as 1528 concerning phenomena which included rappings which answered questions; lights; the levitation of one of the sitters; and similar strange occurrences. Given her considerable interest in the whole subject, Victoria must have been well aware that this sort of thing had reportedly been going on for at least three hundred years.

It is therefore no surprise to learn that she was experimenting with seances and having mediums visit her as early as 1846, long before the cult of spiritualism swept the western world. She constantly asked herself and others close to her: 'Who dwelleth in the dark?'

Queen Victoria seemed to attract to herself people who were interested in the subjects that she was especially interested in. I remember the writer Winifred Graham telling me about the experience of General Sir Thomas Scott which she had heard from the lips of his widow Lady Scott, who occupied a private apartment at Hampton Court Palace — a place full of ghosts!

Soon after starting his military career with the Irish Fusiliers, Sir Thomas Scott was sitting one day alone in front of a fire when suddenly a vision appeared on the blank wall opposite his chair. He saw himself, pictured in the open space by the fireplace, walking up a hill, at the top of which Lord Roberts stood with hands outstretched in welcome. On his face there was a wonderful smile which intimates of 'Bobs' knew well, a smile that helped to make him so lovable and magnetic.

The young subaltern was naturally amazed as he watched this clear, moving picture and could not imagine what it meant; and he was puzzled that he was able to look at it objectively. After a warm congratulatory handshake with Lord Roberts, the vision vanished as suddenly and mysteriously as it had appeared.

Later the happenings, as he had witnessed them in the vision, actually occurred in real life. Scott went to Uganda in his military capacity and, young as he was, he was given command of the troops due to his colonel being ill. Their exciting but dangerous mission was to hunt down a large body of rebels who were trained soldiers, a desperate crowd. For ten months Scott and his men practically lived on bananas. They were at last closing in on the enemy when Tommy

Scott heard that all the rebels' guns were stacked in a fortified compound, ready for a major battle the next day. His quick brain saw the opportunity and, accompanied by two of his men, he planned a secret night raid .

The three men managed to get into the compound and crawling in and out among the guns rendered them unusable. The following morning the mutineers were powerless and Lieutenant Scott and his men captured all of them.

For this splendid piece of work Scott received the D.S.O. and the thanks of Parliament for having 'saved Uganda'. When Scott went to Windsor to receive his D.S.O. from Queen Victoria, Lord Roberts came down the castle hill to meet him with outstretched welcoming hands and the charming smile, exactly as he had appeared in the vision on the wall; a fact that both the Queen and Lord Roberts heard all about with the greatest interest.

Another little-spoken-of acquaintance of Queen Victoria was Frank Buckland, the eccentric surgeon and naturalist. His home near Euston station was a chaotic place full of pet monkeys, a mongoose, a jackass (who let out a wild laugh every half-hour) and pet rats. Buckland must have had a strong stomach for he would eat almost anything: elephant's trunk soup, rhinoceros pie, roast giraffe — he was even credited with having sampled a portion of Louis XIV's embalmed heart!

Buckland had a unique way with animals and wrote about them with an enthusiasm and knowledge unequalled at the time. It was Queen Victoria's occultist Mr White Cooper who urged Buckland to write about his love of nature and the result was the bestseller, *Curiosities of Natural History*.

In 1861 Buckland began a fish hatchery in his Albany Street home and soon set up a museum of fish culture in South Kensington. Queen Victoria went to see it and was so impressed that she invited him to Windsor. In 1867 she appointed him Inspector of H.M. Salmon Fisheries, a post that took him all over the country to inspect the rivers and weirs. He was only fifty-four when he died as a result of the considerable journeying in all weathers that he had undertaken. In his will he wrote: 'God is so good, so very good to little fishes, I do not believe he would let their inspector suffer shipwreck at last. I am going on a long journey, where I think I shall see a great many curious animals . . . this journey I must travel alone.' Queen Victoria enjoyed the company of such an individual.

Cheiro (Count Louis Hamon) has written of the foibles and follies, the shrewdness and the calculating cleverness of Leopold II, King of the Belgians, the man whose father, Victoria's 'Uncle Leopold', had more influence and guidance over her than any other single person — for all his eccentricities, the rakish wig, the three-inch soles to his shoes, the feather boa he was fond of wearing, and his hypochondriac tendencies.

Cheiro tells of having the honour of reading Leopold's hand and revealing to him the number of years he would live. In the right-hand palm Cheiro says he could see years of crowded life and in the left-hand palm 'hereditary pointers that told their own tale of the inherited nature, the weak and strong points that are just as visible on the palm of royalty as on any other hand'. He saw the peculiarities of the Saxe-Coburg dynasty; proud, obstinate, strong in love and hate. The King wanted to know about his physical condition and Cheiro told him that before long some serious trouble would develop in connection with the digestive system and the internal organs. Within two years the King was dead, the cause being a complete breakdown of the digestive organs and intestinal obstruction.

From her earliest recollections and certainly from the time she celebrated her ninth birthday Queen Victoria can be said to have been surrounded by people who were interested in the strange, the unusual and the inexplicable. On her ninth birthday she met Walter Scott who was much interested in hobgoblins and legends and he based some of his works on such subjects, books that Victoria always enjoyed; for years Scott was referred to as 'the Great Unknown' and Victoria would have liked to know that Scott's baronial home, Abbotsford House, is occasionally visited by the ghostly presence of its former owner.

When the Queen's great friend Lady Augusta Bruce said she was going to marry Dean Stanley of Windsor, the Queen was decidedly *not* amused. She hated change, unless she brought it about or was convinced that it was the will of Albert. After Lady Augusta Bruce had spoken to her, Victoria wrote in her Journal: 'it has been my *greatest sorrow* and trial since my Misfortune! I thought she never would leave me!' It was simply the nuisance of Lady Bruce leaving her that annoyed the Queen, not the fact that the Deanery and its precincts were haunted, for she knew that Lady Augusta and Dean Stanley had already experienced some apparently paranormal activity there.

The cloisters near the Deanery have long been reputed to be haunted by the usually invisible ghost of Henry VIII, its presence being evident from the deep groans and sound of dragging footsteps that have been heard shuffling along exactly like someone suffering from severe gout; while the ghost of Anne Boleyn is said to have been seen at a window in the Dean's Cloister. At the Deanery itself ghostly footsteps were heard by Hector Bolitho, the royal biographer, when he lived there. 'I used to hear them at night, walking quickly past my bedroom door,' he told me. Oddly, there were only three steps, but the ghost seemed to take *four* steps down before resuming its unhurried pace but later I discovered that the flooring in this part of the old house had been raised from its early level and in the process one step had been eliminated. Here too a ghostly little boy was often seen in one of the bedrooms.

The Queen's great friend Lord Melbourne frequently saw ghosts and his many first-hand experiences fascinated Victoria. The stories did not frighten her for she had grown up with her mind open to the possibility of such happenings and she had heard too many such tales from too many reliable people to dismiss anything she heard bordering on the paranormal.

Victoria was 'superstitious', as she called it, and was always careful to follow those superstitions with which she was familiar; she liked to think that she would receive a ghost courteously. Nevertheless sometimes she would wake up in the middle of the night, frightened, and to counteract this, when she moved into Buckingham Palace, she quickly had structural alterations carried out so that there was direct access between her bedroom and that occupied by her faithful Lehzen.

Melbourne never abused his intimacy with the Queen, Greville and others tell us, but used it to impress upon her mind 'truth' of every description, including of course his utter conviction that on occasions the ghosts of dead people returned to the land of the living.

Lord Melbourne was in the habit of visiting the picturesque Elizabethan pile, Holland House, much to the irritation of the Queen who decided that the attractive Lady Holland was the real cause of his many visits; indeed the Queen went as far as to tell 'Lord M' that her affection for him was greater than Lady Holland's. By way of answer Lord Melbourne would tell the Queen some of the ghost stories associated with Holland House and as always he won her over for she could never resist a ghost story.

There was a singular story told about Holland House which was already well known in the seventeenth century. The beautiful Lady Diana Rich, daughter of the Earl of Holland, was walking in the fresh air of her father's garden before dinner one evening, 'being then very well', when she met with an apparition of herself, identically dressed, almost as if she were facing a looking glass. About a month later, reports John Aubrey the antiquarian, the Lady Diana died of smallpox. 'And furthermore,' he adds, ''tis said that her sister, the Lady Isabella Thynne, saw the like of herself also before she died.' Later there was yet another similar warning of approaching death and it came to be accepted that whenever a mistress of Holland House met herself, death hovered about her.

Also, it was said, Holland House harboured the ghost of Sir Henry Rich, first Earl of Holland, who walked at midnight, entering the Gilt Room through a secret door, with his head in his hand! The Earl had been executed in 1649 but whether there was any blood dripping from the ghostly head I do not know. There are, however, said to be three drops of blood by the side of the recess near the secret door from which the ghost emerged to walk slowly through the house he had loved and had re-named — three spots of blood that nothing would ever efface.

In 1840 the newly-wed Queen Victoria and Prince Albert went to stay at Woburn Abbey, where Victoria had previously stayed with her mother eight years earlier.

As John, Duke of Bedford, recounts in his book *A Silver-Plated Spoon* (1959) his great-grandmother Elizabeth was one of Victoria's bridesmaids while Anna Maria, Marchioness of Tavistock (who married Francis, the seventh Duke of Bedford) was appointed one of Victoria's ladies-in-waiting and walked in the coronation procession at Westminster Abbey. By 1840 she had become Duchess of Bedford and on display at Woburn there is a spray of orange blossom from the Queen's wedding bouquet and a gold bracelet with a miniature of the Queen set in diamonds, a gift from the bride and groom.

The company in attendance during the visit to Woburn by the Queen and Prince Albert included the Duke of Wellington, Lord Melbourne and Lord and Lady Palmerston. Anna remained a close friend of the Queen all her life and is credited with introducing the habit of five o'clock tea. Anna was almost certainly the mistress of Sir Edwin Landseer, the most popular and prolific animal painter in Europe, a great favourite of Queen Victoria and Prince Albert and a man who is known to have attended seances. The hangings and coverings on the four-poster in the State Bedroom at Woburn are still those used when Queen Victoria slept there.

At Woburn the present Duke of Bedford told me that his introduction to psychic matters came when he was a young man and attended a party given by Lord Tredegar, 'a very old man who was much interested in black magic and the supernatural'. At night, in one of the enormous rooms of his house in Wales, with an owl flying round the room, Lord Tredegar would don cabalistic garb and 'tell fortunes and read characters'. The strange thing was that as soon as he began, the temperature in the room suddenly dropped; everyone present agreed about this, and although the Duke was situated in front of a huge and roaring fire, he found himself shivering. He never forgot that visit to Wales and, like Queen Victoria and her family, he and his family have always accepted the possibility of ghosts.

One of the many manifestations at Woburn, witnessed by all the family and a number of other people over the years, was the persistent and inveterate door-opening phenomenon that, the Duke told me, eventually forced him and his family out of what had been their television room. Times without number a door handle would turn and the door would open and then, after a pause, the door at the opposite end of the room would also open by itself. New locks were fitted and the doors were kept locked but still they opened by themselves; the doors were re-hung so that they opened differently — but still they opened by themselves. Eventually the wing was reconstructed and now there is an open passage where the doors of the television room used to be. 'But the ghost simply turned its attention to other doors,' the Duke said, and he recounted how his son Francis, his wife, the servants and various visitors, including their friend Paul Getty, had all experienced the bedroom doors at Woburn Abbey opening by themselves.

Before the dissolution of the monasteries, Woburn was a Cistercian abbey and the abbot there is said to have been beheaded. His ghost, as Queen Victoria was interested to hear, was still seen from time to time. Years later further excavation was taking place under the abbey to provide an extra staircase for visitors and one evening everyone had left except for one of the cleaning ladies who was sweeping the floor ready for the next day's work. After about ten minutes she came out in a very frightened condition, saying she had seen a monk walking about down there. Everyone laughed and one of the men went down to lock up. Two minutes later he returned, white and shaken, saying he too had distinctly seen the figure of a monk. Oddly enough the digging had taken place in what had once been the monks' burial ground and some of the ancient bones had been disturbed.

I remember the Duchess of Bedford telling me on one of my visits to Woburn: 'Ghosts are quite frequent and mostly friendly at Woburn ... when I first came I did not believe in them ... now I have to believe in ghosts.'

Sir Charles Wood, although a fellow Liberal, was not enamoured of W. E. Gladstone as a leader and in this he found himself in agreement with the Queen. Nor was this the only thing that the Queen and Sir Charles had in common; he went on to become Lord Halifax, a name inseparable from one of the most famous of all collections of true ghost stories, *Lord Halifax's Ghost Book*, which contains a weath of well-authenticated and firsthand experiences of all kinds of ghosts and ghostly happenings.

Queen Victoria was delighted when Sarah Lady Lyttelton accepted a position in 1842 that involved superintending the nursery. Lady Lyttelton had both rank and ability and the Queen liked her and treated her as a friend, not least because of her name. Was it not a well-established fact that a spectre had appeared to the profligate Lord Thomas Lyttelton (or Lyttleton) in 1779 and foretold his death?

During the night of 24 November 1779 Lord Lyttleton had been awakened at his London home by what he thought was a bird fluttering near his bed but when he was fully awake he saw, standing at the foot of his bed, 'the figure of an unhappy female whom he had seduced and deserted and who, when deserted had put a violent end to her existence'.

As the startled Lord Lyttleton watched, the apparition pointed to a clock over the fireplace, its face just visible in the dim light, and the ghostly form indicated that in three days to the minute Lord Lyttleton would die.

Next morning, although shaken by the experience, Lyttleton put a good face on the matter and joked about it to his friends. The following day he went to his country house, Pitt Place, near Epsom, and on the third day he held a large party there. His friends, realizing that he was more disturbed by the vision than he cared to admit, hit on the idea of advancing all the clocks in the house by one hour, unbeknown to Lyttleton. So, believing the fatal hour had passed, Lyttleton relaxed over a few more drinks and saying he had 'bilked the ghost', set off for bed about an hour later. As a church clock struck the real time, Lord Lyttleton collapsed in the arms of his valet and died without saying a word.

A remarkable painting of the ghostly encounter was executed in 1780 and according to Sir Nathaniel Wraxall, an acknowledged authority on the eighteenth-century Lord Lyttleton, it was 'faithfully designed after the description given to the artist by the *valet-de-chambre* who attended Lord Lyttleton and to whom his master related all the circumstances'.

In 1855 the Queen asked Sir Henry Ponsonby to get in touch with the Home Secretary to mitigate the sentence of hard labour that had been passed on W. T. Stead who had been arrested for publishing his exposure of the white slave traffic. The Queen had little general sympathy for Stead, for she could not forgive public revelations about immorality, but she was aware that the famous editor and spiritualist had no doubt about the possibility of the human mind to communicate with other minds, regardless of time and space. The evidence for ghosts, he felt, was to be found on every hand.

Ghost phenomena, Stead said, were not induced but spontaneous and of constant but irregular occurrence. 'What is wanted on the part of the masses is a recognition of the fact that certain phenomena occur which, if diligently noted and carefully studied, may help us to fresh mastery over nature, and to as yet unconceived triumphs over time and space.' It was heady stuff, such as the Queen revelled in.

When Bertie went to Oxford, it was Henry George Liddell, Dean of Christ Church, who urged that the young Prince should take up residence inside the college so he could make friends of his own age, advice that Bertie ignored, taking lodgings in a gloomy private house instead. This same Henry George Liddell was the father of the girl Alice who inspired the Rev. Charles Dodgson (better known as Lewis Carroll) to write *Alice in Wonderland*. Carroll was a Fellow of Christ Church where he spent all his working life. He was interested in spiritualism and it must be likely that either Liddell or Carroll or both of them, knowing of the Queen's interest in such matters, would take the opportunity to discuss the subject with her. She had already told

Lewis Carroll how much she liked *Alice in Wonderland* and that she looked forward to another work from his pen. It seems, according to Ellis Hillman, president of the Lewis Carroll Society, that there were several significant hints that the author was very interested in psychic matters and the paranormal in general and it could well be that the mysterious missing parts of his diaries could have contained references to these activities which his family did not feel should be preserved. It would not be the first or the last time that this sort of thing happened. Certainly Carroll's first biographer, who had seen the diaries before they were mutilated, says unequivocally that Carroll 'took a great interest in psychic phenomena and ghosts'. Lewis Carroll was also interested in dreams, an interest he shared with Queen Victoria, and he is said to have produced at least one poem in what might be called a dream or trance state.

Not perhaps a friend of Queen Victoria but certainly an acquaintance of her eldest son, Edward, Prince of Wales, was Professor Arminius Vambery, a man whose valuable advice on Eastern European matters had resulted in his being made a Commander of the Royal Victoria Order. He was a strange, colourful adventurer who had journeyed for twenty years through the Middle East in disguise, showing considerable courage and a disconcerting habit of repeatedly encountering the inexplicable.

A friend of Henry Irving and Bram Stoker, it is more than likely that Vambery, with his curious tales of places where mystery and intense superstition still reigned — including Transylvania — set in Stoker's mind the idea of what is perhaps the world's most enduring supernatural novel, *Dracula*.

Such tales from a such a man Bertie would have retold to his mother who, as we know, liked nothing better than mysteries and she would have learned more of the Hungarian Arminius Vambery when she met Bram Stoker and Henry Irving on several Royal 'Commands' at Windsor. Stoker reported the private performances to the world's press, with the permission of the Queen, who wrote that 'Mr Bram Stoker may write whatever he pleases about the event'.

In 1902 Bertie, now King Edward VII, wishing to surprise the Kaiser during his visit to England, invited Irving and his company to Sandringham. Irving made the trip, rushing his company from Belfast, where they were appearing, to Sandringham and back in record time.

The redoubtable diplomat, First Marquess of Dufferin and Ava, Frederick Temple Hamilton-Temple Blackwood, delighted the Queen in 1873 when he told her that a deputation of women had demanded the vote since men were seldom fit for work! The Dufferin family have long been convinced of the authenticity of a curious legendary story when Lord Dufferin saw a seemingly ghostly form of a particularly singular aspect. Ten years later in Paris he saw the same figure (or so he thought) as he was about to enter a lift; he recoiled in horror and missed the lift which plunged to the bottom of the shaft killing all those inside. It is a strange story that is difficult to fully substantiate but the present Marquess of Dufferin and Ava has informed me that the story is 'perfectly true'.

In 1878 Mrs Lillie Langtry was presented to Queen Victoria and at the same time met the Prince of Wales (later Edward VII), whom she was to know on intimate terms. Her beauty caused a furore in London society. The daughter of the Dean of Jersey, she died in 1929 in her villa at Monte Carlo where Queen Victoria, who abhorred gambling for high stakes, once went so far as to refuse a bouquet when she learned that it came from a gambling casino.

Lillie Langtry was interested in predictions and she consulted Cheiro on several occasions. An entry in his Visitors' Book reads, 'Cheiro's predictions of my future will influence me in all my dealings — because I am so impressed by the extraordinary precision with which he read my past — Lillie Langtry.'

Later, when she had become Lady de Bathe, she wrote to the seer from 28 Regent Court, Hanover Gate, London, on 15 April 1911:

My dear Cheiro,
I have heard that you have returned to London, and I think it is only fair to tell you how very accurate your remarks were in my case, and the strange fulfilment of what you said would happen during the past ten years.

You told me that I should not be accompanied by my husband to America, although I had planned my tour there expressly for that purpose. I could not see how your words could come true, but the Boer War broke out, and events happened exactly as you said they would.

You foretold a scandal and trouble for me in the States during the tour I was then contemplating. In this I again doubted your accuracy, as I was taking an excellent company, and a play that had been a great London success; but you were right again, for I reached America during a political campaign, and the play in question, *The Degenerates*, by Sydney Grundy, was dubbed immoral, on account of the title, by those who, in such a moment, were glad to seize on anything to further their party interests. I had all the trouble and scandal which you had indicated, being in some cases hounded from town to town.

But perhaps the most curious incident was the following. You told me that in the following month of July, I would have an accident in connection with a horse, which would cause a shock to my nervous system which would take me some time to get over. This happened when my favourite racing mare, Maluma, ridden by Tod Sloane, broke her shoulder in the race for the Liverpool Cup and had to be killed. I must confess, whether people believe it or not, that this affected me so much that it was a long time before I could again get up my enthusiasm for racing.

These are only the things that stand out more clearly than others in the years that have passed since I last saw you, but in minor details even, you were equally true in all you said.

I think it is only fair to write and tell you how accurate you have been. Encouragement does us all so much good in our work! If people could only realize this, the world would be filled with much better efforts.

Believe me, Very truly yours,

Lillie de Bathe.

Queen Victoria said, on the resignation of George Douglas Campbell, eighth Duke of Argyll, over the reintroduction of the Land Bill in 1881, that she had lost her last 'independent and true friend'. She had also lost the one person who could relate promptly any incident of apparent psychic activity at Inveraray Castle, the home of the Dukes of Argyll and the haunt of the strange little 'Harper of Inveraray'.

The Harper is said to be the ghost of a man who was hanged at Inveraray when Montrose's men were hunting the first Marquess of Argyll. Occasionally the Harper is seen but more often just the sound of harp music is heard in the area of the Blue Room. The same sound has been reported for some three hundred years, when no actual harp was in the castle.

When the great Cetewayo , King of the Zulus, after being punished for the Zulu War and then restored to his Kingdom, was brought to England and into the presence of the Great White Queen in 1882, she bowed in response to the Zulu royal salute and in her rather flat and querulous tone welcomed him as a friend. Within a very short time she was questioning him about the witchcraft and occult practices of the Zulus, to which the tribes were still so much a slave. That she was pleased with the interview is evident from the great silver goblet that was her gift to him, inscribed: 'Presented to H.M. King Cetewayo by H.M. Queen Victoria.' She wrote afterwards, 'Cetewayo is a very fine man in his native costume or rather in no costume . . . unfortunately he appeared in a hideous black frock coat and trousers but still wearing the ring round his head denoting that he was a married man.'

Nicholas II, Tsar of Russia, who was married to Queen Victoria's granddaughter Alix, was another person close to the Queen who consulted Cheiro the palmist, seer and numerologist. Unbeknown to Cheiro, the Tsar's date of birth had been among those the Prince of Wales (afterwards Edward VII) had given to Cheiro to work out their 'numbers'. About a year after that interview with the Prince of Wales, a gentleman called to see Cheiro and, producing a sheet of paper covered with Cheiro's handwriting, asked how he had come to the conclusion that 'the man whose numbers and birthdate are shown will be haunted all his life by the horrors of war and bloodshed; that he may do his utmost to prevent them but his Destiny was so intimately associated with such things, that his name would be bound up with some of the most far-reaching and bloodiest wars in history and that in the end, about 1917, he would lose all he loves most by sword or strife in one form or another and he himself would meet a violent death'.

Cheiro's visitor did not reveal that he was in fact the person the notes referred to but he took detailed notes of the explanations that Cheiro offered, paid the usual fee and left. A few weeks later a Russian lady called and among other things told Cheiro that Nicholas II had called upon him recently and she thought he had made a peace convert of the Tsar who was adamant that he would not be associated with war in any shape or form.

In 1904 Cheiro has recounted how he dined with the Tsar and Tsarina at the Summer Palace. A minister had warned him beforehand to avoid all subjects touching on occultism in the presence of the Tsarina who had read widely on the subject and had a dread of the future. As soon as Cheiro saw the Tsar he recognized the man who had come to see him in London. That night Tsar Nicholas asked Cheiro to work out before his eyes the charts of two people after being supplied with the necessary details. Cheiro did so and said both showed the same fate: that 1917 was overwhelmed by dark and sinister influences that pointed inexorably to — the end. Thirteen years later on 12 March 1917 came the Russian Revolution, followed three days later by the abdication of the Tsar, followed on 16 July 1918 by the massacre of the Imperial family.

One evening in 1886 when Lord Randolph Churchill was at dinner with Queen Victoria she wrote afterwards that he had said 'some strange things'. In point of fact the Queen and her Chancellor of the Exchequer had much in common for Lord Randolph was extremely superstitious, especially over the number thirteen, and he attributed many adverse events in his life to the fact that he had been born on the thirteenth of the month. Cheiro has revealed that Lord Randolph Churchill was much interested in the numerologist's account that the number thirteen in ancient times had been venerated. It was the early Christian fathers who had spread the idea that it was an evil number, and they connected it with the thirteen people who sat down at the Last Supper. The Queen would have considered such talk 'very odd'.

Oscar Wilde visited Windsor in 1888 to attend the funeral service of the old German Emperor and to write a report on the event. The Queen allowed Wilde to see the Chapel, and he is said to have been 'most affected'. One wonders whether he had the opportunity of relating to the Queen — or indeed whether she knew — of his great interest in the realms of the occult and the unknown, as is evident from his writings. A few years later he too was to meet the remarkable seer, palmist and writer, Cheiro, Count Louis Hamon.

Cheiro had read Oscar Wilde's hands through curtains with Wilde otherwise completely hidden; at the time he was at the height of his fame with *A Woman of No Importance* running on the London stage. Cheiro was struck by the difference that he saw in the marking of the left hand (denoting hereditary tendencies) and the right hand (showing the developed or attained characteristics); the left hand appeared to him to be that of a king, but the right that of a king who sent himself into exile. While the left hand promised a most unusual destiny of brilliant and uninterrupted success, the right showed this success would be completely broken and ruined by a certain date.

The beautiful Blanche Roosevelt (Comtesse Machetta d'Algri) was a gifted American authoress, poet, painter and singer; she was also a charming and gentle creature who appealed to women as much as to men. Even Queen Victoria, after the Comtesse had been presented at court, requested to see her again. She too had visited Cheiro and would have told the Queen how astonished and amazed she had been at the things Cheiro had told her.

Arthur James Balfour, successively Chief Secretary for Ireland, leader of the Conservative Party in the House of Commons, First Lord of the Treasury, and Prime Minister, shared Queen Victoria's interest in the supernormal; in 1893 he became President of the Society for Psychical Research. The Queen thought him 'singularly charming and agreeable'. Later she wrote of his 'extreme fairness, impartiality, and large-mindedness'; he saw 'all sides of a question' and was 'wonderfully generous in his feelings towards others, and very gentle and sweet-tempered'. When, during the early days of the Boer War, Balfour talked to the Queen of reverses and compromises, she took off her spectacles and said, 'Please understand that there is no one depressed in this house. We are not interested in the possibilities of defeat; they do not exist.' It did not escape the Queen's notice, however, that Mausoleum Day, as the royal family called 14 December, fell in the awful 'Black Week' of the Boer War, when the British generals were defeated. Once, during the bitter struggle, the Queen's eyesight had caused her to misread news of a defeat as one of victory and she had been radiant, aggressive and bellicose; only to learn the truth from Princess Beatrice.

Cheiro's first client in London was Balfour, who did not give his name but said afterwards that the seer, after looking at the palms of his hands, had not made a single mistake in anything he had said of Balfour's past life or of his very intricate character. Subsequently Balfour sent many clients to Cheiro.

Among other things, Cheiro told Arthur Balfour that he could see no indication of marriage and this seemed to please the politician who said: 'I am determined to remain a bachelor to the end and I am glad that you see nothing to the contrary.' On his deathbed the first Earl Balfour, K.G., O.M., was heard to remark, 'I am longing to get to the Other Side to see what it's like.'

After dinner with the Queen at Windsor, Lord Kitchener ('a striking, energetic looking man') told her how he had added Dongola, a province of the Sudan, to her lands; and he brought her a drum captured from the enemy, a Crusader's sword he had found, and the flag from the tower of the captured fortress. These were all added to the trophies from India and Zululand that the Queen possessed.

Two years earlier Kitchener had also paid a visit to Cheiro , which he would surely have mentioned to the Queen knowing of her interest in such matters. Kitchener was to say that Cheiro had been singularly accurate in everything he had told him.

In later years when she was to an extent dominated by Abdul Karim, the Munshi, and much of her time was occupied with her Indian Empire, the Queen decided to have a Durbar Room at Osborne.

The decoration of this room, which can be seen to this day, was entrusted to John Lockwood Kipling, Rudyard Kipling's father and keeper of the museum at Lahore. The Queen was enchanted with the dazzling white plasterwork and fretted woodwork.

Rudyard Kipling had arrived in London in 1889 known only to the literary world, but within three months he was the most popular writer of the day. Kipling was, of course, fascinated by the supernatural, a fact that is clear from much of his writing and from the evidence of R. Thurston Hopkins who knew Kipling well in his latter years. Kipling's sister, Mrs Holland, was a noted psychic who received many messages, through automatic writing, that seemed to emanate from the dead, messages that many people have considered far more intelligent and meaningful than the majority of such scripts.

Today and ever since his death at Batemans in 1936 the ghost of Rudyard Kipling is said to be seen occasionally inside the house he loved and where he lived for over thirty years, while in the garden that he and his wife created, the ghosts of both the great writer and his wife have reportedly been seen.

It is said that when 'Lord' George Sanger took his celebrated circus to haunted Windsor Castle and paraded his animals round the Great Quadrangle, the Queen showed one of her rare snatches of humour. In the dry manner that she reserved for such occasions, she asked him: 'You call yourself *Lord* George Sanger, I hear?' Sanger bowed assent. '*Very* amusing,' commented the Queen.

Yet she was attracted to circuses and performing animals. Alfred

149

Bunn was at one time the undisputed chief of the theatrical world of London, being lessee of both the Theatre Royal, Drury Lane and Covent Garden at the same time. He was not averse to trying anything at his theatres, from German opera to a whole troop of Astley's horses. When he engaged Van Ambergh's performing animals, Queen Victoria paid the theatre a visit on 10 January 1839 when she not only saw the show but went behind the scenes and heard something of the history of the Theatre Royal, including its unique period ghost which seems to date from the eighteenth century and to have become more commonly reported with the passing of years.

The story was related to me by theatre historian W. J. Macqueen Pope who told me he had seen the ghost himself several times. The figure is that of a young man dressed in grey; he has a white wig, carries a three-cornered hat, wears riding boots and has a sword hanging from his waist. The figure is always seen in daylight, between 10 a.m. and 6 p.m., and all witnesses apparently agree on the attire although some say that he has powdered hair and is not wearing a wig, and others report that he is wearing the tricorn hat. Invariably no sound accompanies the appearance or movement of the apparition, which walks leisurely and without hurrying along the gangway at the back of the upper circle and finally disappears at the far end into the wall near the royal box.

'Popie' thought that the young man, whose handsome face with square chin has been clearly seen so many times, probably had a girl friend in the theatre in the eighteenth century. She was possibly a favourite of the theatre manager of the time and the young man may have been ordered out; perhaps an argument and a fight followed, and the young man fell, mortally wounded by a stab from a dagger, his body hastily walled-up in the little passage along which he had walked every night to meet his sweetheart.

This theory is based on the fact that during structural alterations on the upper circle, workmen reported that part of the wall sounded hollow and when it was broken down a small room or part of a passage was disclosed. On the floor lay the skeleton of a man with a Cromwellian-style dagger still embedded between his ribs. A few pieces of cloth were found among the bones, but they crumbled to dust as soon as they were touched. The place where the gruesome discovery was made corresponds exactly with that part of the wall where the ghost has always been said to disappear. 'Popie' told me that there were records reporting the appearance of the ghostly 'Man in Grey' going back more than two hundred years. During the rehearsal of a show one afternoon the ghost walked while there were over a hundred people on stage and seventy of them claimed to have seen it. 'Popie', in his history of the Theatre Royal, Drury Lane, says he wished to put on record that he had seen this apparition 'on numerous occasions'. Queen Victoria was particularly interested to hear that the Man in Grey is regarded as a good omen, for its appearance during rehearsals or during the early days of a run at the theatre invariably seemed to forecast a success for the production; it is never reported before or during the run of a failure. Indeed the Queen soon returned to the theatre to hear more about the Man in Grey, and she returned yet again a week later; in June 1843 the Queen and the Prince Consort attended a Command Performance at that haunted theatre.

Poet Laureate Alfred Lord Tennyson visited the Queen at Osborne House and stayed nearly an hour. 'It was most interesting,' the Queen wrote afterwards in her Journal. By this time the poet, born in 1809 when George III was on the throne, was very old and 'very shaky on his legs' but 'very kind'. Did he, knowing of the Queen's interest, recite his poem *Haunted Houses*, one wonders?

> All houses wherein men have lived and died
> Are haunted houses.
> Through the open doors
> The harmless phantoms on their errands glide,
> With feet that make no sound upon the floors . . .
> The spirit world around this world of sense
> Floats like an atmosphere, and everywhere
> Wafts through these earthly mists and vapours dense
> A vital breath of more ethereal air . . .
> So from the world of spirits there descends
> A bridge of light, connecting it with this,
> O'er whose unsteady floor, that sways and bends,
> Wander our thoughts above the dark abyss.

It must be likely that Tennyson, if the Queen showed any sign of scepticism in a discussion that touched on ghosts, would have spoken to her in the terms that he once wrote: 'It is all very well for you who have probably never seen spirit manifestations to talk as you do, but had you seen what I have witnessed you would hold a different opinion.'

Queen Victoria liked poetry but she was timid and prudish after Albert's death; 'clever scientific people', she found, were 'a positive necessity'. She revelled in scientific learning and experiment. Jupiter, she was told, was as light as cork; the moon was definitely uninhabited; and once Professor John Tyndall, the great physicist and natural philosopher, made lightning for her in test tubes. Tyndall became well known through some early magnetic investigations, a subject that had long interested the Queen. A number of early psychical investigators, including Sir William Crookes and Sir William Barrett, who were both known to the Queen, also conducted experiments in the fields of attraction and the properties of a magnet.

Sir William Crookes, an early Ghost Club President, discovered thallium and acthode rays, invented the radiometer and the spintharoscope, and was the first man to have his house lit by electricity; he made the bulbs himself.

On 31 May 1906 King Alphonso XIII of Spain married Victoria Eugénie, daughter of Princess Henry of Battenberg and granddaughter of Queen Victoria. The posthumous son of Alphonso XII, he was proclaimed sovereign at birth and he fascinated Queen Victoria. He had the unenviable reputation of being a *jettatore* and he was undoubtedly at the centre of a number of curious mishaps.

On the occasion of a state visit to Italy to pay his respects to the new government, an Italian fleet steamed out to meet the King off Genoa. The weather was perfectly clear but when the Spaniards came within sight of the coast the worst storm in years developed, washing four Italian sailors overboard to their deaths, and an air compressor on an Italian submarine in the escort exploded and killed a man.

After this, to the Italians, explicit proof that the King was a *jettatore*, it came as no surprise when an ancient bronze canon, fired in salute as the King entered Naples, exploded and killed the crew. And to crown matters, a naval officer in the reception committee at Naples collapsed and died as soon as he had shaken hands with Alphonso.

The King had long had the reputation of possessing the evil eye but he met occasional humiliations on this score with dignity. In Rome the people muttered '*mal occhio*' as he went by and made the manual gestures which are supposed to ward off evil, and brushed their clothes after he had passed to avoid contamination. A method of protection against the evil eye in Italy consists of touching something made of iron such as a horseshoe or key and it was noticeable that the cheers which greeted the King's public appearances in Italy invariably merged with the jangling of iron. At the end of Alphonso's state visit to Italy the royal train passed the dam holding the waters of Lake Gleno, and the next morning the dam broke, drowning fifty people and making five hundred homeless. The King's reputation was guaranteed!

Once, when Elsa Maxwell, the indefatigable party-giver, gave a dinner for King Alphonso in Venice he found himself the only guest! Twenty titled Italians had refused to attend. The King ignored the empty places and is said to have charmed Elsa Maxwell as much as she charmed him. Queen Victoria, aware that the King had also withstood several attempts on his life, kept herself somewhat aloof and apart from Alphonso but she could not help but be completely captivated by the singular King and his reputation.

One royal biographer states that the Queen liked Cecil Rhodes when she met him and when told, later, that he was a woman-hater, she replied, 'Oh! I don't think that can be so, he was so very civil to me.' One reason she liked him was that he was greatly interested in the study of numbers. Rhodes had always been convinced that the number six had been significant throughout his life but Cheiro calculated that five was his ruling number. He was the fifth son of his father, he had first gone to South Africa on the fifth day of the month, and he was born on 5 July. Cheiro recommended that he carry out important events on either the fifth day of the month or dates producing this number. Rhodes later told Cheiro that he severed his connections with South Africa by resigning on 5 January 1896 and he tried to carry out all important speculations on the fifth, or the fourteenth or twenty-third, the two numbers which add up to five.

Queen Victoria was quite fascinated for she had *almost* been born prematurely on 23 April, St George's Day, during the hectic journey to Kensington that her parents had undertaken to ensure that she was born in England. She had actually entered the world the following month, on 24 May 1819; and she knew that a Gypsy in Malta, long before that eventful day, had prophesied that her father would beget a great queen.

Joseph Chamberlain could hardly be called one of the Queen's friends — after all, she had once called on the government of the day to disavow him: 'He approves of the disgraceful riot at Brimingham!' the Queen had said. 'If a Cabinet Minister makes use of such language . . . he ought not to remain in the Cabinet.' Chamberlain was to be the last minister received by Queen Victoria. Whatever her opinions of him, the Queen was immediately interested to learn that the palmist and seer Cheiro had been to the House of Commons in 1894 to keep an appointment with Chamberlain. There he had pointed to the strong Line of Destiny in the politician's hand (and interestingly enough also evident in the hand of his son, Austen) and was able to pinpoint, through his system of dates, the exact years that Chamberlain would occupy positions of the greatest authority. Cheiro proved to be correct and at the very zenith of his career, in 1906, Joseph Chamberlain was stricken with paralysis and as a complete invalid was compelled to live a life of inactivity until his death in 1914.

Baroness Burnett-Coutts and Queen Victoria were friends for many years — until the 67-year-old Baroness married her former secretary, an American forty years her junior. Queen Victoria was shocked and never again visited the Baroness.

The Queen would have been more than interested to know that the ghost of her one-time friend was seen forty years after her death by a convincing witness. Mr Alan Dent, the well-known theatre and book critic, himself told me that he believed he saw the ghost of Baroness Burnett-Coutts in the Strand one sunny June morning. He noticed an elderly lady walking ahead of him, a somewhat singular figure in Edwardian dress, and he realized that once or twice before he had seen the same figure, but always from the rear. This time he decided to pass the old lady and obtain a front view. As he quickened his steps and passed her, he had a glimpse of a pale complexion and a slight pout as she continued in an unhurried but purposeful way. As soon as he was past her, Alan Dent paused at a shop window and looked round, but of the old lady he had passed only seconds earlier there was no sign. She had completely vanished. Some days later he chanced to mention the event to a friend who lived in Long Acre. He listened carefully to what Alan Dent told him and said he had seen the same figure himself many times, and always from the rear; he had often wondered whether it might be the ghost of Baroness Burnett-Coutts (his father had been one of her coachmen). It must seem likely that she would be seen in the vicinity of her bank in the Strand where she had walked so frequently during her life.

Sir Robert Peel, whom Victoria described as her ideal of what a Prime Minister should be, must, during his many audiences, have told her of his psychic experiences. Both he and his brother were unshakably certain that they saw Lord Byron in London in 1810 when he was in fact lying dangerously ill at Patras. During the same critical period the apparition of Lord Byron was seen by other people and was even seen apparently to write down his name among the inquirers of the King's health.

Interestingly enough, Lord Byron himself had a similar psychic experience when, with others, he saw the apparition of Shelley walk into a wood at Lerici, though they knew him at the time to be several miles away. Byron always claimed he saw the ghostly Black Friar of Newstead on the eve of his ill-fated marriage.

CHAPTER TEN

QUEEN VICTORIA – HER IDIOSYNCRASIES AND APPROACH TO OMENS AND SUPERSTITIONS

All her life Queen Victoria, in common with many members of the royal family, was superstitious and aware of possible omens; her numerous idiosyncrasies nearly all stemmed from superstition in one form or another, and it was with considerable dread that she — and indeed other monarchs and royals — face the approach of 'unlucky days'.

'Thank God and touch wood,' The Queen would begin her letters to members of her family who were recovering from some illness or unhappiness; and whenever she could she would walk four steps downstairs before going up, to prevent bad luck. She always tried to befriend Gypsies to bring herself good luck and it is known that she expressed great interest in the lore and legend of plants and insects — especially queen bees. She searched unceasingly for a solution to the Indian Rope Trick, even offering £1,000 to anyone who could explain it. 'Mysterious Victoria', Henry James called her. An enormous oak tree in Winsdor Great Park, known as Herne's Oak and reputedly the haunt of the legendary 'foul fiend of the forest', was blown down in 1863 and the Queen hurriedly arranged for another to be planted in its place to placate the ghost of Herne, a forest keeper in the reign of Richard II who hanged himself. His ghost was said to appear beneath the shadow of the oak tree whenever disaster threatened the royal family. When the tree was blown down local cabinet makers manufactured furniture from the wood, and other woodworkers and carvers made various small wooden items from the trunk and branches of the famous tree, all of the articles being clearly marked 'Herne's Oak'. All such pieces have long been collectors' items.

Queen Victoria always dreaded the thirteenth and the fourteenth of each month, because the thirteenth, apart from its traditional association with bad luck, was the date that she had her first suspicions that the Prince Consort might die; and the fourteenth was the day on which he did die, a Saturday — the day after a Friday the thirteenth! In 1892 Prince Albert Victor (Eddy), already engaged to Princess May of Teck, died on 14 January — again the dreaded fourteenth. A couple of months later her son-in-law Louis, Grand Duke of Hesse, died on 13 March — 'so near the terrible fourteenth'. Victoria became almost obsessed by these two dates and always feared that something terrible would happen on them. Odd that her Journal, so much a part of her long life, came to an abrupt end on the fourteenth day of a month; 14 January 1901 is blank, the first blank page for sixty-nine years.

Claremont was a place of contrasting memories for Victoria; it had been the scene of some strange meetings between strange individuals; strange happenings had occurred there and even stranger stories had come out of the house, such as the tale that blossomed into a rumour as fantastic as anything the Queen could have imagined.

During her first pregnancy in 1840 the Queen often felt unwell and cried a lot. Prince Albert was alarmed at her gloomy thoughts and saw to it that she left Windsor, where the forthcoming funeral of Princess Augusta was likely to depress her still further, and went to Claremont.

Rumour had it that the Queen expected to die in labour (only a few short months before, she had described having children as 'the *only* thing I *dread*') and she spent a lot of her time at Claremont in the bedroom where Princess Charlotte had died; it was said that she had decided to furnish all the rooms exactly as they had been when that sad event occurred twenty-three years earlier. After the last detail had been attended to in this ghoulish procedure, Queen Victoria, it was said, would follow her cousin to the grave.

There is little doubt that Princess Charlotte's death did prey on the Queen's mind at this time and she made extensive inquiries as to the real cause of death; she had always understood that lack of exercise and a starvation diet had played their part though in her brighter periods Charlotte gloried in healthy exercise and had a hearty appetite. In actual fact the cause of Charlotte's death lay at the door of Sir Richard Croft who did not use forceps owing to a 'mistaken system . . . of midwifery'; as we have seen Sir Richard committed suicide three months afterwards.

On 14 December 1895 Victoria's great-grandson Prince Albert, afterwards King George VI, was born at Sandringham. The Queen was by no means pleased that the baby Prince should arrive on the 'terrible day' and, according to Hector Bolitho, King George V said afterwards that his grandmother referred to the birth as a 'personal affront'. The Queen recorded in her Journal that 'George's first feeling was regret that this dear child should be born on such a day'. George VI also died at Sandringham, in 1952, and his ghost was afterwards reported to manifest there. The house was haunted for years and an exorcism was held in Queen Victoria's time which seemed to placate the 'troublesome spirit' for a time.

In 1876 Princess Alice, the Queen's second daughter, was sent to Eastbourne with her family where they fell ill with diphtheria; her baby Princess May died from the disease on 16 November and Prince Ernest had the illness too and thought he was going to die. His mother, seeking to comfort him, gave what Disraeli later described as 'the kiss of death' and three days later the Prince was out of danger. On 8 December, however, came the news that Princess Alice herself had caught diphtheria. Soon the dreaded 14 December dawned and as always the Queen went to the Blue Room to commune and pray. During the morning she was told of the death of Princess Alice and the Queen never forgot the strange twist of fate that caused the child to be 'called back' to her father on this of all days; that the child who had been such a help and support during her father's last days should pass away on that awful day seemed to the Queen 'almost incredible and most mysterious'.

When Bertie was ill at Sandringham in 1871 and the dreaded 14th approached the Queen virtually gave him up as being past recovery, but 14 December dawned and passed without his dying, much to her surprise. She said Bertie had been on the 'very *verge* of the grave . . . hardly anyone had been known to recover who had been so ill as he was'.

On 13 December he had beome delirious and for hours he would talk in strange languages, sing, swear, whistle, whisper and shout secrets of his many sexual ecstasies; then he would abuse Alix who nursed him untiringly. At one stage he threw anything he could lay his hands on about the room and especially at the Princess; when she next entered the room she did so on all fours, just in case any missiles were in evidence, but it was no use, as soon as she stood up she was floored with a pillow!

During the crisis of his illness he looked wildly about him and asked his mother, 'Who are you?' She was terrified, her customary silent strength completely shattered, and she watched, helpless, as she saw him clutching at the bedclothes, seeming to feel for things that were not there. His sister said she heard the death rattle and indeed Bertie did seem to be at the point of death, but then he was stripped and two bottles of old champagne brandy were rubbed briskly into his body, and Bertie returned from the brink.

The hours passed and Alix sat on by the bed; midnight came and passed and the date was 14 December. In the morning Bertie awoke and called for a drink; the tide had turned. For weeks he remained ill, his pulse and temperature far higher than they should have been, his breath laboured, his hair falling out; he had spasms of violent pain in

157

one hip and a leg swelled alarmingly, but by the middle of February the family and the five doctors attending him were able to say that the Prince of Wales was out of danger.

There was another miracle at Sandringham that winter for Bertie, so it has been said. Frightened of death and drained of sexual desire and energy for other women, he fell in love again with Alix, the woman who had held his hand in his darkest hours. Years afterwards, Alix would refer to those later days, after his illness, as the happiest of her life.

A recent biographer says the Queen was not superstitious in her old age, although in middle age perhaps she was. The fact is that Victoria was superstitious all her life — despite the recent assertion of the Registrar of the Royal Archives to me that 'there is nothing in the Archives to suggest that the Queen was particularly superstitious'. Those who suggest that she was not superstitious rely heavily on the words of Sir Frederick Ponsonby but Ponsonby can hardly be described as or regarded as an impartial observer. He was always well known for his 'respect' and admiration for his monarch and he was grateful to her for the 'clear and unmistakable directions', the way she considered each difficulty, promptly deciding upon it with an accurate knowledge of precedents; her 'love of fairness and justice'; her 'clear sighted judgment', etc., etc.

Queen Victoria always said she once saw the ghost of Queen Elizabeth I in the Library at Windsor and she also saw the famous Green Lady ghost at Crathes Castle; such experiences heightened her interest in these matters. We know that the Queen was sufficiently interested in table-turning to attempt it with Prince Albert in 1853, and the table duly turned *before* the psychic Lady Ely added her hands to the table; and Victoria never forgot several 'psychic experiences' she had. One she related in a letter to the Princess Royal who was recently widowed and was feeling that there was no purpose in living. 'I too wanted once to put an end to my life here,' wrote Queen Victoria. 'But a Voice told me for *His* sake — no "Still Endure".' The experience made such an indelible impression that 'Still Endure' became a familiar motto for the Queen.

Soon after John Brown's death in March 1883, when she was recovering from a fall, the Queen recalled, as she found herself able to get in and out of her carriage by herself for the first time on 13 July, that exactly forty-one years earlier on that date the Duke of Orleans had been killed by falling out of his carriage; a tragedy that Queen Victoria always believed signalled the beginning, and was the indirect cause, of all France's troubles. At all events she took good care not to fall from her carriage! Months later, after administrations from a masseuse, Madame Charlotte Nautet (who was known in court circles as 'The Rubber'), and dozens of other attempted remedies, the Queen was still a very lame and a very sad old lady.

A story of pre-vision is contained in the records of the Society for Psychical Research concerning the death of the Duke of Orleans. The daughter of a Colonel Blanckley had awoken one night convinced that something terrible had happened in France: first, there had been a carriage accident; then a figure seemingly dying, which she recognized as the Duke of Orleans; then a doctor bending over the Duke – then nothing. As soon as it was daylight she wrote it all down. Two days or so later *The Times* announced the death of the Duke of Orleans. Later, visiting Paris, the percipient saw and recognized the place of the accident. She discovered that the doctor who had attended the dying Duke was an old friend of hers and, as he had watched by the Duke's bed, his mind had been constantly occupied by her and her family who were then in Edinburgh.

Various visitors to Windsor and Balmoral and Osborne remarked that the Queen, strong-minded woman though she was, often incurred the displeasure of her consort by bemoaning a broken mirror or some such unlucky mishap as spilling salt. Yet Prince Albert too seems to have had his share of premonitions. In the autumn of 1860, on the last day of their visit to his beloved Coburg, the Prince went for a walk with his brother Ernst and broke down, sobbing, saying he was sure he would never see his birthplace again. He was dead in little more than a year and did not see Coburg again.

A few months after that 'prophecy' Prince Albert was horrified at the death of his new young physician Dr Baly and was 'greatly alarmed' lest the event foretold, predicted or indicated in some mystic way misfortune for himself. During the course of a railway accident at Wimbledon in January 1861 Dr Baly fell through the broken carriage floor and was run over. Prince Albert in the weeks that followed this sudden and unexpected death repeatedly referred to the 'incalculable' loss; Queen Victoria at the time wrote in her Journal with what sounds suspiciously like a reproof for divine sovereignty: 'The only person killed was our valued Dr Baly.'

Nor is it uninteresting to observe that the last sermon Prince Albert ever heard at Balmoral was based on the text 'Prepare to meet thy God'. An unmistakable sign to the Queen, let alone an omen, was when one morning, during his last illness, the Prince Consort heard birds singing one dawn and he thought he was back in the Rosenau, a romantic little *schloss* outside Coburg where he was born. 'I went to my room and cried dreadfully and felt oh! as if my heart must break . . .' wrote the Queen; she *knew* at that moment that she was going to lose the love of her life.

The Queen always regarded dreams with awe and she was constantly wondering whether she would be able to sleep at night and whether she would have nightmares. In her Journal she recorded four events which did give her nightmares. There was the death of Lady Flora Hastings who had wrongly been assumed — by the Queen among others — to be pregnant by the hated John Conroy, whereas the suspicious swelling was the result of a tumour on the liver. Secondly there was the death of her husband, 'dearest dear Albert'. Thirdly there was a naval accident with great loss of life; and fourthly the grim affair of Lord Crawford's embalmed body being stolen by poachers and held for ransom. When Lord Frederick Cavendish (Lucy Lyttelton's husband) and Under-Secretary Frederick Burke were knifed to death in Dublin's Phoenix Park, the Queen's first thought was whether the event would disturb her sleep and give her nightmares! 'Fortunately,' she writes, 'the dreadful event did not haunt me.'

Queen Victoria was horrified at the attempt in 1900 on the lives of the Prince and Princess of Wales and when this was followed by the assassination of King Humbert of Italy, she became convinced that she was next on the list. Yet, when they came, attempts on the Queen's life were seen by her as a clear sign from the Almighty that her life was not yet at an end and that she was destined for a higher service. There was a double attempt on her life in 1842 when John Francis twice pointed a pistol at her on two consecutive days (fortunately the pistol was not loaded on either occasion). The Queen had a presentiment that these attempts might encourage others and sure enough four days later a deformed boy named John William Bean fired a pistol at the Queen but it was loaded with paper and tobacco and not with gunpowder.

The Queen thoroughly approved of the invention of the steam railway train, although in later life she developed a great fear of accidents in any form of transport. There is a story, as we have seen, that a moth once saved the life of Queen Victoria during a railway journey. It was the kind of event that would have intrigued the Queen for it appeared to be a forewarning.

In Queen Victoria's early days old people still believed that the royal touch would cure their ills and there are many stories of people mortally sick who rallied after Queen Victoria touched them; and her victorious journeys among her people always seemed to be undertaken on fine, warm and sunny days and so the 'Queen's weather' became proverbial. It began with her coronation — the weather was perfect for her return from the Abbey; it was also a perfect day on her Diamond Jubilee, and for the vast majority of her public functions in between it was the same story.

Victoria could, when she wanted, relax and romp and play as well as the next person (before she became too old) but then suddenly and seemingly without cause she would stop, even as a young child and turn on that icy stare which said so plainly: 'We are not amused.' She was insecure and emotionally unstable throughout most of her life, but then she did know the depths of sadness and depression in alternation with the heights of joy and merriment. She always felt inferior because of her small stature and quietly sought to surround herself at court with smallish people so that she would not appear unduly short among them. She was always looking for omens and when in 1858 she saw Donati's comet with a star 'distinctly through its tail', she was convinced that the appearance of the comet in that condition heralded war; and sure enough soon there were wars almost wherever the puzzled Queen looked, and more were to come.

The Queen's beloved eldest daughter, Vicky, married to Prince Frederick William of Prussia, later Frederick III, German Emperor and King of Prussia, had suffered terribly in giving birth to a son, Prince William, the future Kaiser William II. It was a breech birth and the child's arm was dislocated; for a time both the child's and his mother's lives were in danger. Although his mother recovered and had many more children, Willy never had the full use of his shortened and withered left arm. It seemed to Queen Victoria that the cold, blue little arm of the boy, which was often skilfully concealed when he had grown up, was an ill omen, a branding almost by the devil, a mark for all to see that Willy was different. How right all that turned out to be; odd that it should be Willy who would hold the old Queen in his arms as she died.

When she attended the first day of the Great Exhibition on 1 May 1851, the Queen wore the fabulous Koh-i-Noor diamond, certain that it would bring luck to the exhibition. She was more than gratified when she saw an article in *The Times*, which she cut out and preserved, likening the stupendous opening to the concourse of all peoples on the Day of Judgement!

Queen Victoria was not a little disturbed when she heard about the difficulties with some Gypsies who had an encampment on the hill where it was proposed that Alexandra Palace should stand. The humble life of the vagabond Gypsy, 'the chief ornament of the Portsmouth Road', had always appealed to her. As a thirteen-year-old girl she had designated a camp for them at Claremont, sending them blankets and soup and listening to their stories; she was utterly convinced that true Gypsies were 'chosen people' and harm would come to those who treated them harshly.

When the Gypsies were eventually evicted by the builders from the site of Alexandra Palace they put a curse on the building that would occupy the area of their camp, saying, 'May death and destruction befall the place and everything associated with it.'

Queen Victoria heard all about the Gypsies' curse and was not surprised when the palace burned down in 1874, the year after it was opened. Rebuilt in 1875, it was eventually put to various uses including the housing of internees, Government offices and BBC television studios but it was always something of a white elephant and when new plans for its use were in full swing it again burnt down, in 1980. Two railway lines were laid over the years to serve the building; one to the palace gates was closed in 1963, the other into the palace itself was closed earlier, in 1954. There are even stories of a complete train and its occupants being buried in a landslide and the story goes that it is buried there where various 'inexplicable' sounds and disturbances have been reported from time to time. The Queen would probably have said, 'What can you expect?' and she would hardly have approved of the recent plans for a multi-million pound scheme to rebuild the palace into a major leisure complex.

Queen Victoria did not approve of secret societies and Bertie had a verbal wigging from his mother when she learned that he had been initiated into the Order of Freemasons; it was more than disapproval, she had a horror of such organizations.

Another idiosyncrasy was a tendency to be careful with money and when the Prince and Princess of Wales first stayed at Windsor they discovered, to their amusement more than anything else, that lumps of sugar per cup of tea were strictly rationed — and that lavatories were supplied with only squares of newspaper . . .

After the death of Prince Albert deep mourning was not lifted even for the wedding of the heir apparent a year and a quarter after the Prince Consort's death. The Princesses and Ladies of the Household at Windsor were ordered to limit themselves to grey, lilac or mauve; and as Vera Watson puts it in her volume *A Queen at Home* (1952), this was not the only 'ghostly presence' of Albert at the wedding. The Queen paid Alexandra's travelling expenses to England for the wedding, carefully selecting Lieutenant Grey and Colonel F. Seymour to meet the Danish royalty 'and make further arrangements for the embarkation on the Royal Yacht, as those who had the honour of being sent in 1840 to bring their beloved Prince to England for his marriage'. The Queen was not particularly happy about paying any expenses to the Danes over the marriage and she queried whether since the Danish party would be travelling on Danish railways and a Danish royal steamer as far as the frontiers, she was expected to pay for that part of the journey as well.

On the eve of the wedding the Queen took Bertie and Alix to the mausoleum. She joined their hands together in front of the marble effigy and said: 'He gives you his blessing and I give you mine'. At the wedding Jenny Lind sang the *Chorale* for which the Prince Consort had composed the music and as she began the Queen raised her eyes to Heaven . . . and as the first verse ended she burst into tears.

King Frederick's presents included a necklace containing 2,000 brilliants and 118 pearls from which hung a facsimile of the Dagmar Cross. In this was set a fragment reputed to be part of the True Cross and a piece of silk taken from the grave of King Canute – all talismans of good fortune. In fact, Princess Alexandra nearly always wore a choker, usually of jewellery, round her neck to hide a scar. Stockmar, who was not happy about the wedding plans of Bertie and Alix since it did not fit in with his plans, hinted at sinister reasons for the blemish on her neck. The scar was said to be the result of a doctor's experiment for a cold cure but Stockmar said he suspected scrofula and added, 'Not a step further otherwise a disaster can occur of which the consequences cannot be foreseen.'

The royal wedding at Windsor on 10 March 1863 was the first since that of Henry I in 1122 and St George's Chapel was bathed in sunlight as the guests began to filter in. Lady Spencer entered in a spectacular dress once worn by Marie Antoinette; Lord Palmerston somewhat lowered the tone by combing his hair in the middle of the ceremony; and Disraeli loudly proclaimed his success at being present and having obtained a ticket for his wife – there had been no intention of inviting 'Dizzy' but Palmerston persuaded the Queen otherwise. It was one time when the Queen did forgive and forget and in later years she came to think a great deal of Benjamin Disraeli – too much, some people thought.

The Queen herself, by way of contrast to the lords and ladies in their magnificent attire, wore her widow's weeds with a long veil to her cap, her only ornament the Order of the Garter. She insisted on watching the ceremony from the Catherine of Aragon closet and even refused to attend the wedding breakfast.

The newlyweds were to spend their week-long honeymoon at Osborne, the vast and silent Italianate mansion fashioned out of the dead Prince Consort's dream. After a tiresome and tiring journey and an exhausting wedding, Bertie and Alix eventually arrived at Osborne. They were alone at last – or were they? A hat here, a despatch box there, a pen ready for use: everything that had once belonged to beloved Albert remained as it had been when he left the island for the last time. It was as if he had just gone out of the door and would be back at any moment. This was as the Queen wished it. Wondering and apprehensive, the couple walked hand in hand across the cold mosaic floors and began their life together.

Some people regarded as ominous the fact that Alix's first child, Albert Victor, was born prematurely and weighed only three and three quarter pounds. In fact all her six children were born prematurely, including the last, Alexander John, in 1871, who only lived one day. After that Alix stayed out of Bertie's bed and was relieved that child-bearing for her was over. It had left her deaf and lame and none of her children were half as strong as Victoria.

During the course of a grand tour in 1869 when Bertie and Alix visited Vienna, Cairo, Constantinople, Athens and Corfu there were several amusing incidents. Bertie accepted an invitation to dine at a harem where Alix was puzzled as to the purpose of a large divan, covered with cushions, which stood in the centre of an otherwise empty room . . .

Princess Alexandra loved to distribute money to beggars and to help the poor and at the First Cataract on the Nile naked men rode water logs, seeking alms. They scrambled from the river, 'clothed only by the right hand', the left holding the log on their shoulder, and as Alexandra held out a coin to each their right hands shot out to take the money. It was an embarrassed Alexandra who returned to her cabin that day!

But it was at Wadi Halfa that the Princess collected the oddest item among all the souvenirs that she sent back to Sandringham — a ten-year-old Abyssinian boy whose father and mother had remarried and were no longer interested in him. Selim knew a few words of English and was delighted at the idea of belonging to the Prince and Princess. He duly arrived at Sandringham where, for a time, he aroused considerable interest and amusement; but when he broke one of Bertie's guns he was sent away, not back to Egypt or even to Barnardo's but, almost certainly at the suggestion of the superstitious Queen, to a clergyman who specialized in exorcising 'devils'!

With a degree of apparent surprise Elizabeth Longford (in *Victoria R.I.*, 1964), allows herself to say: 'Princess Victoria's gift for predicting her future was never more apparent than on her sixteenth birthday: "I feel that the two years to come till I attain my eighteenth," she wrote on 24 May, 1835, "are the most important of any almost . . ."' In fact Victoria had flashes of prediction and premonitions all through her long life.

She certainly seems to have had a premonition about General Gordon's death. Almost a full year before Gordon was speared to death the Queen wrote to Gladstone: 'The Queen trembles for General Gordon's safety. If anything befalls him, the result will be awful'. And the night before her coronation the Queen slept badly because she had, she wrote, 'a feeling that something very awful was going to happen'. As we have seen, several things did go wrong. But still the coronation was a never-to-be-forgotten spectacle with thousands of her loyal subjects lining the streets and the Queen wrote in her Journal that she would 'ever remember the day as the proudest of her life'. The Queen also had fears and misgivings and sleepless nights before the Silver Jubilee celebrations, but they went off well.

Always fascinated by numbers, Victoria was captivated for some unknown reason by the year 1888. She found it a very strange number to write. 'Never can it be written again!' she announced with typical illogicality. Would her fears about the year 1888 prove to be unfounded? Well, it was the year that saw the death of the old Emperor of Germany, and the illness and death of the new Emperor, 'dear, darling Fritz', her daughter Vicky's husband. He was succeeded by William II, or 'Kaiser Bill' as he was known.

Some of the old Queen's pronouncements were prophetic without her knowing it. Writing to Lord Salisbury in 1890, after Heligoland had been given to Germany, she said.

> It is a very bad precedent. The next thing will be to propose to give up Gibraltar; and soon nothing will be secure, and all our Colonies will wish to be free.

CHAPTER ELEVEN

DEATH
– THE LIFELONG OBSESSION

Queen Victoria, by any standards, was an unusual woman. Most people would think it very odd for a wife with an apparently adoring husband, a caring mother, a large dutiful family and countless relatives near and far to be so affected by the deaths of such people as Lord Liverpool, a kindly and much-respected family friend who died in 1851, and the Archbishop of Canterbury who died in 1846, that she complained of feeling 'more and more alone'.

Part of the explanation may have been the Queen's instinctive and firm if unconscious determination to make the most of any death that remotely affected her. It has been argued that her isolated and almost rootless childhood caused her to endeavour to put down roots for the rest of her life, often where roots should never have been planted; and when any of these foundations (solid to her but shaky in fact) disappeared with the death of the person concerned, she somehow found new life through the sadness and loneliness of her own past reflected by the death of others. She said, in 1850, that the death of Sir Robert Peel whom she disliked, 'such a cold, odd man', was like losing a father.

Victoria always enjoyed sitting up late at night; she loved mysteries and never ceased to dwell on the oddness of death and the wonderful life after death when, she was sure, it was easy for some people to return and affect the lives of those still living. She loved any stories of death and dying and revelled in the last words of King George IV who, clasping his doctor's hand, had said: 'My boy, this is death'. Victoria puzzled hour after hour as to what exactly had caused him to say what he did and what happened to him immediately afterwards.

Many people might consider the years when a number of one's friends and relations pass through the valley of death as black and dismal years but for Victoria there were compensations, for not only did death itself fascinate her but also the mourning, the formality —

all the trappings and procedure of death seemed to give her a new lease of life. Vampire-like she thrived on the dead but this is not to say that she was unaffected by death; merely that, perhaps unconsciously, she enjoyed it.

On that 'dark day' when the old Duchess of Kent died, the estrangement between Victoria and her mother that had marked the first years of the young Queen's reign had long been over if not forgotten, and the old lady had lived contentedly enough at Frogmore.

Both Victoria and Albert hurried from Buckingham Palace when her illness took a turn for the worse and they were with her when she died. (Victoria always liked to be in at the death just as she liked to be present at births.) At the death of her mother Victoria's grief was unbounded and its extravagance and her apparently total loss of control were the forerunners of the nervous collapse that followed Albert's death later the same year. The Queen was adamant that Frogmore was to be kept 'just as dear Mama left it' and this also foreshadowed what was to happen after Albert's death. Later, in her not always reliable Journal, she wrote of 'the weeping which day after day is my wlecome friend' and revealingly adds: 'the approval of the manner in which I have shown my grief, is quite wonderful'. She seemed to gain consolation not only from feeling grief, not only from displaying it so that other people were aware of her grief, but also from the knowledge that people approved of her exhibition of grief.

In the same year young King Pedro of Portugal, the son of Victoria's cousin Ferdinand, whom Victoria had once said she loved like the dearest of brothers, together with his younger brother, died of typhoid. Later the same month came the news about the Prince of Wales's affair with the young actress Nellie Clifton — a black day indeed! Then on 14 December Victoria sat beside her husband's sickbed while their children and some of the household came quietly into the room to bid the Prince Consort 'Goodbye'. At 10.45 p.m. he died, Victoria holding his hand. Her blackest year was almost over but her fascination with death and the possibility of an afterlife, especially Albert's continuation in it, was to continue unabated for the rest of her long life.

Queen Victoria seemed to think there was something loyal and reverent and right about leaving a dead person's room as it was at the time of the occupant's death and we constantly see her approval of this practice. After the death of her lovely first cousin Princess Victoire, Duchess of Nemours, Queen Victoria returned to the room where Victoire had died and was 'delighted' to find 'all has remained as she left it'. Revisiting the room a year later she found spread under a glass case locks of her cousin's beautiful hair.

Even Lord Brougham, notwithstanding that he was an associate of the hated John Conroy, seems on occasion to have had a similar outlook on certain matters to the Queen. His daughter Eleanor died when she was only nineteen and he kept her room untouched and as she had left it all his life. Incidentally Lord Brougham, who has been described as one of the hardest-headed persons that ever lived, a Lord Chancellor, trained from his youth to weigh evidence, recounts a remarkable experience in his memoirs:

A most remarkable thing happened to me, so remarkable that I must tell the story from the beginning. After I left High School I attended with my close and most intimate friend classes in the University. We did not always attend the same class but on our walks together to and from classes we frequently discussed many grave subjects, including, among others, the immortality of the soul and a future state.

This question, and the possibiity of the dead appearing to the living, were subjects of much speculation, and we actually committed the folly of drawing up an agreement, written with our blood, to the effect that whichever of us died first should appear to the other, and thus solve any doubts we had entertained of the life after death. After we had finished our education my friend went to India, having obtained an appointment there in the Civil Service. He seldom wrote to me and after the lapse of a few years I had nearly forgotten his existence.

One day, while lying in a warm bath and enjoying the comfort of the heat, I turned my head round, looking towards the chair on which I had deposited my clothes, as I was about to get out of the bath. On the chair sat my friend of years ago, looking calmly at me! How I got out of the bath I know not; but on recovering my senses I found myself sprawling on the floor. The apparition, or whatever it was, had disappeared.

The vision had produced such a shock that I had no inclination to talk about it or indeed to mention it to anyone but the impression it made on me was too vivid to be easily forgotten and so strongly was I affected by it that I wrote down the whole story, with the date 19 December, and all the particulars, as they were fresh before me. No doubt I had fallen asleep, and that the appearance presented so distinctly before my eyes was a dream I cannot for a moment doubt; yet for years I had had no communication with my old friend, nor had there been anything to recall him to my recollection. Nothing had taken place concerning India, to the best of my knowledge, or with my friend or his family or anyone connected with him that might have provoked me to have such a dream.

I recollected quickly enough our old discussion and the

bargain we had made and I could not discharge from my mind the impression that my friend must have died and that his appearance to me was to be received by me as proof of a future state; the complete date was 19 December 1799. Soon after my return to Edinburgh there arrived a letter from India announcing the death of my friend and stating that he had died on 19 December 1799.

After the Prince Consort's death at Windsor Castle the Blue Room was meticulously photographed so that it might be cleaned as necessary but always put back as it had been on the night he died. A bust of the Prince was placed between the two beds which he had shared in his last hours and Victoria slept in the bed she had occupied when he had slept beside her; often in the years that followed she would clasp to herself one of his night-shirts and a cast of one of his hands would be within her reach.

Over the uncreased pillow she hung his portrait crowned with a wreath of evergreens. Her handkerchiefs and her writing paper, already heavily bordered in black in memory of her mother, were altered so that the mourning borders were increased. A photograph of Victoria and her family was taken grouped around the bust of Albert and each evening a clean nightshirt for the Prince was laid on his bed and hot water was provided and a clean towel.

Soon rumour after rumour said the Queen was mad. Fuel was added to the fire in this respect when Lord Clarendon, mentioning a possible Opposition attack on the government of the day, was shaken and astonished when the Queen tapped her forehead significantly and whispered the warning: 'My reason, my reason', indicating that any political crisis might send her insane. Some journalists even went so far as to say that some people 'in aristocrat circles' said the Queen was convinced that her husband was still alive and available to her wishes and demands and needs.

At Windsor the Prince Consort's body, said the Queen, was to be buried in a great Romanesque mausoleum, brilliant with mosaics, crowned with copper and sporting four bronze angels extending their wings to support his marble effigy on the sarcophagus which was to be wide enough for her to join him when her now unhappy days were over.

When Lord Canning died soon after Lady Canning, the Queen wrote in a letter to Lady Clanricarde: 'How enviable to follow so soon the partner of your life; how I pray it may be God's will to let me follow mine soon.'

Before she left Windsor for Osborne, five days after Albert's death, the Queen walked down to Frogmore and chose the site where the mausoleum was to be erected, 'for us'. She really felt that by the time the mausoleum was completed she would be inside it beside her beloved Albert; one wonders what she would have said and done had she known that she had forty years of widowhood stretching ahead of her.

She did not intend the mausoleum to be a sombre death chamber but rather a bright monument to Albert's glorious life. And after that was all planned the Queen turned her attention to building Albert memorials wherever she thought they would be appropriate. Apart from the massive national memorial at Kensington, there were to be statues and memorial stones and plaques and monuments all over the country so that nothing he ever did would be forgotten; there was even to be a mark to indicate where Albert had shot his last stag! The Queen believed that the Frogmore mausoleum would be unique not only among Albert memorials but among all memorials to the dead in that it banished gloom and radiated life and hope; it was to be a testament to her belief and conviction that there was a life after death and that that was something to celebrate . . . and still every night Victoria prayed for death to take her to join Albert.

So Victoria fled to Osborne. She and Albert had begun negotiations for purchasing Osborne House, then a small property, in 1843. They built the present structure from money they had saved; it was to be where they could be safe from the 'inquisitive and often impudent people'. Today its overcrowded rooms, replete with every kind of family memento and gift that came to the Queen from every part of the world, catches in some strange way the unmistakable atmosphere of a life long departed; an expectant, waiting feeling that frightens as much as it comforts.

For a long time after the death of Prince Albert only two people had admittance to the Queen, Princess Alice, the Queen's eldest daughter, and Lady Augusta Bruce, perhaps the only real woman friend the Queen ever had. Princess Alice received nothing but praise for her calm demeanour through this difficult period while Lady Augusta, moved by both pity and loyalty, came to be guardian, custodian and keeper in the sinister and macabre air that pervaded and was encouraged at Osborne — something of which remains to this day. For weeks and months, during the day and at night, the Queen would be heard wailing and moaning by anyone who passed along the corridors; small wonder that members of the court, wandering about the house with no orders and nothing to do, subscribed to the growing rumour that the Queen had gone mad. One Privy Councillor declared that she 'was no longer concerned with earthly things'.

During those hushed, grief-stricken days, weeks and months, the Queen, during rare moments of thinking about the living, issued orders that were to last until her own death four decades later. A photograph of the corpse of Prince Albert lying on his death bed was to be hung a foot above the pillow on the unoccupied side of every bed in which the Queen would ever sleep; the Prince's rooms at Osborne, Windsor, Buckingham Palace and Balmoral were to be kept exactly as they were on the night he died, and so on.

During those dark days the Queen was not really among the living and the problem for her advisers was how to bring her down to earth. Five months after her husband's death she wrote to the Queen of Prussia: 'I lived only through him, the Heavenly Angel . . . my only wish is to join him soon . . . I try to comfort myself by knowing that he is always near me, although invisible.' To her Uncle Leopold she described how, when in trouble, she would go to the bed where Albert had died and pray 'to be guided by my darling to do as he would wish'. She related that invariably a calm would come over her and she knew that her anguish was 'seen and heard'.

In the drawing room at Osborne today there are somewhat macabre replicas of the limbs of the royal children as infants and a marble carving, executed in 1843, of one of Queen Victoria's hands. The Royal Librarian at Windsor tells me that this was a common practice of the era and not an eccentricity of Queen Victoria but there are few examples of the habit outside Osborne. Upstairs each room has a view of the sea and dotted everywhere, like white pebbles on a seashore, are small statuettes and busts and little crimson cushions with more marble hands and feet of the Queen's children. The Horn Room is another of the many fantastic rooms at Osborne, containing furniture where every item is composed of antlers. Osborne has a strange atmosphere of life and death; if Victoria had had her way everything there would have been frozen into an emotionally moving mirror of death.

In Kensington, near where the Queen was born, she decided that her husband would have his finest monument; here he would be sculpted in gold, holding the catalogue of his wonderful exhibition, and sheltered by a canopy in the Oriental and Gothic style that he so admired. Overnight, it seemed, following the death of Albert, Victoria changed from a comparatively happy 42-year-old wife and mother to a solemn, unhappy-looking woman whose tears were never far away; she pledged the rest of her life to sorrow and mourning and to seeking the answer to the question of life after death and its manifestations.

Weeks after the death of Prince Albert, Lord Clarendon talks of the Queen repeatedly going into every detail of the Prince's illness, of his appearance before and after death, on and on and on — although such revelations invariably threw her into 'a paroxysm of grief'. He noticed too that the children, perhaps to please their mother, were 'always talking about dear Papa'. Clarendon himself, without any encouragement on his part, was ushered into the rooms of the 'beloved dead' and there was expected to gaze in awe at the untouched room but instead found himself looking in astonishment at one of the Prince's 'open pocket handkerchiefs on the sofa'.

The sudden void in her life caused Queen Victoria to become very difficult in several ways. Often irritable, sometimes ominously silent, she also had irrational changes of mind. When the beautiful Alix, whom Victoria almost loved, went home to Copenhagen to prepare her trousseau for her marriage to the Prince of Wales, the Queen underwent one of her sudden changes of mind. Thoughts of the forth-coming wedding became almost a nightmare to her: 'I dread the whole thing . . .' she wrote. 'It is for me far worse than a funeral . . .'

As the marriage approached the Queen became more and more distraught and disturbed, seeking one way and another to delay the event, even down-grading it at the expense of the first anniversary of the death of Prince Albert and the anniversary of her mother's death: death was beginning to become dominant and all-important to Queen Victoria.

On other fronts too she sought to delay the marriage: there were dis-agreements over the actual date, the place, the colours of the dresses, the names of those who were to be invited, who of those present would be invited to stay at Windsor, when the bride was to arrive — in fact there were disagreements over just about everything and everyone.

Eventually the date of 10 March 1863 was settled upon, a date that fell in Lent. Predictably the Church protested, to which the Queen, with a finality that could not but be admired, completely stifled all further disapproval by asserting that the event was a religious ceremony and not a variety performance! She also pointed out without mincing words: 'In my young days there was no Lent.'

But still the Queen could not bear the thought of celebrating a wed-ding so soon after the death of Albert. In the end she had a covered way specially constructed so that she could reach the dark Catherine of Aragon Closet, high above the altar, without being seen. And, as we have seen, it was from that sombre place in the splendour of St George's Chapel, fifteen months after the death of Albert, that the Queen observed the wedding of her son and heir. Afterwards, instead of attending the wedding breakfast, the Queen ate alone. Then, after the guests had departed, she drove to the mausoleum and there prayed in the 'beloved resting-place' and felt 'soothed and calmed'. In the shade at Frogmore on that sunny day the Queen, as on so many occa-sions before that date and afterwards, found release for a time from the awful grief that seemed to be destroying her.

The Queen never missed an opportunity to exhibit her grief. In 1850 when the first Queen of the Belgians had died, Victoria wrote to her Uncle Leopold, the King of the Belgians, that she wished to be with him, 'to cry with you and to talk with you of her . . . to be able to mingle our tears with yours over her tomb . . .' It was a sincere expression of grief but it was also a pandering to the morbidity of the situation.

Everything to do with death fascinated Victoria. She was much taken with the stained-glass window in the Belvoir mausoleum depicting the faces of four dead Rutland infants, which she saw, and spent a long time studying, during her visit in 1835.

There are entries too in her Journal of solitary visits to the family tombs at Windsor where melancholy thoughts swept over her: '. . . so many near and dear ones lying under the stones she walked upon, so many walking above who would soon be underneath.' Both Victoria's father (whom she never knew) and his father George III were buried by night in the family vault at Windsor and the Queen often attempted to relive the funerals she had never attended, recalling to her mind what she had been told; how, for example, her father's enormous coffin was conveyed with great difficulty into the family vault after becoming jammed in the entrance.

Victoria spent much of her life, although she was not conscious of the fact, in looking for a father-figure. She found several and when they died she literally revelled in their deaths in a way that later generations find difficulty in understanding but to her it was simply another way of showing that such men were almost of as much use and value to her when they were dead as they were when they were alive.

In a strange almost incomprehensible way she was a divided person, especially in the matter of her interest in death. On the one hand she had to be near it and treat it almost as entertainment, while on the other hand she looked at it with a cold calculating eye, always seeking to discover more and to probe deeper. Thus even her own brushes with death she treated in a detached way, almost as though she were uninterested although the opposite was true. In June 1850 the Queen had just left Cambridge House, after visiting her dying Uncle Adolphus, when a demented man reached forward and struck her across the face with a heavy cane. She sat perfectly still as though, if this were death, she would meet it with her eyes open and observing everything as it happened. For days her head was 'green and brown from the blow' but she was chiefly concerned with the fact that she had not been badly hurt, although everyone else was puzzled as to why, for by all accounts she should have died in the attack, had he wanted to kill her. The Queen regarded the whole episode as a message: her time to die had not yet come.

For a long time following the death of Prince Albert Victoria was not a popular Queen; rather she was seen as an embittered recluse with no interest but herself and the death of her husband. Only her second daughter, Princess Alice, was really aware of the great dark cloud of misery that enveloped the Queen; others could only guess at the extent of her sadness and measure it by her strange whims and fancies and sudden changes of mood and lack of interest in everything about her. Gradually the darkness of her outlook deepened into paranoia and she developed obstinate and unalterable obsessions. One was that Bertie was responsible for Albert's death. Another was that whatever Albert had wished or planned should take place. Yet another was that she utterly refused to believe that Albert had completely left her — witness the nightshirt and the hot water and the readiness of all his things.

She seemed almost to go out of her way to be unpredictable and from time to time issued distinctly odd orders. When Bertie and Alix were engaged she issued a firm order that they were not to be allowed to be alone together; she gave her formal assent to the marriage two months after the engagement and then she suddenly turned completely against Alix's parents. When Alix first came to visit her, the Queen was full of praise and kindness and the young Princess made quite an impression when she burst into tears as Victoria rambled on and on about her life with Albert. The Queen never forgot that performance although in later years Alexandra would smile at the memory of the time she had been sent 'on approval' to Osborne, as if she were a package of goods.

It is another quirk in the strange and complex character of the Queen that in the midst of all this preoccupation with death she had time to think of men. She never concealed her admiration for men's figures and quite often felt more than a little in love.

One wonders what she thought, if indeed she knew, of Charles Dickens's 'hopeless passion' for her and his intended bizarre request. He wrote to his friend T. J. Thompson (who was in love with Dickens' wife for years):

> and I am raving with love for the Queen . . . we sallied down to Windsor, prowled about the Castle, saw the corridor, and their private rooms, nay the very bed-chamber lighted up . . . I have heard that she reads my books and is very fond of them. I think she will be sorry when I have gone. I should wish to be embalmed and to be kept (if practicable) on the top of the triumphal arch at Buckingham Palace [the Marble Arch, then in front of the palace] when she is in town and on the north-east turrets of the Round Tower when she is at Windsor.

Thirty years later, in 1870, the Queen invited Dickens to Buckingham Palace but by that time he was no longer in love with the puffy-faced and portly Queen and the conversation seems to have been mainly about class division although he doubtless related to the Queen some of his many psychic experiences. There was the fulfilment of a vivid dream (the Queen was very interested in dreams); the apparition of his much-loved sister-in-law Mary Hogarth; the ghost of his dead father and the remarkable premonition of a ghost story that turned out to have actually happened.

This singular event had occurred nine years earlier, in 1861, following the publication of some of his ghost stories in *All the Year Round*. One story told of a fictional artist who travelled on 13 September from London to a stately home in the country. On the train the artist fell into conversation with a sad-looking young lady who seemed to know exactly who he was, and who asked him to observe her closely because one day he might be asked to paint her portrait from memory.

She alighted at the station before his, remarking as she did so, 'We shall meet again soon.' Sure enough, when he reached his destination he discovered to his astonishment that she was a fellow-guest. Seated beside her at dinner that evening he spoke to her several times and assumed that she was an old friend of the family. Next morning, when he asked after her, he was told that he was the only guest and he then discovered that he alone had seen the young lady!

For more than two years the artist was baffled by the mystery and he could not forget the young girl's mournful face . . . and then he met a complete stranger who asked him whether he could paint a portrait from a verbal description. The man said his beloved and only daughter had died two years before, on 13 September, and there was no picture to remember her by. The artist needed no description for he remembered the date all too well and he quickly sketched the features of the young lady he had met on the train. Her father was astonished at the perfect likeness.

When Dickens published this story in his magazine he received a startling letter from a real artist who claimed that the basic story was fact, not fiction, and had happened to him! Even the date, 13 September, was correct. Had Dickens unknowingly written a ghost story that had actually happened? He checked and rechecked the real artist's account of his eerie experience and was so impressed by his findings that he published a follow-up to his ghost 'story'.

By 1874 there was a persistent rumour that Queen Victoria had committed suicide. The palace replied with a statement that she was 'quite well'. In fact the sixty-year-old Queen was in better health than she had been ten years earlier and there are far fewer references in her Journal to the sufferings she experienced from her 'nerves', although there are indications that she suffered severe headaches; there are several allusions to her 'poor head' and to the feeling that it was going to burst.

The shadow of death was never far from Victoria nor did she want it to be, although she would have been the last person to admit such a thing. In 1878 her daughter Alice, who had so comforted her after

Albert's death, died, by an odd quirk of fate, on the anniversary of her father's death. Lady Augusta Bruce, later Lady Augusta Stanley, one of the Queen's most trusted friends who had also helped the Queen after Albert's death, had died a couple of years earlier. In March 1879 the year after Princess Alice's death, a grandson, one of Vicky's sons, died from haemophilia.

In 1884, when her son Leopold died, the Queen wrote in her Journal, 'I am a poor desolate old woman, and my cup of sorrow overflows. Oh God in His mercy, spare my other dear children . . .' but Frederick died in 1888 after reigning as Emperor of Germany only ninety-nine days. In 1895 Prince Henry of Battenberg, the husband of Victoria's 'Baby', Beatrice, died. As Dorothy Marshall puts it, 'During the last years of Victoria's life death seemed to hover perpetually. It was the penalty of marrying young and living to old age.' But in the midst of death the Queen still looked for evidence of life after death.

Once, at Nice, Victoria received that queen of actresses, Sarah Bernhardt. Brought up in a convent, Bernhardt went on to leave all that far behind her and become the greatest actress of her day. In 1892 she had an interview with Cheiro the palmist and seer who saw only her hands, a heavy black lace mantilla covering her head and face. Purely from an examination of the hands Cheiro described brilliant success, artistic conquests and triumphs but also some trials and eventually a long-drawn-out tragedy before the end. When he had finished, the actress revealed her identity and said in that sweet voice of hers, 'It is the most wonderful thing I have ever known, wonderful, wonderful, wonderful . . .'

Cheiro took an impression of Sarah Bernhardt's right hand and his remarks about it are of considerable interest — or so Victoria thought. Even the shape of the hand, he said, was in accordance with her artistic temperament while all the principal lines were strangely clear and straight, indicating that she marked everything she undertook with an unmistakable personality all her own. The two lines that rose above the wrist and proceeded upward to the base of the second and third fingers (the Line of Fate or Destiny, and the Line of Sun or Brilliancy) were extremely unusual and indicated the extraordinary success she would enjoy in her acting profession from her very earliest years. She had in fact made her debut at the age of fifteen when she entered the Paris Conservatoire. Unfortunately both these strong lines appeared to break up in the latter years, before they reached the base of the fingers, and this indicated a definite period of tragedy before death.

In 1915 (when she was seventy) an accident led to the amputation of one of Sarah Bernhardt's legs and for the remaining eight years of her life, although she could no longer walk or stand unaided, she played at the Front, toured America and acted in London. She died on the verge of bankruptcy in Paris in 1923 where she agreed to pose for a cinematograph company, although she knew that death was near. Propped up in bed she played her last part and as the crew left her room she sank into a coma from which she never awakened. The irony of it all was that the film company failed and the money that might have paid for her funeral never materialized. Nevertheless nearly a million francs worth of flowers followed her hearse to the grave. Queen Victoria would have been fascinated and repelled at the same time had she known that the French actress, of mixed French and Danish parentage and of Jewish descent, would be buried in the rosewood coffin she herself had designed and with which she had travelled all over the world for more than thirty years.

In June 1893 the Queen was appalled and frustrated with grief at a sensational naval disaster. For some inexplicable reason Admiral Sir George Tryon had turned his flagship *HMS Victoria* into the path of *HMS Camperdown* commanded by Admiral Markham, with the result that the *Victoria* sank to the bottom of the Mediterranean carrying with it Tryon himself and more than half of his men. 'Too awful!' wrote Queen Victoria in her interminable Journal. 'Too dreadful to contemplate!' And she sent a letter of condolence to Lady Tryon, refraining from referring to Tryon's last recorded words: 'It was all my fault.' One of the surviving officers reported that as the ship went down he heard Sir George cry out that it was all his fault and, with a young midshipman standing beside him – the lad had refused Sir George's order to jump overboard to possible safety – the Admiral went to his watery grave.

What interested Queen Victoria, once she recovered from the shock of having lost a ship, was the remarkable experience of Lady Tryon. On the afternoon of 22 June 1893 Lady Tryon was giving one of her 'At Home' parties at their London house. That sunny afternoon the cream of society chatted and gossiped among the elegant furniture: military gentlemen in colourful uniforms, dandies in tight-waisted frock coats and ladies resplendent in their frills, laces and jewels. Suddenly there was a hush in the buzz of conversation as a commanding figure in naval uniform walked into the room without being announced, strode straight across the room – the guests drawing aside to let him pass – and promptly vanished! He was recognized by everyone present as Sir George Tryon.

At that precise moment, it seems Admiral Sir George Tryon was drowned in the wreckage of his flagship, *Victoria*. The reason behind the collision remains to this day one of the great naval mysteries of all time.

In her last years the Queen was to change some of her ideas about death and mausoleums. She no longer felt, she said, that 'dear ones' were bound to the place 'where their cast-off garments lay' but were in fact '*everywhere* near you'. Perhaps at last she was prepared to acknowledge what she had always believed but up to that point was afraid to admit, even within the confines of her Journal.

The time came when she had to be carried up the steps of the mausoleum at Frogmore but she still felt impelled to visit it; death continued to fascinate her. Knowing of her interest in such matters her daughter in Germany wrote to her after the Dowager Empress Augusta died in 1890, describing in great detail the body of her mother-in-law lying in state:

> The poor Empress lay in her coffin which looked like a bed it was so covered with flowers. You would have thought she was just going to a fête or a soirée, her face was so calm and peaceful and had grown younger. There seemed not a wrinkle, and the eyes that used to stare so and look one through and through were closed which gave her a gentler expression than I ever saw in life. Her false hair in ringlets on her brow, the line of the eyebrows and eyelashes carefully painted as in life — a golden myrtle wreath on her head and an ample tulle veil, very well arranged, flowing and curling about her head and neck and shoulders hiding her chin, her hands folded, her bracelets on and her wedding ring. The cloth of gold train lined and trimmed with ermine which she wore for her golden wedding was well folded and composed about her person and over her feet, and flowed far down the steps in front. She looked wonderfully well and really almost like a young person. I felt that if she could have seen herself she would have been pleased.

Death, when it came for Victoria, came quickly. On 14 January 1901, in her eighty-second year, there was a blank page in her Journal for the first time in sixty-nine years — and on that awful date the 14th too. The old Queen would not have missed the significance of that.

A couple of days later Victoria was mentally confused, she had difficulty speaking and the next day a heart specialist was called to Osborne and the family were advised of the severity of the situation. The Prince of Wales arrived on the 19th and a bulletin was issued saying the Queen was not 'in her usual health'. Next day she seemed unchanged but at midnight she began to sink but rallied and asked the doctor in attendance: 'Am I better at all?' He told her, 'Yes.' 'Then may I have Tudi?' the Queen asked. The little pet Pomeranian was brought in and lay for a while on the dying monarch's bed.

She hardly moved for the rest of the day but showed some sign of listening when Randall Davidson, Bishop of Winchester, recited her favourite hymn, 'Lead Kindly Light': 'And with the morn those angel faces smile — Which we have loved long since and lost awhile.' The angel face that Victoria had last seen forty years before was, she knew, waiting to welcome her — at last. Death, the last great mystery that had obsessed her for half a century, claimed her and she went willingly, supported by her grandson the Kaiser of Germany whose good arm held her while she breathed her last.

After lying in state in the Albert Memorial Chapel the family took her to the 'dear mausoleum' where at last she joined her husband.

CHAPTER TWELVE

THE ROYAL FAMILY'S INTEREST
IN THE PARANORMAL

It is an interesting fact that most, if not all, members of Britain's royal family since Queen Victoria have been and are interested in various aspects of the paranormal, be it ghosts and hauntings, mediums and spiritualism, spirit healing or alternative medicine.

It is small wonder that many of the royals are interested in ghosts since so many royal residences are reputed to be haunted. Buckingham Palace is supposed to be haunted by a private secretary of King Edward VII who committee suicide; Windsor Castle has the royal ghostly forms of Henry VIII, Elizabeth I, Charles I and George II — and according to reports the Queen herself likes to be made aware of alleged sightings. Queen Elizabeth II is said to have caught sight of the ghost of John Brown, Queen Victoria's confidant, some ten years ago at Balmoral. Sandringham is reputed to have several ghostly 'presences': a bloated panting apparition whose activities warranted a service of exorcism a hundred years ago; an invisible 'something' that moves objects; 'hollow footsteps' in deserted corridors — all are an accepted feature of Sandringham. Glamis Castle, ancestral home of the Queen Mother and birthplace of Princess Margaret probably has a dozen different ghosts and the last Earl of Strathmore told me that he is sure there are mysteries still to be uncovered there; Osborne House has, appropriately enough, the ghost of Queen Victoria herself; St James's Palace and Kensington Palace are also haunted; and so the list goes on and on.

Medium Bertha Harris said to me in 1976: 'I can tell you that the royal family have always had a deep interest in spiritualism — but it would not do for them to admit it.' She claimed that King George VI visited her 'many times', the introduction being made through the royal portrait artist Sir Oswald Birley, a friend of the King. Birley's wife was one of Bertha Harris's clients and a fellow spiritualist and Bertha showed me a copy of Sir Oswald's portrait of the King signed by the artist. Once, during the Second World War, there was an air raid during the time that the King was consulting Bertha: 'We all shot under the table . . . fear is a great leveller! I found myself on my knees peering into my Sovereign's eyes inches from my face!'

Bertha Harris told me that her clientele had included Queen Mary and King George VI, the Duke of Windsor and Mrs Simpson, King Paul and Queen Frederika of Greece and many other famous people. She said Queen Mary (who was virtually bald, which may have had something to do with her well-known frigidity and reserve) often consulted her and she was able to relay messages from her dead husband, George V. There was no pretence of love between them when they married but they grew to love each other to the extent that when they were apart George would feel ill. His son, George VI, Bertha was able to advise and seemed to help on many occasions; she told me she could see his agonizing death but she did not mention that to him. She told King Paul and Queen Frederika that their son, then a small boy, would grow up to become King but would lose his throne and live the life of an English gentleman, which certainly came true.

King George II of the Hellenes, a great-grandson of Queen Victoria, was also much interested in spiritualism and he sat with medium Estelle Roberts in London on many occasions and was very sympathetic to trance manifestations and clairvoyant messages. His uncle Prince Christophere of Greece revealed in his published memoirs that a medium had predicted 'much of the dark future of the family through wars, revolt and exile'. Another royal client for Estelle Roberts was King Paul of the Hellenes, a cousin of Prince Philip, and his wife Queen Frederika who also sat with Bertha Harris.

Princess Marie Louise, a granddaughter of Queen Victoria and great-aunt to Queen Elizabeth II, was seemingly treated for six years by the healer Harry Edwards. After her first visit in 1950, when she was suffering from arthritis, Edwards said, 'the arthritis was taken away; her left shoulder became free and she could move her knees without pain. Apart from some inconvenience in her thumb joint, she never complained again about arthritis.' Princess Marie Louise was deeply interested in spiritualism and both she and her aunt Princess Beatrice visited mediums and received a number of evidential messages. Harry Edwards also claimed to have successfully treated the Earl of Athlone, a great-uncle of the Queen and two other members of the present royal family.

King George V, whose ghost has been reportedly heard and seen at Sandringham, where he died, seems to have been interested in the whole realm of psychic activity. When he was sent an alleged message from his mother Queen Alexandra, after her death, he replied to the correspondent personally, saying, 'It was so kind of you to send me such an inspiring message from my dear mother . . .' and he added, significantly, 'My mother is constantly with me, watching and guiding my private affairs.'

The *Flying Dutchman*, probably the most celebrated ghost ship, although there are many others, was convincingly sighted by no less than thirteen witnesses in 1881, among them a boy cadet, Prince George, later King George V. His diary records the appearance in a matter-of-fact and utterly convincing fashion, showing that already the Prince accepted the possibility of such manifestations:

> At 4 am *The Flying Dutchman* crossed out bows. A strange red light as of a phantom ship all aglow, in the midst of which the masts, spars and sails of a brig 200 yards distant stood out in strong relief. She came up on the port bow where also the officer of the watch from the bridge saw her, as did also the quarter-deck midshipman who was sent forward at once to the forecastle. But on arriving there was no vestige nor any sign of any material either near or right away to the horizon, the night being clear and the sea calm.

Standing alongside Prince George when he saw the ghost ship was his elder brother, the ill-fated Prince Clarence, then heir to the throne.

The formal entry in the ship's log reads:

> July 11, 1881. During the middle watch the so-called *Flying Dutchman* crossed our bows. She first appeared as a strange red light, as of a ship all aglow, in the midst of which light her masts, spars and sails, seemingly those of a normal brig, some two hundred yards distant from us, stood out in strong relief as she came up. Our lookout man on the forecastle reported her as close to our port bow, where also the officer of the watch from the bridge clearly saw her, as did our quarterdeck midshipman, who was sent forward at once to the forecastle to report back. But reaching there, no vestige nor any sign of any material ship was to be seen either near or away to the horizon. The early morning, as the night had been, was clear, the sea strangely calm. Thirteen persons altogether saw her but whether it was the *Flying Dutchman* or one of the other few alleged phantom ships which are reputed to haunt this area must remain unknown. *Tourmaline* and *Cleopatra*, which were sailing on our starboard quarter, flashed signals asking whether we had seen the strange glow, and if we could account for it.

The legend of the *Flying Dutchman* goes back to 1680 and in the archives of the Ghost Club there are reports of sightings in 1823, 1866, 1890 and 1939. During the Second World War Admiral Karl Doenitz,

Hitler's former Commander-in-Chief of U-boats, included in one of his reports a sighting of the mysterious ghost ship:

> Certain of my U-boat crews claimed they saw the *Flying Dutchman* or some other phantom ship on their tours of duty . . . when they returned to their base the men said they preferred facing the combined strength of Allied warships in the North Atlantic than know the terror a second time of being confronted by a phantom vessel.

There is a tradition that the *Flying Dutchman*, herself a cursed ship, is a harbinger of doom or misfortune to those who see her. In his diary the future King George V goes on to say:

> At 10.45 am the ordinary seaman who had first reported the *Flying Dutchman* fell from the foretopmast cross-trees on to the forecastle and was smashed to atoms. At 4.15 pm after quarters, we hove to with the headyards back and he was buried at sea. He was a smart royal yardman and one of the most promising young hands in the ship and everyone feels quite sad at his loss.

Whatever the explanation there can be no doubt that for over three hundred years varied and reliable eye-witnesses have reported seeing a ship moving over the sea around the Cape of Good Hope, a ship with a strange square, squat hull, a high poop and an ancient rig.

Queen Elizabeth II, who is said to have read with interest the quarterly Newsletter of the Churches Fellowship for Psychical and Spiritual Studies, has long been a fervent believer in homoeopathy. Kay Kiernan, a psychic healer, treated the Queen for an injured shoulder and she said afterwards, 'the Queen was very interested and asked many questions'. The same healer treated Princess Margaret and Princess Alexandra. Incidentally the Queen and Princess Margaret seem to be telepathically in rapport and when the Queen and her sister played charades as children Princess Margaret once said, in response to being congratulated on the apparent skill shown, 'It's quite easy if Lillibet and I are doing it because there is a kind of telepathy between us.'

There seems no doubt that the Queen Mother and other members of the royal family have consulted mediums, in fact the evidence is overwhelming, but from time to time when there is publicity about the matter Buckingham Palace issue statements that such reports as have reached the Press are untrue. Sometimes they go to extraordinary lengths to obtain denials of previously accredited stories as happened a few years ago to Tom Corbett, the society clairvoyant. Why should there be such a fuss? Probably because as head of the Church of England the Queen must take seriously any suggestion involving the royal family with a person claiming to possess occult powers. The palace cannot forget the constitutional crisis in Holland when Queen Juliana reportedly consulted a faith healer.

According to Gordon Adams, a former son-in-law of medium Lilian Bailey OBE, as reported by Tony Ortzen in his book *When Dead Kings Speak* (1985), the Queen Mother successfully made contact with the dead King George VI through Lilian Bailey, the sittings being made through speech therapist Lionel Logue who treated George VI for his speech defect.

It is through Lionel Logue, for one, that we know there were diaries of Queen Victoria relating to her sittings with John Brown. They were destroyed, the King told Logue, except for one which was found in the archives at Windsor and which he, the King, read with much interest. 'My family is no stranger to spiritualism,' he reportedly told Logue.

Lionel Logue accepted spiritualism and believed that he received remarkable evidence for survival after the death of his wife. At the first seance when Logue, Lilian Bailey and Hannan Swaffer were involved, the medium did not know the identity of Logue and was puzzled when she saw the spirit form of King George V. Addressing Lionel Logue she said, 'He asks me to thank you for what you did for his son.' Logue replied, much to everyone's surprise, 'I quite understand.'

Logue claimed that he discussed many times with King George VI his conviction of the truth of life after death and described the many seances he had attended, and he never met any hostility. After the death of George VI, Logue, who seems to have been a natural psychic, believed that he received messages from the dead King and he was asked to transmit one of these messages to Buckingham Palace, but his health broke down and it is said that he was never able to convey that particular and personal message.

Lilian Bailey, who was awarded the Order of the British Empire for secretarial services during the First World War, received a legacy on Logue's death — a chair that had been used many times by King George VI when he attended speech therapy treatment.

As far as the present royal family are concerned they are obviously taught to be very careful in what they say and they usually confine their public utterances about the paranormal to such subjects as alternative medicine. During the course of a radio phone-in on 2 September 1985, Princess Anne revealed that she was brought up on a certain amount of homoeopathy and when she travels she always takes with her a first aid kit of homoeopathy which has provided all she has ever needed; she has found, over the years, that in some ways homoeopathy is remarkably effective. Princess Anne is a patron of the Society of Osteopaths.

Dr Mervyn Stockwood, former Bishop of Southwark, who has sat with mediums and shown a healthy interest in the paranormal for many years, is said to have had lengthy conversations with Prince Charles on various aspects of the subject but especially his deep interest in spiritual healing. The Prince of Wales's interest in such matters is widely known and he has been seen as putting pressure on the University of Wales to establish a Chair in Parapsychology. For some years now he has championed alternative medicine and even aimed a blow at the very heart of orthodox medical treatment by referring to his feelings about the matter in a speech to the British Medical Association.

There are those who maintain that Prince Charles has personally explored the world of spiritualism and hoped to contact Lord Louis Mountbatten, his much-loved Uncle Dickie who was murdered by political terrorists. As far as I am aware Buckingham Palace has never officially denied this story but the Prince did say, during the course of a television interview in 1985, that he had never used an Ouija board but, he was very interested in spiritualism and such matters and he put in a very sensible plea for a more open-minded approach to these things.

Tom Johanson of the Spiritualist Association of Great Britain has written about Prince Charles and his interest in psychic matters in the *Spiritualist Gazette* saying, 'He has often stated to the Princess he strongly senses the presence of his uncle who he is convinced is anxious to communicate.' Other published stories have said that the Prince would spend considerably more time experimenting with the psychic world 'if it wasn't for his other commitments'; and that when he and Princess Diana visited Lord Mountbatten's home for a charity ball, the Prince is said to have remarked, 'When I danced with Diana it was as though Uncle Dickie was guiding me around the dance floor.'

Princess Diana, it has been stated, thought that the idea of Prince Charles 'being constantly followed around their home by the ghost of Uncle Dickie is too frightening to think about' but, it has been said, Prince Charles is collecting books on paranormal subjects and is determined to alter Diana's opinion.

Lord Mountbatten's house, Broadlands, was the venue for many seances in Victorian days when the house was owned by Lord and Lady Mount-Temple. Lady Mount-Temple became a spiritualist following the death of her mother in 1861 and among the frequent sitters at her seances was John Ruskin, the artist, philosopher and man of letters. Professor Van Akin Burd unearthed the story of these sittings during the course of research on Ruskin among the Mount-Temple papers at Broadlands.

There have been repeated reports that Princess Michael of Kent consults clairvoyants and in particular a psychic practitioner named Peter

Lee; and it has been revealed that the Hon. Angus Ogilvy has had 'spirit' healing from Lady Michaela Denis Lindsey (the former Michaela Denis who was widely known for her wildlife films made in co-operation with her late husband Armand Denis) and that the healing sessions have been attended by Angus Ogilvy's wife Princess Alexandra.

According to Lady Michaela, the crippling pain in Angus Ogilvy's back ceased as soon as the healer's hands located the seat of the trouble and her patient's pain 'vanished for the first time since he injured his back twenty years earlier.'

Prince Philip is one member of the present royal family who has been named as taking part in seances and other methods of alleged communication with the dead. Some years ago it was reported that during the course of a visit to Prince Franz Josef II and his wife Princess Gina of Liechtenstein (who were said to be very interested in attempting to foresee the future and were in fact often uncannily accurate), several members of the royal family, including Prince Philip, Prince Charles and Princess Anne, took part in a session of purported foreknowledge with a local fortune-teller.

Prince Charles's addresses over the years contain statements that we can all study profitably. In a recent one, for example, he said:

> Don't underestimate the importance of an awareness of what lies beneath the surface of the visible world and of those ancient, unconscious forces which still help us to shape the psychological attitudes of modern man. [and again] . . . that invisible aspect of this universe, which although unprovable in terms of orthodox science, as man has devised it, nevertheless cries out for us to keep our minds as open as possible and not to dismiss it as mere hocus-pocus, for it can mean much to those whose inner lives may be transformed through contact with these extraordinarily gifted people.

Buckingham Palace have several times admitted that Prince Charles, Prince of Wales, writes his own speeches.

Two final quotes from Prince Charles: 'Paranormal activity is an interesting area to study', and 'If we skirt round issues all the time how do we get anywhere?' How indeed.

CHAPTER THIRTEEN

QUEEN VICTORIA, THE ENIGMATIC – HAS SHE RETURNED AND WHAT WAS SHE REALLY LIKE?

We know that the ghost of Queen Victoria has been reportedly seen on several occasions at Osborne house but this may well be some kind of atmospheric photograph — a recording of the old Queen at the house she loved best; an impression caused by a combination of circumstances and events that reappears on certain occasions and under certain conditions. It need not necessarily be evidence of the 'return' of Queen Victoria.

There are scores of mediums who have claimed to receive messages from Queen Victoria long after she was dead but here the quality of the mediums and the quality of the messages leaves much to be desired. Occasionally, however, one comes across something that makes one wonder.

Queen Victoria's daughter Princess Louise was convinced that her mother spoke to her through the mediumship of Leslie Flint, the direct-voice medium, and one could argue that Princess Louise would have been likely to know her own mother's voice and could hardly have been mistaken, so perhaps this is more interesting.

Another sitter with Leslie Flint was John James, a former house steward to Princess Louise at Kensington Palace; so we have an independent witness who might be acceptable. James was a regular sitter with Leslie Flint and on one occasion Queen Victoria purported to 'come through' and she thanked James for giving healing to her daughter. Only then did the royal servant reveal that he had helped to relieve Princess Louise's arthritic pains on several occasions: no one knew anything about that until the old Queen in her inimitable way referred to it.

Another reported appearance of the ghost of Queen Victoria is at Windsor and it dates from a curiously poignant episode in her life and in the history of Windsor Castle. The outstanding memory for practically everyone present at the brilliant wedding of Bertie and the lovely Alexandra was not the dazzling ceremony or the colour and the pageantry, but rather the strange kind of cage, high above the altar in St George's Chapel; a forbidding, dark and mysterious place draped with purple velvet that would draw back silently at the wish of the stricken Queen within. Dressed in black with only the bright blue streak of the Order of the Garter to relieve it, her white expressionless mask of a face would occasionally look out at the spectacle below her. But then she would draw the curtains as soon as she thought she saw someone looking at her, only to peer forward again for another look. This strange procedure continued throughout the ceremony and there have been visitors to St George's Chapel in recent years who have asked about the white-faced lady sitting alone in the dark recesses of Catherine of Aragon's closet. No human occupant is there but perhaps the Queen does return occasionally to look down on the passing throng of sightseers as she might well do were she still on earth.

During recent years some curious 'proofs' of the existence of ghosts have come from Margo Williams, the Isle of Wight psychic. Margo first discovered in 1976 that she could hear the voice of a ghost speaking to her at a place where a haunting had been reported by other sensitive persons. The ghostly voice usually related the reason it haunted that particular spot. This strange phenomenon developed over the years to the extent that not only did the ghosts tell their tales of woe but often they gave instructions for unearthing physical objects which had belonged to them or had been closely connected with them. Such artefacts include coins dating back to the beginning of the eighteenth century and pieces of jewellery, china and ornaments, as well as a few small items of gold, silver and ivory. Margo now has a collection of some three hundred such items.

Margo Williams does most of her work in the open countryside accompanied by two or three people as witnesses, including her husband, Walter. Depending on the accuracy of the ghostly instructions the discovery of items by searching or digging can take anything from ten minutes to a couple of hours; but witnesses to such activities have included newspaper reporters, photographers, librarians, historians — in all some forty independent witnesses. Once the lost item has been recovered the ghost voice often speaks to Margo again, sometimes merely to thank her and to ask her to look after the property but nearly always saying they can now continue onwards 'through the tunnel' or 'towards the light'. I recently asked Margo and Walter Williams, who I visited on the Isle of Wight during the early days of Margo's mediumship, whether they had ever come across anything concerning Queen Victoria. This is their reply; it is a verbatim report of the allegedly paranormal communication:

Up a path near Niton, Isle of Wight. Everyone says how cold it is as they walk past here. It is not cold, they are not realizing that I am crying out to them. My name is Emily and when the last breath left my earthly body I was in a tunnel and at the end was a bright light but I had to come back as I think I was a traitor. I told Queen Victoria a lie and to tell a falsehood to a queen must make one a traitor. I could see colours coming from people and as I loved painting flowers and countryside scenes I would try to mix my watercolours to match their shades. I found by making a round circle of colour a face would appear that people would recognize as a loved one who had passed on. Unfortunately it soon disappeared. I only told my friends of this but one of them worked at Osborne House as a servant in the kitchen and she told someone who in turn told the Queen. I was sent for and this sad lady who ruled over us actually spoke to me and bade me sit on a stool and paint her own colour. I had my brush and watercolours and started to mix the silver grey I saw coming from her. I painted on a piece of paper the coloured circle and then the worst happened, nothing at all! No face, nothing! I immediately showed it to the Queen and said I could see the face of Prince Albert who she dearly loved and mourned. She said she could see nothing but I lied to her saying that only sometimes could the face be seen by other people. She was overcome with joy and thanked me and then the next horror occurred; the brush that I had laid upon a small table by my side fell on to the carpet and being wet with paint, it left a mark. I was so embarrassed and apologised but the Queen was so happy to think that I could see her husband's face, she said the mark on the carpet did not matter at all. Strangely enough I then lost the gift of seeing faces in the coloured circles that I drew and in fact it never happened again after my visit to Osborne House.

A few days later a servant called at my home with a very small gift; it was an ivory brush-rest, so that never again would I drop a paint brush! I treasured this and always took it with me when I went to paint country scenes. We left that part of the Island and came to live this side. I came up here painting and near where you are now, by the bushes and rocks, I dropped my brush and rest; I found the brush but not until I came back from the tunnel and returned here could I see the little ivory brush-rest. Please find it and at the same time you may find a ring which I saw a woman drop nearby, a ring which had my initials on it.

The ivory brush-rest was found and also a gold ring with the initials

E.M. The ghost voice then spoke again to Margo:

> The sun is shining and I feel free to go towards the light. You found the Queen's gift to me which I so carelessly dropped. I held myself back because of my feelings of guilt; I should not have lied to the great lady. I am glad you found the ring as well as I called to the woman who dropped it but she did not hear me and did not seem at all worried. I felt it was a sign as it had my initials on it; that one day someone would hear me and it was you. Thank you for your attention and your hard work digging for my treasure. I am floating now towards the light.

Other mediums have reported that the dead Queen Victoria has communicated through them, and there are other strange manifestations too. The pond at North Tawton in Devon, for example, is supposed to fill itself when a national calamity is imminent and it reportedly did so before the deaths of George IV, Edward VII, George V and Queen Victoria. On a more personal note, I wonder whether the old Queen tried to get through at a seance held at a haunted house near Evesham in May 1985, when a party of members of the Ghost Club spent a night there. I was deeply involved in researching this book at the time, although those taking part in the seance did not know that, and they reported that they had been astonished at the violent interruption of the seance they were conducting when the initials of Queen Victoria repeatedly came through, with such absolute compulsion and almost frightening force that one experienced member felt she had to leave the room. She came and talked to me about the next book I was writing and then it all came out. The implication was that Queen Victoria did not want me to do this book. Perhaps she would not have wanted it; I don't know, but I do know that once I had heard about this apparent attempt at communication and having made up my mind to go ahead with the book, things gradually became easier and more and more material came my way.

What kind of woman was Queen Victoria? What was she really like? The only true answer must be that Britain's longest reigning monarch was a very complex character.

Queen Victoria was a law unto herself and she would not tolerate opposition; indeed when she was thwarted by her ministers and it looked as though she was not going to get her own way, she several times threatened to abdicate and move to Australia with her family. She trusted her instincts implicitly and always thought she could tell which men were good and which were evil. She was utterly dedicated to the service of her country and her peoples but she was not above pleading illness of one sort or another to get out of an embarrassing situation or an unwelcome engagement.

Queen Victoria was something of a spendthrift in some ways, as her Hanoverian forebears had been; she found the opposite sex very attractive all through her life — another Hanoverian trait; and like many small women she preferred tall men. Her favourite people were those who were witty, romantic, uncomplicated and mysterious; and the most important ingredient was unquestionably 'mysterious' for she truly loved mysteries, enjoyed being mystified, and even made mysteries where none existed. A case in point is the curious incident when she passed over Sir William Harcourt after Gladstone's retirement in favour of Lord Rosebery. By mistake the unfortunate Harcourt was ushered into the presence of the Queen — and was promptly dismissed. Years afterwards Rosebery asked the Queen whether this had in fact happened. 'Yes, that was terrible,' she replied. 'No one knows to this day how it happened — no one can explain it.'

She would go out of her way to talk to people who had had an inexplicable experience and she expressed considerable interest in such activities as the restoration work at St Peter Vincula in the Tower of London, the scene of a number of reported ghostly appearances, and in such perennial mysteries as the Indian Rope Trick. For years a certain royal physician and his descendants used a verterbra from Charles I's severed neck, set in gold, as a salt cellar, until Queen Victoria heard about it and ordered the bone returned to the royal coffin.

All her life Queen Victoria was devoted to dogs and in her eyes cruelty to animals was an unpardonable offence. When Eos, the Prince Consort's favourite greyhound, was accidentally shot, the Queen was consumed with anxiety, far more upset than the Prince, as invariably happened in any matter that concerned him; Eos in fact made a satisfactory recovery. Sir John Conroy, it seems from material now available, only once redeemed himself in her eyes. In 1833 he presented the Duchess of Kent with a King Charles spaniel named Dash. Soon Victoria was dressing 'dear sweet little Dash' in a scarlet jacket and blue trousers; she gave him three rubber balls for Christmas and two pieces of gingerbread decorated with holly and candles! When she felt unwell Dash spent 'his little life' in her room. Victoria loved dogs and horses in particular (generally regarded as the two most psychic animals); she certainly found them more reliable than some of her human companions.

Although only five feet two inches in height the Queen was always physically robust; she was also often excitable and irritable and frequently suffered from moods of depression. She had a quick and hot temper and when she suddenly flew into a rage about some trifle (she admitted herself that great events made her quiet and calm and only little trifles fidgeted her) she was quite capable of hurling accusations and suspicions and even physical objects at 'dear Albert', although she bitterly regretted such outbursts later. There are stories of such exhibitions resulting in Albert going to his room and locking the door; of the Queen following and banging on the door demanding to enter saying, 'The Queen demands entrance'. Only when she had quietened down and said 'It is your little wife who wants to come in' would Albert open the door. During such outbursts the Queen would become almost hysterical which frightened her because she thought her grandfather George III had died insane and she was haunted by the fear that if pushed too far she too might lose her reason.

Mentally the Queen was far from robust and indeed she suffered several nervous breakdowns, both when she was young and when she was mature. Through much of the 1860s she was mentally unbalanced, having moods of deep depression, suffering visions of strange imagination and enduring periods of extreme hysteria so that those about her never knew in what mood she might be.

For a long time following the death of her mother loud noises set her on edge and she would shut herself away, hugging the grief to herself. After the death of Albert she prayed every night, long and earnestly, that she would not long survive the husband who had been — and still was, she felt — everything to her. Friends spoke openly of her 'morbid melancholy' and at least one doctor stated that her mind was 'far from satisfactory'.

After Albert became Chancellor of Cambridge University the Queen acquired a passion for going about incognito. She used to indulge in moonlight walks with Albert along the college 'backs', a veil over her tiara and a mackintosh over her orders and ribbons being considered sufficient to preserve her anonymity. After attributing Albert's illness to 'worry and heartbreak over the Prince of Wales, and his exhausting journeys to Cambridge' she never visited the town again.

She loved to wear the Garter on all possible occasions and was very fond of jewellery and much interested in the origin of the royal jewels. The crown traditionally used at coronations was the St Edward's Crown which weighs over five pounds. When this was considered to be 'unsuitable' for the young Queen, she was interested to learn that a brand new Crown of State was to be made for her coronation using historic jewels from the Imperial Crown, including the Black Prince's ruby, worn by Henry V at Agincourt, and the oldest Crown jewel of all, a sapphire taken from the finger of Edward the Confessor when his tomb was opened in the twelfth century.

The Keeper of the Jewel House at the Tower of London at that time received no salary and was dependant upon the coppers paid by visitors who came to see the Crown Jewels, then housed in the haunted Martin Tower. Interest in the new crown being understandably considerable, the Keeper, Edmund Swifte, looked forward to an improvement in his income, a financial increase being welcome as Mr Swifte had a family to provide for. Unfortunately for him the jewellers who made the new crown, Rundell, Bridge and Rundall, put the crown on show in their shop in Ludgate Hill, an event which drew large crowds to their premises. Mr Swifte wrote to the Lord Chamberlain's office pointing out the loss of his 'hopes and prospects' but his pleas fell upon deaf ears and the crown continued to be on view at the manufacturers.

It was this same Edmund Swifte who was at the centre of two of the strangest stories ever to come out of the Tower of London. It should be appreciated that Swifte was an intelligent and highly respected officer. He was the man who questioned the sentry who claimed to see the figure of a huge bear emerge from beneath the arched doorway of the Martin Tower one midnight in January 1815. The sentry lunged at the form with his bayonet, only to find the weapon pass through the form without hindrance and embed itself in the stout door; whereupon the sentry fainted and was found by some of his comrades. When Swifte questioned the soldier next day the man was still 'trembling and haunted by fear', and according to contemporary evidence he was a 'man changed beyond recognition'. Within two days he was dead. Queen Victoria asked to be acquainted with all the details of this strange event.

Edmund Swifte was the centre of a strange encounter himself in October 1817 as he and his family were having supper in the dining room of the Martin Tower. Those present with Mr Swifte were his wife, their eldest child, a boy of seven, and Swifte's sister-in-law. Swifte was on the point of offering his wife a glass of wine when she suddenly exclaimed, 'Good God! What is that?' pointing above her husband's head. He looked up and saw a cylindrical object, like a glass tube and about the thickness of his arm, hovering between the ceiling and the table. It appeared to contain two dense fluids, white and pale blue, the colours incessantly mixing and separating within the cylinder. Swifte and his wife watched the object for perhaps two minutes and then it began to move slowly round the table, following an oblong path and passing in front of Swifte's sister-in-law, his son and himself but pausing behind Mrs Swifte, near her right shoulder. Suddenly Mrs Swifte shrank down, covering her shoulder with both hands and shrieked, 'Oh Christ! It has seized me.' Swifte quickly picked up a chair and struck out at the object, whereupon it completely vanished. Edmund Swifte and his wife, in common with many people who experience apparently inexplicable experiences, had to face considerable scepticism from friends and other people but they adhered steadily to the story; as long as forty-three years later their account remained factual, unembroidered and convincing, and has always puzzled psychical researchers. Queen Victoria was among the few who did not pour scorn on the story at the time she heard it.

Queen Victoria never forgot and she never forgave. She refused to be painted by Sir John Millais, who painted such well-known pictures as 'Bubbles' and 'The Boyhood of Raleigh' and portraits of Tennyson, Gladstone and Disraeli, because she understood that he had seduced his future wife when painting her; yet she determinedly saw to it that King William IV's ten illegitimate children were provided for.

Immediately after her marriage to Prince Albert, Queen Victoria insisted that she could not be away from London for more than two or three days because as Sovereign she must remain at the heart of things to see and hear all that was going on; a point of view in sharp contrast with her many years of seclusion at Osborne after Albert's death. Among the Queen's most lasting memories were long conversations at Osborne and at Windsor about the unseen world, its reality and its nearness.

What did the Islanders think about Queen Victoria and her love of Osborne and their island? Well, as Brian Vesey-Fitzgerald puts it: 'Queen Victoria brought great prosperity to the Isle of Wight . . . but as a place of quiet beauty she ruined it for ever.'

For years the Queen continued to embrace her strange, confused wish for both privacy and power. *The Times* once published a paragraph stating that workers at the Woolwich Arsenal had been warned they would be arrested if they looked out of their windows while the royal carriage was passing.

Queen Victoria possessed an indifference to cold and when she first moved into Buckingham Palace all the chimneys smoked so no fires could be lit; everyone shivered — except the Queen. In days past the coldness of Kensington never seemed to affect her and in days to come the chilliness of Balmoral and even Osborne, dreaded by most of her court, appears to have left the Queen completely unaffected. It is an interesting fact that many mediums and psychic people are curiously insensitive to temperatures.

Physically Queen Victoria is perhaps best but unflatteringly described as a dumpy figure with a poor complexion, protruding eyes, a droopy mouth and an authoritarian bearing; she also had a cold, withering stare that could silence anyone, except John Brown, and like many blustering people she looked up to those who stood up to her. Throughout her life Victoria never lost the habit of lowering her head (perhaps to try to hide her receding chin) in spite of the fact that the resourceful Lehzen used to pin a sprig of holly to the front of her dress when she was a girl to encourage her to hold her head up! In later life Queen Victoria has been described as a 'majestic barrel of a woman'.

She was also a bully and seemed to weave an hypnotic spell over some people. Lady Ely, the second Marchioness of Ely and the Queen's

194

Woman of the Bedchamber, was a small, pretty woman who lisped and stammered. She would deliver the Queen's instructions in a 'mysterious whisper' and, being essentially a reserved person, the Queen bullied her unmercifully. However even Lady Ely had her uses; she seemed to be psychic and often took part in the table-turning sessions that Victoria and Albert conducted with some success.

As a girl Victoria could be enchanting but already she was decidedly self-willed. When she saw an old man trying to shelter from the rain she told the footman to 'run to that poor man with an umbrella, he is very old and will catch cold'; and her lifelong obstinacy is evident from the story of her music teacher who chided her one day, for she was not a very successful pianist. 'There is no Royal road to music, Princess,' he said. 'You must practise like everyone else.' Victoria shut the piano lid with a bang. 'There,' she said, 'you see, there is no *must* about it.'

As a young child, when she was about to borrow a toy from some friends, her nanny was heard to say, 'If you give it to the Princess, it will be broken in a minute.' Even in those days she was conscious of her small stature and used to complain, 'Everybody grows but me . . .'

As she grew into her teens Victoria was permitted to widen her reading and it is recorded by Elizabeth Longford (*Victoria R.I.*, 1964) that *The Conquest of Granada* by the American Washington Irving 'set her wandering in imagination through the mysterious Orient' (although why this should be so is not entirely clear); in any case, 'These are all Phantom Castles,' wrote Victoria. 'Which I love to form'.

No one could describe Victoria as a helpless cringing female although in her early widowhood she endeavoured to pass herself off as such for, combined with her intense obstinacy once her mind was made up, she had an innate need for someone in her life, preferably male, on whom she could lean.

Nature had endowed Victoria with a clear and charming voice when she wished to use it. Throughout her long life people commented on the clear and bell-like tones with which she delivered her public speeches. Ellen Terry described Victoria's voice as 'like a silver stream flowing over golden stones'.

Elizabeth Longford has pointed to 'the toughest of all virtues, truthfulness' as something shared by our present Queen and Queen Victoria, but Victoria's word was not always to be relied upon. She told her private secretary that Palmerston had accused Louis Philippe, King of France, of stealing the Cabinet key from under her pillow during a visit she made to the Chateau d'Eu and reading the despatches; but no despatches were sent to her there. The Queen did not like Palmerston and never lost an opportunity of putting a bad word against him; she laughed heartily at the rhyme: 'If the devil had a son, Surely he'd be Palmerston.'

One of the best known anecdotes concerning Queen Victoria is that when she learned at the age of eleven that she was in line for the throne, she said solemnly, 'I will be good.' In later years when she was asked whether the story was true she said, according to Hector Bolitho, 'Of course not. How could I say such a thing.'

Soon after the accession of Queen Victoria a number of biographies emerged and the 'I will be good' legend was born; her tyrant of a mother was portrayed as a kind, wise and good parent who brought up the Princess entirely on her own. By the end of Victoria's reign there were quite a few different versions of the Queen's life but none of them mentioned those long periods of unpopularity which the monarchy suffered during her reign, none of them referred to her father's mistress or her mother's probable liaison with Conroy. Then the Greville memoirs appeared and Queen Victoria was shocked to discover that the diarist disclosed suspicions of her mother's adultery with Conroy, strongly supported by the Duke of Wellington whom she had described as 'very dear and nice' and of whom she had once said 'There is one individual for whom I entertain a decided preference, and the individual is the Duke of Wellington'. Victoria had believed that no one outside the family circle had been aware of these happenings. After the Queen died the *Creevey Papers* appeared and revealed her father's years of enjoyment with Julie St Laurent; his great unhappiness at having to enter formal marriage with the Queen's mother, and much gossip about his manners and conduct.

The Queen always had a tremendous appetite for one so small; but by all accounts she ate with astonishing speed, always being the first to finish, and the first to be served of course. The instant she had finished a course and laid down her cutlery, John Brown, standing behind her, would signal for her plate to be removed, which was followed by the prompt removal of the still half-full plates of most of the guests!

During the autumn of 1835, when she was on holiday at Ramsgate, the Princess Victoria suffered a serious illness that confined her to her room for five weeks; an illness variously described as 'bilious fever', 'an attack of typhoid fever' and 'a mere indisposition'. Today's medical opinion is that the Princess suffered from tonsilitis, septic tonsils, but it could well have been a nervous collapse, brought on by strain, physical as well as mental. Thererafter Victoria was advised to take exercise in the fresh air, to keep on the move indoors, to use Indian clubs to 'improve the figure and promote good circulation' and to masticate every mouthful of food thoroughly. These sensible measures seem to have done the trick and she suffered no further attacks. Perhaps her illness brought her physical rest and mental relief at a time when it was most needed; perhaps she was the victim of poltergeist activity. At all events, and not surprisingly, Victoria thereafter had the greatest respect for commonplace and natural or 'alternative' medicine, a trait that has been followed by most of the royal family since her reign.

Towards the end of 1838 Queen Victoria was worried about her health and increasing weight. She fought many fruitless battles over diet for she liked all the wrong foods: sweet ale, hot wine and water, highly flavoured food, and so on. When it became common knowledge that the Queen was ordering her dresses larger, she countered by saying that she 'couldn't endure tight clothes'.

Her worry about other aspects of her health was probably attributable to her ancestry: she feared for her eyes (George III, who was thought to have been mad, had suffered with his eyes) and her tendency to plumpness she probably inherited from her aunts. What was more worrying was that, for a period, she became very lazy and disliked washing (also inherited) and even took to taking her bath at night instead of before dinner so that she did not have to dress again! And then there was the maid who was dismissed for nearly giving her mistress ringworm.

Another illness that completely confused and puzzled the Queen was haemophilia, the mysterious disease that is as old as man, is shrouded in legend and has overtones of being an hereditary curse. Haemophilia was called the royal disease for it appeared in the ruling houses of Britain, Russia and Spain. It remains to this day a mysterious and chronic disease, both the cause and the cure being unknown.

Queen Victoria repeatedly said haemophilia was 'not in our family', by which she presumably meant the House of Hanover; it must therefore, she asserted, have come through the Coburgs, who in any case were subject to most of the diseases then known. The Queen's youngest son, Leopold, died of haemophilia in 1884; her daughters Alice and Beatrice were both carriers; in fact of course it is now known that Victoria herself, unknowingly, was a haemophilia carrier for seemingly a spontaneous mutation had occurred, either in the genetic material of Victoria herself or in the X chromosome passed to her at conception by her father. Of her daughter Alice's eight children, two of the girls, Alix (Alicky who was married to Nicolas II, Tsar of Russia) and Irene (who married Prince Henry of Prussia), were carriers. Alix's brother Frederick, called Frittie, was a haemophiliac. At the age of three Frittie and an elder brother were romping in their mother's room one morning while she was still in bed. The windows which reached to the ground were open and Frittie tumbled out and fell twenty feet to the stone terrace below. No bones were broken and at first he seemed only shaken and bruised but bleeding in the brain had begun and by nightfall Frittie was dead.

Victoria was surprisingly liberal in many ways and although her benevolence was usually reserved for the weak and the poor (and animals), she always had a somewhat inexplicable tolerance for the man — or the woman — who took too much drink; a tolerance possibly stemming from John Brown and his habit of drinking more than was good for him. Perhaps the Queen saw John Brown in every drunken person she encountered or perhaps she knew what the weakness was like for she was by no means averse to a drop of the hard stuff herself.

When a man who tended the lamps at Windsor Castle was so drunk one evening that he fell, dropped a lighted lamp and endangered the castle, the Master of the Household sent a written report of the matter to the Queen but by way of reply she merely wrote 'Poor man' on the account.

The Queen was a supporter of marriage with a deceased wife's sister; she tolerated Roman Catholics, as long as they were not converts; and she was completely free of any racial discrimination. People of all colours were equal in her eyes. On the other hand she had no patience with 'women's rights' and was genuinely horrified at the idea of women doctors although she herself was brought into the world by a woman, with a male doctor in attendance. She was very shocked and found it 'beyond her comprehension' when her daughter Princess Alice took up medical studies and anatomy!

A creature of contradiction, the Queen, despite her dislike of the process of human birth, invariably insisted on being present at the births of as many of her grandchildren as possible. She also became interested in hospitals during the Crimean War and laid the foundation stone for, among others, St Thomas's Hospital where she was intrigued to peruse the copious files devoted to the ghostly Grey Lady of St Thomas's.

Victoria was, if not a many-sided individual, certainly a two-sided person. As Sir Frederick Ponsonby recounts in his memoirs, the Queen could be a dragon to the household in her old age, while at Osborne, within the family circle and especially in the company of some of her twenty-nine grandchildren, she was often (but not always) a sweet and charming old lady, and much loved by practically all the family. At the same time, some of Queen Victoria's grandchildren dreaded staying with her.

It has been genuinely thought that Victoria did not like children but this is not entirely true; she did not care for young babies and she thought they looked like frogs but once the 'frog stage' was behind them and the children were older she loved them dearly, especially her firstborn, the Princess Royal, who was always the favourite. When her first child was born Dr Locock, who was in attendance, said, 'Oh Madam it is a Princess', to which the Queen replied coldly, 'Never mind, the next will be a Prince.'

By and large the daughters of Queen Victoria were, like their mother, lively and pretty until they reached puberty, when they soon became fat and plain and inclined to have spots, probably the result of too much rich food.

In later life the Queen was sympathetic to the trials and tribulations of the poor and she was interested in improving housing conditions, especially sanitation (after all, she reasoned, if Windsor town had not been full of open sanitation ditches, the Prince Consort might never have contracted typhoid). She even visited Parkhurst prison and a workhouse at Windsor but there were limits to her benevolence. Firmly believing that those who touched pitch became defiled, she frowned on people and societies who were concerned with helping prostitutes; she even withheld her approval from the Salvation Army.

She was really much more interested in matters pertaining to death than matters pertaining to life and as Ronald Pearsall has pointed out (*The Table-Rappers*, 1972), 'the fact that Queen Victoria and her consort experimented with table rapping gave spiritualism a cachet, but her particular clique was considered decidedly passé compared with the salons of the fashionable society hostesses . . .' With or without the undoubted interest of Queen Victoria, spiritualism grew and spread during the Victorian era into the worldwide religion that it has become today.

More than one of the biographers of Queen Victoria has remarked upon the sessions of clairvoyance, the presence of mediums and weird ceremonies in the Blue Room with John Brown in trance, the Queen's regular praying for the dead and of course Brown's second sight which the Queen unquestionably accepted. She never forgot those warning words of John Brown as the royal party was about to leave Balmoral in the autumn of 1861, when Brown said he hoped they would all be well through the winter and return safe 'and above all that you may have no deaths in the family'. Within weeks King Pedro of Portugal and Prince Ferdinand had passed from this world and soon Albert too was dead.

As time passed the Queen became convinced that the dead Albert was still near her and available for advice and comfort. When the Crown Prince of Prussia and Queen Victoria's daughter Vicky decided to withdraw for the time being from public life because they had doubts about accepting the throne if Fritz's father King William abdicated in his favour, Queen Victoria immediately invited them to England. 'Albert, she *knew*, would agree . . .' She could hear his voice saying 'They shall come here!' And this was no literary turn of phrase for by this time she was certain that she *could* her Albert's voice on occasions. Victoria frequently visited the great mausoleum that she had had erected to Albert's memory and she dragged every visitor there. After a visit on 16 June 1865 she wrote. 'I knelt and prayed by the beloved shrine . . . I feel more and more that my beloved one is everywhere, not only there . . .'

No sovereign in the past has done more for the theatre than did Queen Victoria and she always took an interest in new developments. In November 1896, in the Red Room at Windsor, she saw the cinematograph pictures that had been taken at Balmoral several weeks earlier. She thought the so-called 'animated pictures' were 'wonderful, the people, their movements and their actions, all as if they were alive . . .'

Poetry, the Queen claimed, she liked 'in all shapes'. She recommended Elizabeth Barrett Browning's *Aurora Leigh* to the Princess Royal, despite its 'dreadful coarseness'. She had a weak spot for Mrs Browning but one wonders what she thought of Robert Browning's *Mr Sludge, the Medium*, for the Queen was known to be irritated by scepticism in psychic matters. When faced with it she would show her mournful face with its drooping mouth and fix the culprit with her stony stare until he or she felt *very* uncomfortable.

Some writers have asserted that the Widow of Windsor was as close if not closer to her husband in death as she was in life. Repeatedly the Queen wrote that Albert was 'perfection in every way, in beauty, in everything. Oh how I adore and love him!' It would seem that even physical death could not separate them and that she was conscious of Albert's presence for the rest of her life.

Queen Victoria loved drama and never missed the opportunity of exploiting a situation or revelling in an unusual combination of circumstances. She always enjoyed the strange and the mysterious and during a visit to Emperor Napoleon III and the Empress Eugénie in 1855 for example, as Elizabeth Longford has remarked: '. . . there was something delightfully mysterious in his manner which immediately appealed to her . . .'

Queen Victoria could have been a diarist of the first rank. She seems to have had total recall and thought nothing of writing an entry of more than two thousand words at the end of a long day. By the end of her life she had filled some 122 volumes; a record of people, places, events and emotions without parallel in history. Unhappily very few of these Journals still exist. Her youngest daughter Princess Beatrice was appointed by Queen Victoria to be her literary executor and some years after the Queen died the Princess, activated by devotion to her mother and with the best possible motives decided that the Journals were not suitable for general distribution and consumption and she destroyed almost all of them. Only the early, closely supervised, diaries were completely spared. In the middle of a volume for 1837, when Victoria came to the throne, for example, half the pages have been wrenched out and the volumes that followed have disappeared. There is one little mystery that Queen Victoria would have appreciated: some years ago a closely guarded collection of books and papers were preserved in a library at Kensington; they were under lock and key and one of the staff at the time tells me that even the Librarian was not permitted entry. One day everything was removed.

It is perhaps the omissions in her early Journals, which her mother and governess saw regularly in those days, that give the best clues to Victoria's private feelings and opinions. The great tussles she had with Conroy and the rows with her mother are never mentioned. Sadly, very little of her interest in the strange and mysterious is evident from her available Journals which are merely copies of some parts of the original Journals but there is considerable contemporary evidence for this early and enduring interest. Even the sceptical Elizabeth Longford has to admit that the Queen had 'a weakness for the *outré* ever since her childhood'.

The last four years of the Queen's reign were lived in increasing shadows, but she enjoyed her Golden and Diamond Jubilees. On 22 June 1897, Jubilee Day, the Queen was seen by one observer to be a little old lady with weak eyes and faltering legs wearing a shawl and using a parasol to shelter her from the sun — inevitably it was 'Queen's weather'.

From 1889 her sight began to fail and she would write of never knowing such murky weather at Windsor, making it necessary to have candles at the luncheon table . . . no one argued with her, even then. Soon she had severe sciatica and nights without sleep made her feel drowsy in the evenings, sometimes almost too sleepy to write her Journal. Once she wrenched her wrist badly when she fell at the mausoleum, and more and more family deaths saddened her as the years passed.

Most of her old friends were already dead. Lady Augusta, Lady Ely, Lady Churchill, her devoted private secretary (when the body of 'Beloved Jane' was conveyed to the mainland the Queen endured agonies lest the ship should founder . . .), Henry Ponsonby, Dean Stanley, John Brown, Disraeli and a host of others, not to mention the family. Even her dearest daughter Vicky looked as though she might race her mother to the grave . . . Victoria was old and frail, her eyesight failing, her rheumatism troublesome. Her nights were restless and her days consumed with compensating sleep. To top it all, the shadow of war hung over the nation.

The old Queen, as everyone now called her, struggled to keep going but by the turn of the century she admitted that she felt so unwell and so weak that she entered the New Year sadly. Her lifelong zest for life and knowledge had gone but her dogged determination kept her alive a little longer. Then on 13 January the Journal that she had kept so faithfully for nearly seventy years ceased. On 19 January a bulletin was issued saying she was not in her usual health; on the 22nd, surrounded by her children and grandchildren, Queen Victoria died.

Before her death she had left minute instructions for her funeral, which were carried out to the letter. She made her last slow journey to Frogmore and there she was laid in the mausoleum where so often as a broken-hearted widow she had sought and found strength and comfort. At last she was united with her dead Albert. On the sarcophagus their marble effigies lie side by side for all the world as though they are asleep and will awaken at any moment.

It has never really been explained how it was that while the Prince of Wales stood in great distress at the foot of his mother's deathbed, the Queen died in the arms of the German Emperor, that wicked grandson for whom she always had a soft spot. Afterwards it was this same grandson, Willy, and not one of her own children who took charge of everything. It was he and not an undertaker who measured the Queen for her coffin, and who summoned the Duke of Connaught to help him and Dr Reid lift the corpse into the coffin.

A few weeks before he died the Prince Consort had said to the Queen: 'We don't know in what state we shall meet again; but that we shall recognise each other and be together in eternity I am perfectly certain.' In all the forty years of her widowhood, while the world about her moved restlessly towards doubt and cynicism, the Queen had believed what her husband had told her, with all her heart. She deserved it to be true.

SELECT BIBLIOGRAPHY

Ashdown, Dulcie M., *Queen Victoria's Mother*, Robert Hale, 1974.
Bedford, John, Duke of, *A Silver-Plated Spoon*, Cassell, 1959.
Bolitho, Hector, *The Reign of Queen Victoria*, Collins, 1949.
Cheiro (Count Louis Hamon), *Confessions of a Modern Seer*, Jerrold, 1932.
Cheiro's Mysteries and Romances of the World's Greatest Occultists, Herbert Jenkins, 1935.
Corti, Egon Caesar Conte, *The English Empress*, Cassell, 1957.
Crane, Jane, *Queen Victoria and the Royal Glen*, ERD, 1984.
Cullen, Tom, *The Empress Brown*, Bodley Head, 1969.
Day, James Wentworth, *The Queen Mother's Family Story*, Robert Hale, 1967.
Duff, David, *Alexandra: Princess and Queen*, Collins, 1980.
Fodor, Nandor, *These Mysterious People*, Rider, 1934.
Fodor, Roger, *Dearest Child*, Evans Bros., 1964.
—— *Queen Victoria*, Collins, 1951.
Greenhouse, Herbert B., *In Defence of Ghosts*, Simon and Schuster, 1970.
Lord Halifax's Ghost Book, Geoffrey Bles, 1939.
Herbert. B. H., *Railway Ghosts*, David and Charles, 1985.
Howarth, Stephen, *The Koh-i-Noor Diamond*, Quartet Books, 1980.
Iremonger, Lucille, *The Ghosts of Versailles*, Faber and Faber, 1957.
Longford, Elizabeth, *Victoria R.I.*, Weidenfeld and Nicolson, 1964.
—— *Elizabeth R.*, Weidenfeld and Nicolson, 1983.
Magus, Philip, *King Edward the Seventh*, John Murray, 1964.
Marshall, Dorothy, *The Life and Times of Victoria*, Weidenfeld and Nicolson, 1972.
Maxwell, Sir Herbert, *Sixty Years a Queen*, Harmsworth Bros., 1897.
Pearsall, Ronald, *The Table-Rappers*, Michael Joseph, 1972.

Pearson, Margaret M., *Bright Tapestry*, Harrap, 1956.

Plowden, Alison, *The Young Victoria*, Weidenfeld and Nicolson, 1981.

Plowman, Thomas F., *In the Days of Victoria*, John Lane, Bodley Head, 1918.

Price, Harry, '*The Most Haunted House in England*', Longmans, Green, 1940.

The Private Life of Queen Victoria (by one of H.M.'s servants), Arthur Pearson, 1902.

Stead, Estelle W., *My Father*, Thomas Nelson, n.d.

Stead, W. T., *Real Ghost Stories*, Grant Richards, 1905.

Tisdall, E. E. P., *Queen Victoria's Private Life*, John Day, 1962.

Underwood, Peter, *Dictionary of the Supernatural*, Harrap, 1978.

—— *Gazetteer of British Ghosts*, Souvenir Press, 1971.

—— *Gazetteer of Scottish and Irish Ghosts*, Souvenir Press, 1973.

—— *Haunted London*, Harrap, 1974.

—— *This Haunted Isle*, Harrap, 1984.

Victoria, Queen, *Leaves from the Journal of Our Life in the Highlands* (edited by Arthur Helps), Smith, Elder, 1868.

—— *More Leaves from the Journal of Our Life in the Highlands*, Smith, Elder, 1884.

Walker, Oliver, *Proud Zulu*, Werner Laurie, 1949.

Watson, Vera, *A Queen at Home*, W. H. Allen, 1952.

Woodham-Smith, Cecil, *Queen Victoria: Her Life and Times, 1819–1861*, Hamish Hamilton, 1972.

Wymer, Norman, *Dr Barnado*, Longman, 1962.

INDEX